WITHDRAWN

The Case Method
at the Harvard Business School

For if education may be defined in a word, that word is controversy. Where concord reigns, learning withers; where conflict rules, it flourishes.

— DONALD MOFFAT, in *Fair Harvard*

The Case Method at the Harvard Business School

PAPERS BY PRESENT AND PAST MEMBERS OF THE FACULTY AND STAFF

edited by MALCOLM P. McNAIR
Lincoln Filene Professor of Retailing

with the assistance of ANITA C. HERSUM, *Research Staff*

GRADUATE SCHOOL OF BUSINESS ADMINISTRATION
GEORGE F. BAKER FOUNDATION
HARVARD UNIVERSITY

1954

McGRAW-HILL BOOK COMPANY, INC.
New York   Toronto   London

The cases reproduced in this volume have all been previously copyrighted, that of the Conmay Company by the McGraw-Hill Book Company, initially on publication of Cabot and Malott's *Problems in Public Utility Management* (1931), and the others by the President and Fellows of Harvard College.

Of the individual papers included in this volume, three are reprinted from other publications: "An Introduction to the Use of Cases," from *The Case Method of Instruction* (McGraw-Hill, 1931); "Because Wisdom Can't Be Told," from the *Harvard Alumni Bulletin* (October 19, 1940); and "The Case Method in College Teaching of Social Science," from *The Journal of General Education* (January, 1949).

The quotation facing the title page is from *Fair Harvard*, Photographs by Samuel Chamberlain with Text by Donald Moffat. Cambridge, Harvard University Press, 1948.

THE MAPLE PRESS COMPANY, YORK, PA.

This volume is dedicated to

MELVIN T. COPELAND

Foreword

Because of the ever-growing interest in the case method of instruction and research in business administration, I welcome the publication of this volume. This book is addressed particularly to teachers and academic administrators who have wondered what the case method is and how it is used at the Harvard Business School. In some part it is addressed also to students, who in many instances encounter difficulty in making the transition to the case method from other, more usual methods of instruction. In the broader field of the general application of the case method, this volume should serve the same useful purpose as the one edited by Kenneth R. Andrews last year devoted particularly to the use of the case method in the teaching of human relations.

For more than thirty years the case method of instruction has been one of the major distinguishing characteristics of the educational program of the Harvard Business School. The seeds of this development were originally planted during the administration of Edwin F. Gay, the first Dean of this School. These seeds did not grow and flourish, however, until my immediate predecessor, Dean Wallace B. Donham, took office in 1919. Dean Donham's training in the law and his own wide business experience gave him the conviction that the case method was the sound approach for instruction in the Harvard Business School. His inspiration and enthusiasm stirred members of the Faculty to undertake the arduous pioneering necessary to make a success of this new and daring educational venture. Dean Donham recognized that the development of the case system for teaching business would be a slow and expensive process. The law schools had the decisions of the courts, the medical schools had hospital cases and clinical records, and the scientific schools had their laboratories and records of experiments. In contrast, there were nowhere any records of the process of making business decisions. Therefore the development of the case system in the Business School had to take the slow and hard way; in fact, to borrow a word from the late Lawrence Henderson, it had to take the "pedestrian" approach. This was true literally as well as figuratively, because those who gathered cases had to go out to the businesses themselves to record the actual situations.

Throughout the period from 1908 to 1942 many men contributed greatly both to developing the educational philosophy underlying the case method and to working out solutions to the many practical problems inherent in its use. No man, however, did more in both these areas than Melvin T. Copeland, and I am pleased indeed that the editor of this volume has seen fit to dedicate it to "Doc" Copeland.

Since the early 1940's heavy emphasis has been placed here at the Harvard Business School on extending the case method to such fields of growing importance as human relations and the social responsibilities of business leadership, on relating other teaching methods, notably the research assignment, the written problem analysis, and the specially prepared factual note, to the case method, and on expanding our research program substantially beyond our immediate needs for teaching materials.

As a product of this long period of development, the case method stands as the signal contribution of the Harvard Business School to education in the profession of business administration. A profession is not like a highly specialized discipline, which often salutes the newness of small discoveries rather than their importance to mankind. For new ideas and for progress a profession must depend in large part on the effective utilization of scholarly accomplishment in other fields. The dependence of business upon science and technology is clear. In the social sciences we are accustomed to think of economics as our source discipline. But we must not conceive of business education as simply consisting of applied economics. We must look to all the social sciences for insight usable in defining the scope of administration and for aid in teaching those professional skills that will promote the attainment of good managerial results. Sociology, psychology, anthropology, political science—these are as important to us now and for the future as is economics, the field from which we still need to derive a theory recognizably useful as an account of and a guide to business activity.

It is one of the great strengths of the case approach that, by its emphasis on the process of business decision making, it forces this needed synthesis of a variety of social disciplines. The student is placed in the position of the businessman who must act, who must before he acts weigh the bearing on his problem of a variety of different considerations, both short-run and long-run in character, but who must in any event make a decision and implement it. The distinguishing characteristic of the case method in the classroom is the extent to which the responsibility for this analytical sifting of pros and cons and for arriving at a definite decision is undertaken by the student himself.

But the case method is also an important tool of business research and has been increasingly so employed at the Harvard Business School, where our research activities rest on the plan, we believe unique among universities, of providing at all times that one-third of our Faculty members shall be given full time to engage in research important to them. For the years ahead the opportunities for significant and indeed pioneering studies are endless. We need more study of the traditional and basic functions of business. For it is the hard core of competent day-to-day operation of business on which depends the continued existence of our type of industrial society. We need extension of the two new fields now permanent parts of our curriculum— human relations and social responsibilities of business leadership. We must arrive at a better understanding of the essential power in our many centers of initiative, power stemming from a risk-taking, daring, and adventurous spirit. Research must contribute to the achievement of stabilized employment coupled with high productivity and a full economy independent of defense spending and proof against unpredictable fluctuations. We must explore and attempt to master the human and technical problems of making both our markets and our technological skills freely available to the rest of the world. Constant inquiry is at the heart of a professional approach to business administration. In no small measure it is the spirit of the case method that will power our Faculty to maintain this constant inquiry.

DONALD K. DAVID, *Dean*
Harvard Graduate School of
Business Administration

Editor's Preface

This volume originated in a series of discussions some years ago among three men, James W. Culliton, now teaching at the University of Notre Dame, Stanley F. Teele, Associate Dean of the Harvard Business School, and Malcolm P. McNair, long a member of the Business School Faculty. Deeply interested in the case method of teaching business and aware of the growing attention paid to it in other institutions and in other fields of teaching, these men felt keenly the lack in print of a fully rounded discussion of the case method. An earlier book, entitled *The Case Method of Instruction*, edited in 1931 by Cecil E. Fraser, was long out of print; during the intervening years, moreover, there had been many significant developments in case pedagogy.

Therefore a series of steps was agreed on, including an essay contest for younger members of the Business School staff, to culminate in a new book made up of papers written by many different individuals. Shortly thereafter Professor Culliton left the Harvard Business School to initiate a significant experiment in the use of the case method under conditions quite dissimilar from those at Harvard; at the same time Dean Teele, carrying a heavy load of administrative duties, found it possible to give only intermittent attention to the project of this volume; and therefore the editorial task devolved upon the third member of the trio. Nevertheless, the impetus for the volume and the general plan for its development and organization owe a great deal to the original discussions among the three individuals.

Some comments on the general plan of the book may be helpful. The decision to have a book written by many men rather than one was a logical consequence of the fact that the case method is so varied, so diverse, so adaptable to the nature of the individual course and to the personality of the individual instructor that no single person can portray it accurately. Indeed, the only discernible common thread running through these varied dissertations on the case method is the emphasis on student participation in the educational process, on the extent to which the student is expected to carry the ball—assessing the facts, making the analysis, weighing the considerations, and reaching a decision.

The book opens with three different statements of the philosophy of the case method, one written some twenty years ago by Arthur Stone Dewing, the second written more than a dozen years ago by Charles I. Gragg, and the third written more recently by the editor. These broad statements are followed by a paper narrating the development of the case method at the Harvard Business School written by Melvin T. Copeland, the man most familiar with the story.

There next appears a series of cases, together with commentaries, to serve as concrete illustrations of what the book is talking about. These cases and commentaries are followed by a group of brief statements by recent graduates reflecting the impact of the case method on them as students. Transition then is made to the point of view of the instructor; and his activities under the case method become the focus of the next four papers, with attention given both to broad pedagogical concepts and to the practical small details. Closely associated with these classroom aspects of the case method is the use of cases as the subject of written assignments, that is, the so-called "business reports" that have long been a feature of the program at the Harvard Business School. Hence a paper on this topic is included.

Next comes the matter of course organization, with papers devoted to two quite different methods of organizing a case course. A logical addition at this point, then, is the look which the authors of the next paper take at the administrative environment conducive to successful case teaching.

The use of cases is not confined to the academic classroom. As the next papers indicate, cases not only constitute an important tool of business research but increasingly are being used by business itself in executive development and supervisory training.

Attention then is turned to the possibility of the wider use of cases in undergraduate schools, and finally the volume ends with three papers directed to specific aspects of getting cases written.

The volume is titled *The Case Method at the Harvard Business School* because all the authors either are presently or have at one time or another been connected with the Faculty or Staff of that School. It is possibly worth mentioning that the views of these individuals on the case method have been developed by contact with two quite different groups of students. For the full period of more than thirty years, cases have been used at the School with young men in their early and middle twenties, typically graduates of colleges in this country or foreign countries, bringing with them a great variety of undergraduate educational backgrounds, including liberal arts, engineering, agriculture, and commerce. Also for some ten years cases (in many instances exactly the same cases) have been used in the Advanced Management Program with experienced businessmen, men in their early or middle forties, coming from many different industries and companies and ranging in educational background from grammar school graduates to holders of doctoral degrees. One of the most striking facts about the case method at the Harvard Business School has been its successful use with these two highly diverse groups.

Encouragement and assistance for this editorial project have come from many sources, inspiration from Dean Donald K. David, former Dean Wallace B. Donham, and especially from Melvin T. Copeland, Professor Emeritus as of July, 1953, to whom the volume is dedicated. As already indicated, the debt is large to those who originally expected to be collaborators in the undertaking, Dean Teele and Professor Culliton. A word of thanks needs to be said also to the individual contributors, many of whom substantially rewrote their papers in order to meet the space limitations of this volume. The tasks of preparing the manuscript for the publisher and reading the proofs have been assumed by my editorial colleague, Mrs. Anita C. Hersum.

MALCOLM P. McNAIR

Contents

*One of the earliest and clearest statements of the general educational
theory underlying the use of the case method in business teaching was
written some twenty years ago by Arthur Stone Dewing,* then Professor
of Finance at the Harvard Business School. The sharp distinction which
Professor Dewing makes between the kind of education that aims
primarily at imparting factual knowledge and the kind that has as its
objective the training of men to take administrative action is basic to the
case method of teaching.*

An Introduction to the Use of Cases

ARTHUR STONE DEWING

Any formal educational method, whatever its practical handling may
be, must rest on some recognizable foundation of educational theory.
In spite of the never-ending conflict of educational methods, a conflict
arising to some extent from the peculiar demands of each age and to
some extent from the eternal conflict of human ideals, there appear to
be two, and only two, essentially different theories of education. Of
these theories individual opinions represent varying combinations and
varying stresses of emphasis.

One theory assumes that education should consist of a brief survey
of the important facts accumulated by man through the ages. The
educated man is the erudite man. Just as the biological development
of the human individual is a brief recapitulation of the evolution of the
species through eons of time, so the education of the individual should
consist of a brief recapitulation of the objective experience of the race
since time immemorial. General education is general accumulation.
Special education consists, of necessity, of a more intensive and exhaustive cataloguing of the results of experience along a certain direction. Specialized education in chemistry is the mastery of the facts of
chemistry brought up to the immediate present. The young chemist
passes over in a few years' time the results which the workers of chemistry have accumulated through centuries of groping and specialized
research. Education in business, according to this theory, should consist of a recapitulation of the results of business experience arranged,
catalogued, systematized, and then presented without the lumber of
discarded precedents. The business student would have thrown before
him, with kaleidoscopic rapidity, the final and definite results of what

---

* This paper is here reprinted from Cecil E. Fraser, ed., *The Case Method of Instruction* (New York: McGraw-Hill Book Company, Inc., 1931).

long experience has taught to be, on the whole, the best and most expedient methods of business conduct.

This method has great advantages. Above all, it is efficient; it is also economical of the time, the energy, and the patience of instructor and student. Further, this method produces brilliant results. A student trained under it seems to possess a sureness, a precision, a firmness of grasp remarkable for the relatively short time which he is compelled to spend in acquiring his knowledge. This efficiency and success can be obtained easily and cheaply without disrupting the present educational methods. The teacher need only learn second-hand the facts of his subject. When he has cast these into some kind of pedagogical order, he is possessed of the tools of his trade capable of producing a finished product after the modes of an approved technique.

The other method starts with an entirely different purpose and ends with an entirely different result. It does not assume, in the first place, that education consists of imparting a brief recapitulation of human experience; it does assume, however, that education must afford the training to enable the individual to meet in action the problems arising out of new situations of an ever-changing environment. Education, accordingly, would consist of acquiring facility to act in the presence of new experience. It asks not how a man may be trained to know, but how a man may be trained to act. It is concerned with precedents only so far as they lead to initiatives. It deals with the oncoming new in human experience rather than with the departing old.

Human thinking and the new in human experience are indissolubly bound together. The essential characteristic of all modes of thinking is that in the process somehow something new is introduced. Whether we examine thinking from the point of view of psychology or from the point of view of theory of knowledge, the conclusion is inevitable that where thinking occurs there is an element of newness involved and without this element of newness there is no thinking. If this is correct, then the accumulation of human experience is inevitably the taking of what is given rather than the creation of what is new. If we teach people to deal with the new in experience, we teach them to think. In fact, power to deal with the new and power to think are pragmatically the same, even though logically the two expressions may not have the same connotation.

As an ideal of educational method teaching people to think has none of the conspicuous advantages of teaching accepted truths. As a method it is crude and clumsy in execution; it is inefficient, in that no scale of accomplishment can be established and empirically applied; it lacks the technical excellence ordinarily associated with good teaching and the finished art of the pedagogues. Nevertheless, the use of cases as the basis of teaching presumes a confidence in the second of these educational theories, and, if the fullest opportunities of case instruction are realized, the whole method becomes nothing but the practical application of the theory that the power of thinking and not the acquisition of facts is the ultimate of our educational ideals.

Progress in organizing and reducing human actions to law and order must be judged according to different standards than progress in the natural sciences. Within the precincts of the natural sciences, so-called facts are subject to empirical tests—the more complete and more universal these tests, the nearer they are presumed to approach the truth. Likewise, in the sphere of religion, tradition prescribes certain ostensibly permanent answers to the question of Pontius Pilate. But when one attempts to reach fixed and certain facts, not to say truths, underlying human actions, one is confronted with an intricate and disordered heteronomy of happenings apparently devoid of order or causal relation. The situation is at its worst—or, perhaps, most complex—stage when we attempt to discover order and scientific precision among the events of social economics.

Some fifteen or twenty years ago a president of the American Philosophical Association, in his annual address, selected a modern corporate security as the most complex fact of our contemporary human consciousness. If not the most complex, it is at least so complex that a science of finance is now very, very far distant from the ideal of certainty and predictability associated with the natural sciences. It is, at best, no further along than Thales trying to deduce order out of the movements of the heavenly bodies without any conception of celestial mechanics. Such is the predicament of the social scientist; such is the problem of the discovery of truth underlying human action. And, in his narrower field, such is the task of the teacher of finance who would lead his students to think through the variety and multiplicity of financial happenings and discover probabilities that are likely to occur at best three times out of five.

Cases should be used with the clear consciousness that the purpose of business education is not to teach truths—leaving aside for a moment a discussion of whether there are or are not such things as truths—but to teach men to think in the presence of new situations. There should not be a single problem in use which is not capable of at least two intelligent solutions, and it would be surprising if any group of experienced businessmen could offer an unequivocal solution with unanimous accord to any one of them. They do, however, have this outstanding value. They are analogues of exactly the kind of problem that is confronting the businessman at the present time. How surely he is able to think through to some intelligent solution will determine the extent of his individual success and his contribution to the economic prosperity of the country. Neither rests on a command of established precedents or on the uncritical allegiance to the experience of others.

Teaching by the case method is class discussion of possibilities, probabilities, and expedients—the possibilities of the combinations of very intricate facts, the probabilities of human reactions, and the expedients most likely to bring about the responses in others that lead to a definite end. Such discussion rests on the nice balancing of probable results; and in this balancing a teacher has little to contribute except a broader appreciation of the springs of human action than his pupils are likely to have developed and perhaps a greater knowledge of economic theory and its applications to contemporary business. This economic theory should have been wrought out of American industrial conditions and not represent merely re-echoes of an economic theory based on the agricultural England of the middle nineteenth century. In any event, all a teacher can hope to do is to develop, first, an appreciation of the almost infinite complexity of modern business problems, second, the hopelessness of reaching a definite and unequivocal solution, and, third—like the Hegelian trichotomy—the solution of this dilemma by some carefully reasoned but, in the end, common-sense line of action. Knotty business problems are usually best met by the simplest and most aggressive response and the one covering the longest range of time. Impatience of results is a deadly sin of business as well as of the teaching of business.

It is interesting sometimes to reflect on the reasons that lie at the foundation of the marvelous success of America in the field of economic achievement. Like the Tyrians of old, we have erected a civilization on the successful working-out of problems in connection with the mastery of our material environment; and in acquiring this mastery we have devised new methods, constructed new tools, and created for ourselves a new social order. At the basis of these achievements lies the distinctive power of the Puritan fathers, of the western pioneers, and of the modern business executives to grapple with new problems with courage and poised minds and without dependence on the guides of precedent and tradition.

Throughout the ages, man has been forced to meet the conditions of his ever-changing social environment and to resort to increasingly intricate modes of thought. The hierarchy of complex changes which passes under the name of civilization has given to the individual at once a simpler natural environment and a more complex social environment. More and more he has gained control over natural law, and more and more social law has gained control over him. This increasingly complex social environment, into which the young businessman is thrown, requires resourcefulness, mental courage, confidence in the untried—in short, exactly those qualities which in the space of three centuries brought into existence a new nation and a new economic order. πάντα ρεῖ, and the ideal of our business education ought to be to teach young men to meet the oncoming flow of things with the courageousness and resourcefulness of their forefathers.

*Writing some ten years after Professor Dewing, Charles I. Gragg,
who had sat in Professor Dewing's classroom as a student, contributed what is today generally regarded as the classic exposition* of
the relationship which the case method requires of teachers and students.
His emphasis on the active participation of the student in the educational
process sets the criterion by which the genuine case method can be distinguished from the spurious.*

Because Wisdom Can't Be Told   CHARLES I. GRAGG

So he had grown rich at last, and thought to transmit to his only son all the
cut-and-dried experience which he himself had purchased at the price of his
lost illusions; a noble last illusion of age. . . . —BALZAC

It can be said flatly that the mere act of listening to wise statements and
sound advice does little for anyone. In the process of learning, the
learner's dynamic cooperation is required. Such cooperation from
students does not arise automatically, however. It has to be provided
for and continually encouraged.

Thus, the key to an understanding of the Business School case plan
of teaching is to be found in the fact that this plan dignifies and dram-
atizes student life by opening the way for students to make positive
contributions to thought and, by so doing, to prepare themselves for
action. Indeed, independent, constructive thinking on the part of students is essential to the sound operation of the plan. This result is
achieved in two ways.

In the first place, students are provided with materials which make
it possible for them to think purposefully. For the benefit of those unfamiliar with Business School cases, it is merely necessary to explain that,
as now used, a case typically is a record of a business issue which
actually has been faced by business executives, together with surrounding facts, opinions, and prejudices upon which executive decisions had
to depend. These real and particularized cases are presented to students for considered analysis, open discussion, and final decision as to
the type of action which should be taken. Day by day the number of
individual business situations thus brought before the students grows
and forms a backlog for observing coherent patterns and drawing out
general principles. In other words, students are not given general
theories or hypotheses to criticize. Rather, they are given specific facts,

*This paper was first published in the *Harvard Alumni Bulletin* for Oct. 19, 1940,
and is here reprinted, in slightly condensed form, by permission of the author and
the editor of the *Bulletin*.

the raw materials, out of which decisions have to be reached in life and from which they can realistically and usefully draw conclusions. This opportunity for students to make significant contributions is enhanced by the very nature of business management. Business management is not a technical but a human matter. It turns upon an understanding of how people—producers, bankers, investors, sellers, consumers—will respond to specific business actions, and the behavior of such groups always is changing, rapidly or slowly. Students, consequently, being people, and also being in the very stream of sociological trends, are in a particularly good position to anticipate and interpret popular reactions.

In the second place, the desired result of student participation is achieved by the opening of free channels of communication between students and students, and between students and teachers. The confidence the student can be given under the case system that he can, and is expected to, make contributions to the understanding of the group is a powerful encouragement to effort. The corollary fact that all members of the group are in the same situation provides the student with exercise in receiving as well as in giving out ideas. In short, true intercommunication is established.

In these facts lies the answer to the unique values of the case system, and from these facts also arise certain difficulties encountered in its use. It is not easy for students to accept the challenge of responsible activity in the face of realistic situations. Nor is it always easy for teachers to preserve the needed open-mindedness toward their students' contribution. Nevertheless, the very existence of the assumption, implicit in the case system, that students are in a position to and will exert themselves to think with a lively independence toward a useful end in itself provides a real stimulus. By the same token, the stage is so set as to simplify the teacher's task of encouraging students to participate actively in the process of learning. The students are given the raw materials and are expected to use them. The teacher, for his part, has every opportunity and reason to demonstrate an encouraging receptivity as well as to inform and guide.

Thinking out original answers to new problems or giving new interpretations to old problems is assumed in much undergraduate instruction to be an adult function and, as such, one properly denied to students. The task of the student commonly is taken to be one chiefly of familiarizing himself with accepted thoughts and accepted techniques, these to be actively used at some later time. The instruction period, in other words, often is regarded both by students and by teachers as a time for absorption.

Thus many students entering graduate schools have become habituated to the role of the receiver. The time inevitably arrives, however, when young people must engage in practical action on their own responsibility. Students at professional school have a little time, at the [Harvard] Graduate School of Business [Administration] two years, to achieve the transition from what may be described as a childlike dependence on parents and teachers to a state of what may be called dependable self-reliance.

If the hearts of the young men entering a graduate school of business administration could be clearly read, it is likely there would be found in many a cherished hope that upon graduation they would find positions of authority and power awaiting them. This is a carefully guarded hope, because for some reason there is a general feeling that it is an unseemly one for young men to harbor. Yet, although the students who possess this hope may be said to be unrealistic under conditions as they exist, they cannot be said to be other than logical. For if a young man more or less permanently is to occupy a humble position in the business hierarchy, he can make better use of two years of his time than spending it at a school of business administration. The apprentice system is open to the young man who wishes to enter business in a fuller way than it is to the young man who seeks to work in the field of law or of medicine, for example. Except in a few instances, such as the plumbing and electrical trades, there are no restrictions similar to those imposed by bar or medical examinations as to who can start in business. And, if a young man who is to spend his life as a salesman, floorwalker, clerk, or minor official has several years to devote to acquiring background, he is likely to find that study of sonnets, or operas, or fishing, or philosophy will be more sustaining to his soul than a broad knowledge of business operations.

The work of a graduate school of business consequently must be aimed at fitting students for administrative positions of importance. The qualities needed by businessmen in such positions are ability to see vividly the potential meanings and relationships of facts, both those facts having to do with persons and those having to do with things, capacity to make sound judgments on the basis of these perceptions, and skill in communicating their judgments to others so as to produce the desired results in the field of action. Business education, then, must be directed to developing in students these qualities of understanding, judgment, and communication leading to action.

Furthermore, since young men who contemplate entering a graduate business school customarily have an alternative opportunity to enter business immediately, the business school must be able to do more for its students than could be accomplished in a corresponding period of actual business experience. Formal professional education necessarily postpones the time of responsible action. Yet a principal object of professional education is to accelerate the student's ability to act in mature fashion under conditions of responsibility. A young man who completes a professional course is expected to demonstrate a more mature judgment, or to demonstrate mature judgment at an earlier period, than the young man who enters upon a career of action without benefit of formal training. The presumption in this situation obviously must be that it is possible to arrange programs of training in such a way as to do more than offset the effect of prolonging the student's period of ostensible immaturity.

It would be easy to accept the unanalyzed assumption that by passing on, by lectures and readings, to young men of intelligence the accumulated experience and wisdom of those who have made business their study, the desired results could be achieved. Surely, if more or less carefully selected young men were to begin their business careers with the advantage of having been provided with information and general principles which it has taken others a lifetime to acquire and develop, they might be expected to have a decided head start over their less informed contemporaries.

This assumption, however, rests on another, decidedly questionable one: namely, the assumption that it is possible by a simple process of telling to pass on knowledge in a useful form. This is the great delusion of the ages. If the learning process is to be effective, something dynamic must take place in the learner. The truth of this statement becomes more and more apparent as the learner approaches the inevitable time when he must go into action.

We are all familiar with the popular belief that it is possible to learn how to act wisely only by experience—in the school of hard knocks. But everyone knows that, from a practical point of view, strict adherence to the literal meaning of this belief would have a decidedly limiting effect upon the extent of our learning. Time is all against it. So we all try to tell others what we know or what we think we know. A great part of our educational system, perhaps necessarily, rests on this basis. It is the simple, obvious way of passing the torch of culture from hand to hand.

Entirely aside from the seemingly sound logic of this course, there exists a natural and strong tendency for people to tell others what is what—how to think, or feel, or act. Often this tendency seems, to the one having it, like an urge to duty. A friend of ours, for example, may remark that he is worried because he doesn't seem to be getting anywhere with the president of the company. "He doesn't seem to know I'm around," our friend explains. Ah ha! We know the answer to that one and will tell our friend how to solve his problem. "Look here, old boy, the trouble with you is you are too shy. Just speak up, loudly and firmly. Tell him what's what. The old buzzard won't ignore you then!"

It is possible that our desire to pass on our knowledge springs in part from the fact that such activity places us, for the time being, in the superior position. From our earliest beginnings there have been people around to tell *us* what to do, to pass on to us their experience and wisdom. There is no little gratification in turning the tables. For a while we will be the parents and someone else can be the child. It is only necessary to listen to a six-year-old lecturing a three-year-old to see vividly the strength of this urge.

Teachers, since it is their avowed objective to extend the knowledge boundaries of others, are particularly beset by the temptation to tell what they know—to point out right paths of thought and action. The areas in which their help is called for are ones they have penetrated many times. They have reflected, presumably, upon their subjects from all angles. They feel that they know the answers and, with unselfish abandon, they are willing to tell all. Their students thus will be saved all the time and effort it would have taken them to work things out for themselves, even granted they ever could work out such excellent answers.

Yet no amount of information, whether of theory or fact, in itself improves insight and judgment or increases ability to act wisely under conditions of responsibility. The same statistical tables covering all aspects of a business may be available to every officer of the organization. Nevertheless, it does not follow that it makes no difference to the business which officer makes the decisions. Likewise, the whole body of generally accepted business theory may be equally familiar to all executives, yet the decisions reached by the various individuals are unlikely to be the same or to have equal merit.

We cannot effectively use the insight and knowledge of others; it must be our own knowledge and insight that we use. If our friend, acting solely on our advice, undertakes to tell the president what is what, the chances are he will make himself conspicuous but not impressive. For him to use our words effectively, granted our diagnosis of the situation is sound, they must become his own through a process of active thought and feeling on his part. Then, if he agrees with us, he will be able to act as we suggest, not on our advice, but from his own heart. The outstanding virtue of the case system is that it is suited to inspiring activity, under realistic conditions, on the part of the students; it takes them out of the role of passive absorbers and makes them partners in the joint processes of learning and of furthering learning.

The case plan of instruction may be described as democratic in distinction to the telling method, which is in effect dictatorial or patriarchal. With the case method, all members of the academic group, teacher *and* students, are in possession of the same basic materials in the light of which analyses are to be made and decisions arrived at. Each, therefore, has an identical opportunity to make a contribution to the body of principles governing business practice and policy. Business is not, at least not yet, an exact science. There is no single, demonstrably right answer to a business problem. For the student or businessman it cannot be a matter of peeking in the back of a book to see if he has arrived at the right solution. In every business situation, there is always a reasonable possibility that the best answer has not yet been found—even by teachers.

Exercise of mature judgment obviously is inconsistent with a program of blindly carrying out someone else's instructions. Moreover, no matter how worthy those instructions may be, they cannot cover every exigency. Tommy's mother says: "On your way home from school never cross the street until the policeman tells you to and, when he does tell you to, run." Perhaps one day no policeman is there. Is Tommy to wait forever? Or, perhaps a driver fails to observe the policeman's signals. Is Tommy to dash under the speeding wheels?

So far as responsible activity in the business world is concerned, it is clear that a fund of ready-made answers can be of little avail. Each situation is a new situation, requiring imaginative understanding as a prelude to sound judgment and action. The following sad limerick, aimed at describing what might happen to business students without benefit of cases, has been contributed by a friend who prefers to remain anonymous.

> A student of business with tact
> Absorbed many answers he lacked.
>   But acquiring a job,
>   He said with a sob,
> "How *does* one fit answer to fact?"

A significant aspect of democracy in the classroom is that it provides a new axis for personal relationships. No longer is the situation that of the teacher on the one hand and a body of students on the other. The students find their attention transferred from the teacher to each other. It is not a question of dealing more or less *en masse* with an elder; it is

a question of dealing with a rather large number of equals and contemporaries whose criticisms must be faced and whose contributions
need to be comprehended and used. Everyone is on a par and everyone is in competition. The basis is provided for strong give and take
both inside and outside the classroom. The valuable art of exchanging
ideas is cultivated, with the object of building up some mutually satisfactory and superior notion. Such an exchange stimulates thought,
provides a lesson in how to learn from others, and also gives experience in effective transmission of one's own ideas.

Under the case system, the instructor's role is to assign the cases for
discussion, to act as a responsible member of the group delegated to
provoke argumentative thinking, to guide discussion by his own contributions and questions toward points of major importance, and, if he
chooses, to take a final position on the viewpoints which have been
threshed out before him. The more powerful are the student arguments, the heavier is the burden on the instructor; he must understand and evaluate each contribution, many of which are new to him,
regardless of how thoroughly he has studied the cases or how many
times he has used them with previous classes. To the instructor, every
class meeting is a new problem and a new opportunity both to learn
and to help others to learn. The important question under these circumstances is not whether the student pleases the instructor but
whether he can either support his views against the counterattacks and
disagreements of others in the group or, failing to do so, can accept
cooperatively the merits of his antagonists' reasoning.

For both teachers and students, the disciplines of the case method of
learning are severe. Sometimes the shock is devastating to young men
who previously have been dominated by patriarchal instructors and
thus have been faced merely with the relatively simple task of more or
less passive reception and verbatim repetition of facts and ideas. Not
all students can bear the strain of thinking actively, of making independent judgments which may be challenged vigorously by their contemporaries. Many people will always prefer to have answers handed
to them. Teachers, for their part, particularly those unused to the system, sometimes find it straining to leave the safe haven of dogmatism
and meet their students on a democratic plane. The inherently dramatic and challenging character of the case system, however, although
it may produce anxiety and confusion for the newcomer, also arouses
his deep interest and leads him to make the effort required for
adjustment.

In making the adjustment to the democratic disciplines of the case
system, students typically pass through at least three objectively dis-

cernible phases. The first phase is that of discovering the inability of the individual to think of everything that his fellow students can think of. In many instances, to be sure, the challenge to original thought is pleasing from the first. Yet perhaps more often confusion and a feeling of helplessness set in: "But it's so discouraging to prepare a case as well as I can and then listen for an hour in class to other students bringing out all sorts of interpretations and arguments that I had never thought of."

The second phase is that of accepting easily and naturally the need for cooperative help. During the last half of the first year and the first half of the second year, students learn to draw more and more fully upon each other's ideas in the working out of problems. Competition for high academic standing grows more keen, to be sure, but the mutual giving and taking of assistance ceases to be a matter of secret anguish. The young men are making common cause and thereby learning the pleasure of group pooling of intellectual efforts.

The third and final phase in the march toward maturity usually comes well on in the second year with the recognition that the instructors do not always or necessarily know the "best" answers and, even when they do seem to know them, that each student is free to present and hold to his own views. When this phase is reached, the student is ready to make independent progress and to break new ground on his own account. He is operating as a responsible member of the community, taking help, to be sure, from both contemporaries and elders, but making his own decisions without fear of disapproval or search for an authoritative crutch to lean upon. An outstanding effect of the case system, in other words, is to put upon students the burden of independent thinking.

No method is foolproof. A badly handled case system cannot but be an academic horror. Improperly handled, a case is merely an elaborate means for confusing and boring students. If, moreover, the teacher insists on being a patriarch—if he is sure he has the right and only answers and visualizes his task as one of forcing the students, the case facts, and *his* answers into an affectionate rapport—it will be found that the out-and-out lecture system is infinitely less costly and less straining to everyone concerned. Such authoritarian use of cases perverts the unique characteristics of the system. The opportunity which this system provides the students of reaching responsible judgments on the basis of an original analysis of the facts is sacrificed.

In addition to the possibility that the case system will be misused, and so become merely a wasteful way of telling the students what the teacher thinks, it must be recognized that the case does not provide a perfect replica of a business situation. In the properly conducted class using business cases, the students are put in the position of the executives who must arrive at definite conclusions to be followed by specific actions whose merits will be tested by resulting developments. Yet there is no escaping the fact that the students' decisions are not tested in this way. As Winston Churchill is reported to have remarked on one occasion, there is a great deal of difference between being responsible for an order which may lose several valuable ships and expressing an opinion without such responsibility. It is too much to expect that anything except experience can be exactly like experience.

Nevertheless, a training period which allows students this relative irresponsibility has great advantages. The serious student gets the essential background for responsible decisions without the risks to himself and to his firm which are inseparable from amateurish action. He is led to active consideration of a tremendous number of diverse and related real situations, which it would take him at least a lifetime of experience to encounter, and he is thus given a basis for comparison and analysis when he enters upon his career of business action.

The case system, properly used, initiates students into the ways of independent thought and responsible judgment. It confronts them with situations which are not hypothetical but real. It places them in the active role, open to criticism from all sides. It puts the burden of understanding and judgment upon them. It provides them the occasion to deal constructively with their contemporaries and their elders. And, at least in the area of business, it gives them the stimulating opportunity to make contributions to learning. In short, the student, if he wishes, can act as an adult member of a democratic community.

As for the teacher, the case method of instruction provides him richly with the basic means of research. Not only does the existence of a stream of recorded business experiences enable him to keep in touch with business life and to make continuous necessary modifications in his inductions and general conclusions. In addition, the relations which the case system sets up between himself and his students give the teacher the continual benefit of fresh, imaginative points of view which always hold the possibility of true advance.

Some observers have looked on the case method as merely an extension of the doctrines of progressive education, an application of the pragmatic approach, an opportunity for self-expression. It is not to be denied that there are points of analogy, in the emphasis on learning rather than teaching, in the responsibility placed on the individual to do his own thinking, in the recognition that there may be more than one answer to a situation. But a case teacher who looked only at these surface similarities and concluded that he need assume no responsibility after turning a class loose on a case would be decidedly out of step with the thinking of most members of the Harvard Business School Faculty. An expression of this thinking appears in the following paper by Malcolm P. McNair.

Tough-Mindedness and the Case Method

MALCOLM P. MCNAIR

William James, a great teacher of philosophy at Harvard during the early years of this century, made the useful distinction between people who are "tough-minded" and people who are "tender-minded." These terms have nothing to do with levels of ethical conduct; the "toughness" referred to is toughness of the intellectual apparatus, toughness of the spirit, not toughness of the heart. Essentially it is the attitude and the qualities and the training that enable one to seize on facts and make those facts a basis for intelligent, courageous action. The tough-minded have a zest for tackling hard problems. They dare to grapple with the unfamiliar and wrest useful truth from stubborn new facts. They are not dismayed by change, for they know that change at an accelerated tempo is the pattern of living, the only pattern on which successful action can be based. Above all, the tough-minded do not wall themselves in with comfortable illusions. They do not rely on the easy precepts of tradition or on mere conformity to regulations. They know that the answers are not in the book.

There never was a time when this quality of tough-mindedness was more needed. We are in a new and strange kind of war. Just because the shooting war is no longer on the front pages, we shouldn't delude ourselves. The cold war is a real war. And we have been losing it, in Korea, in Indo-China, in the Middle East, in Africa, in South America, in the NATO countries. It would be tender-minded to assume that there is any possibility of peaceful cooperation with the

* This paper is adapted from an address given on Feb. 25, 1953, at the first meeting of the executives registered for the 23d Advanced Management Program at the Harvard Business School.

Soviet state as presently constituted. To quote Charles Malik,[1] the Lebanese Envoy to the United States:

> Obviously I cannot get along with one whose whole being not only contradicts mine, but is bent on destroying mine. Therefore when anybody in the West says or has said simply "We can get along with Communism," then one of four propositions is true: (1) either he is a Communist himself; (2) or he is an appeaser; (3) or he does not know what he is talking about; namely, he does not know the nature of the thing with which he can get along; (4) or—and this is the most grievous thing—he does not know the supreme values of his own heritage which Communism has radically rebelled against and desires to extirpate.

Why is it, to paraphrase an observer's interpretation[2] of statements made by General Eisenhower in early 1951, that we of the Western world, who have 90 per cent of the world's skilled, literate, educated manpower and whose institutions and governments are dominated by free men, nevertheless find ourselves in the worst crisis of our history, divided among ourselves, wrangling in confusion, and visibly having lost the power of initiative to our enemies?

Is there a connection between this situation and the fact that an increasing number of the plain people of America are entertaining growing doubts about the character of education in our colleges and are wondering why it seems to be true that college graduates are more likely to prove to be traitors to their country than are ordinary day laborers? I suspect that there is such a connection. Admittedly many of the people who entertain these doubts are not in a good position to know what they are talking about, and it is equally true that demagogues have not scrupled to make political capital by inflaming this popular distrust on the basis of the irresponsible bahavior of a very small minority of college faculty members. Naturally, when such attacks are loosed on the academic citadel, a host of zealous defenders of intellectual freedom dash to the ramparts, and the din of battle becomes almost deafening.

But in the clamor of charge and countercharge, not much is being done to allay the growing feeling of uneasiness that all is not well with college teaching. The indictment lies mainly against the teaching of the social sciences. In contrast to the brilliant achievements of natural science and the deep satisfactions evoked by the study of the humanities, the study of the social sciences seems to produce neither leaders

---

[1] Quoted by permission of *The Christian Century* from the issue of Jan. 17, 1951.
[2] *Intelligence Digest* (Kenneth de Courcy, ed.), Vol. 13, Chap. 4, March, 1951.

nor understanding; worse, it seems to lead altogether too often to an abdication of moral responsibility.

What is the matter with education in the social sciences? I do not profess to be much of an educational philosopher, but it seems to me that some of our difficulties stem from the fact that too many of us in education have forgotten all about William James's admonition to practice tough-mindedness. At the same time too many of us have followed too slavishly another doctrine of James and, more particularly, of his disciple John Dewey, namely, the doctrine of pragmatism and relativism. Largely in our lifetime, we have witnessed the triumphant spread throughout the field of education of this doctrine of pragmatism and relativism, the notion that knowledge is primarily instrumental, that there is no absolute truth, that each person must carve out his own philosophy for himself. This kind of doctrine applied to education, unless the application is thoroughly tough-minded, leads all too often to eclecticism and neutrality on moral principles. Too many colleges and college faculties today fail to be leaders in the great moral struggle of our time. Too often they are neutrals and even take pride in being neutrals, because this is the position which the pragmatic philosophy has made fashionable over the past half century.

Thus it is that all the colleges and universities of this country have traveled a very long way indeed from the injunction laid on Harvard by the Massachusetts General Court in the year 1827:

The president, professors and tutors of the university at Cambridge . . . shall exert their best endeavors to impress on the minds of children and youth committed to their care and instruction the principles of piety and justice and a sacred regard for truth, love of their country, humanity and universal benevolence, sobriety, industry and frugality . . . and those other virtues which are the ornament of human society and the basis upon which a republican constitution is founded; and they shall endeavor to lead their pupils, as their ages and capacities will admit, into a clear understanding of the tendency of the above mentioned virtues to preserve and perfect a republican constitution and secure the blessings of liberty as well as to promote their future happiness, and also to point out to them the evil tendency of the opposite vices.[1]

I venture to say that this failure of higher education today on the moral and spiritual side is one of our greatest handicaps, one of the sources of our greatest weakness in the struggle in which we are engaged, because the average college graduate comes out confused and

[1] An Act to Provide for the Instruction for Youth, Commonwealth of Massachusetts, *General Laws*, Tercentenary ed., Chap. 71, Sec. 30, p. 861.

skeptical, not to say cynical. His view is that you take your choice; pragmatism rules supreme; knowledge is something that you use; so long as you know how to milk the cow, that is all that is necessary; there are no moral truths in the social sciences.

It is true that the great minds from whose writings and teachings this pragmatic liberal tradition in education has developed were themselves for the most part well aware of moral values. They assumed that freedom of inquiry would lead every person to discover those moral values for himself. But I think perhaps they did not emphasize sufficiently the degree of tough-mindedness required on the part of both instructors and students if freedom of inquiry was to produce these results.

Personally, I challenge the point of view that there are no truths in the social sciences. I am certain that there is a hard core of truth in respect to man in his relation to God and in his relation to his fellow men. There are truths there which underlie the whole development of Western civilization. They are truths that have been discovered not only by Christianity but by Judaism, by the great moral philosophers of Greece and Rome, and by the great philosophies of the Orient as well. The truths are there. We don't teach them any more.

Even in the political sphere there is a hard core of truth with respect to those institutions and arrangements which best implement the dignity of man, the moral position of man in the universe. You can find those political truths most eloquently stated in such documents as *The Federalist Papers* and other annals of this great American experiment, which, incidentally, the liberal tradition in education has made it fashionable in recent years to sneer at and deride as flag waving. And therefore, as Dr. Malik says, we of the West no longer know the supreme values of our own heritage.

How do we get education in the social sciences back on the track? At an earlier stage in our country's history the line of distinction between teachers and preachers was almost nonexistent, and no doubt the worthies of the Massachusetts General Court in laying their admonitions on the Harvard College of the 19th century assumed that the ends they desired could be accomplished by the preaching of moral truths. Today we know that this kind of education is not effective. Professor Gragg in his eloquent essay "Because Wisdom Can't Be Told" epitomizes the problem when he says flatly that the mere act of listening to wise statements and sound advice does little for anyone. In repudiating preaching as an educational method, however, it is not necessary to go all the way to the other extreme, as too many teachers of social science seemingly have done. A significant middle ground is that taken by Ralph Barton Perry in his book *The Citizen Decides*,[1] from which I should like to quote to you the following excerpts:

The extent to which the teachers of social science prepare their students for citizenship is . . . limited by their self-imposed code. As in other subjects, such as philosophy and literature, in which it is likewise respectable to entertain different opinions, teachers hesitate to teach their students how to choose among them, and hesitate themselves to choose.

But thought is applied to action through *decision*. Giving students ideas without enabling them to draw conclusions is like giving them sharpened tools without teaching them what to do with them. There are many fields of inquiry in which it is impossible to reach exact and certain results. As a matter of fact, it is impossible to reach exact or certain results in most of the important affairs of life. . . .

.   .   .   .   .

I am suggesting three things. First, that our minds are meant to guide our action. Second, that our minds cannot guide our action unless we make them up. And third, I am suggesting that we are obliged to make up our minds on many fundamental matters, including politics, as best we can, without conclusive evidence of a sort which the question theoretically requires.

What should the teacher try to do about it? I suggest that there is what might be called an "art of decision"—an act of commitment following an interval of non-commitment. The teacher should help his student to learn this art. First, he should practice it himself. The teacher who makes no decisions is evading the hardest part of the task. It is comparatively easy to raise doubts, to point out the ignorance and conflicting evidence that beset the mind on every side. It is well to do this—an honest and trained mind will do it. I would not abolish or disparage the critical part of teaching. But doubt should be regarded as the prelude to belief; or, as we say, criticism should be constructive, and not merely destructive. If beliefs are demolished, they should be built again, or others built in their place. If this is not done, the vacuum will be filled by authority, hearsay, or superstition.

And then, having exhibited the art of decision, the teacher should help his students to reach their own decisions, to make up their own minds. This is something very different from proselytism. It is respectful of other minds; it is both scrupulous and modest. But at the same time, it is responsible. It is an attempt to assist those whose minds have been awakened to doubt, but are suffering from indecision through being ignorant of the way in which to make decisions.

By this time, no doubt you are wondering what all of this discourse on educational and moral philosophy has to do with you as business

[1] *The Citizen Decides: A Guide to Responsible Thinking in Time of Crisis* (Bloomington, Ind.: Indiana University Press, 1951). Excerpts from Chap. VI, "The Academic Community of Freedom," quoted by permission of the author and the publisher.

executives and as students here at the Business School during the next 12 weeks in this Advanced Management Program. Let me put it this way: you, as businessmen and citizens, have many important decisions to make, probably more decisions than you realize. While many of these decisions will be on what seem to be strictly business problems, you will probably be surprised to find how many of your decisions in the years to come will be on political and moral issues, either affecting the relation of your business to the community or affecting your position as a citizen.

Immediately ahead of all the businesses in this country today are many tough decisions, and some of the toughest are those that are not on strictly internal problems. Let me cite a few: There is a pressing problem squarely imposed on the business community by our national necessity to gain allies in the Western world against the threatened program of the Kremlin. We want those allies; we deem that they are necessary for our safety. But experience now amply demonstrates that we cannot buy that kind of friend by a program of foreign spending; we have got to make it possible for the NATO countries to trade with us, or else the entire NATO setup is going to fall apart. Therefore we must in particular situations impose hardships on certain domestic industries by lowering the tariff walls which presently protect them. How can these decisions be made in a way that will occasion the least dislocation of the domestic business structure and at the same time accomplish our purpose of putting a sound economic foundation under the Western world?

Or consider some more specifically domestic problems: The new Administration has taken office with a mandate to halt inflation and at the same time to preserve the economic gains of all groups. The obstacles in the way of accomplishing such a dual objective are well illustrated by the current situation, in which agricultural prices are falling and housewives at long last are beginning to get the benefit of lower retail food prices while congressmen from farm districts are protesting loudly and demanding a strengthening of the agricultural price support policy which has already led to the accumulation of unwieldy surpluses. A program of economy in government spending is projected; but seemingly the only place where any substantial cuts in expenditure can be effected is in the defense budget, and any postponement of adequate military preparedness is difficult to reconcile with the world situation today. Furthermore, even before a balanced budget has been achieved, there is great pressure on Congress to reduce taxes. Along with the program of restricted government spending, this Administration also is pursuing a hard money policy. Therefore money is getting tighter and interest rates are rising. But what will these higher interest rates do to building and industrial expansion generally?

Foremost in many minds is the challenge to business management to prevent any serious business letdown. We got past the much-feared war-end reconversion problem in 1946 without any serious recession; and we got past the minor readjustment in 1949 without any real difficulties. But suppose that, in 1954 or 1955, defense spending, investment in new plant and equipment, and the construction of new housing all slide off simultaneously. Then what? We are now at a peak, but prices are falling and government policies are pointed at contraction and mild deflation. Can other spending, particularly consumer spending, be boosted enough to prevent a serious decline in income and employment? Those considerations are squarely up to business management.

And there are many other challenges to be met by businessmen today. There is the challenge to business management to overcome the lingering social distrust of business. Evidence still exists of widespread misunderstanding and in some quarters actual hostility toward the concepts of profits and private investment. There is continuing skepticism of the operation of economic forces in free markets; and the persistent notion is still held by not a few persons that over-all planning by some superior or selected group can produce better social results than the unfettered forces of consumer choice and free endeavor. Also among the staffs of the various commissions in Washington it remains an important tenet of public policy that business bigness is dangerous and must be either broken up or tightly controlled. Thus we see frequent legislative and judicial attacks on bigness and alleged monopoly, attacks which often at bottom are really attacks on socially effective competition.

Likewise, let us not forget that business management always faces a challenge to keep abreast of new methods and advances, to take advantage of scientific developments, to bring forth new and improved products, and to work out long-run reductions in costs and prices. Particularly, business management faces a challenge to make distribution more effective and likewise to make it better understood. Many people today are disturbed by the fact that typically more than half of the consumer's dollar goes to pay for distribution costs as opposed to production costs. No doubt the appropriate question here is not whether distribution costs are too high but whether distribution is socially effective, but the challenge is nevertheless real.

All this adds up to the fact that there never was a time when skilled administration, i.e., the making of sound decisions and the effective carrying out of those decisions, both in business and in government, was more important; and that, I think, is a basic reason why your companies have sent you men here to this Advanced Management Program. Skilled administration, whether in public or in business affairs, calls for tough-mindedness. Again, I repeat that the toughness I am talking about is toughness of the intellectual apparatus. I don't mean getting tough with your competitors, or getting tough with your labor force, or even getting tough with the Communists. I mean tackling your administrative problems and tackling the larger problems of public policy in a tough-minded way that is not satisfied with easy answers.

That kind of tough-mindedness is the keynote of the training which we are trying to develop in this Advanced Management Program. You have often heard the statement that knowledge is power. Too frequently this is interpreted to mean that knowledge *confers* power. Nothing could be less true, I think, than that *passively* acquired knowledge confers any power on the recipient. This is something which many college graduates have to learn to their sorrow when they get out into the world. When we say "Knowledge is power," we mean something quite different. We mean that true knowledge consists of power, power to tackle a problem, to break it down, sort out the facts, see what must be done, and then get it done.

Now that kind of power can't be conferred; it has to be acquired; and it has to be acquired by painstaking personal effort. That is why we shall ask you to travel the hard route of the case method instead of the easy route of the textbook and lecture method. We shall expect you to dig things out for yourselves, because real education is a process of drawing out the student's mind, not of pouring in the instructor's ideas. The value lies, not in what you will dig out, but in the power that you will develop by digging. In the Business School you will find that there are no answers in the back of the book; in fact, for the most part, there isn't even any book. We shall not tell you; we shall expect you to study the case and then tell us. And then we shall question you, probing, challenging, insisting on respect for facts and likewise respect for logic and consistency. In this way we shall get you to sort out the pertinent facts, determine the matters at issue, formulate critical questions, reach answers to those questions by weighing evidence and pros and cons, and finally decide what you would do if you were the person who had to make the decision.

For this kind of education, tough-mindedness is necessary, tough-mindedness on the part of both students and instructor. It is the instructor's job to see that the men in the class settle down to a tough-minded analysis of the facts and issues, following logical paths of reasoning and judgment to appropriate decisions and conclusions. Even where the subject matter under consideration comprises the vitally important area of human relations, there is still the need to treat opinions and emotions as facts that can be subjected to the appropriate logics of human relations. Naturally, in the examination of many business situations and particularly in the examination of those situations where the reactions of people are important, it is frequently necessary for a class at the outset of the hour to blow off a certain amount of steam, that is, to give expression to those emotions and opinions which may leap to the front on the initial contact with the case material. But after that initial period of catharsis, it is incumbent both on the members of the class and on the instructor to come to grips with reality in an orderly way which leads to decision or to the equally important conclusion that in the particular situation no decision is yet possible. In other words, effective case discussion is an exercise in decision-making; and whether the issue be administrative, economic, political, or moral, the quality of tough-mindedness is a prime requisite.

Now if we, that is, you and all the Faculty together, are successful in this kind of learning, i.e., this mastery of the art of decision-making, you will not go away from here under the illusion that the Business School has provided you with any "answers," any body of specific knowledge, any set of formulae, or any ready-cut pattern of behavior that will enable you immediately to become more successful administrators. On the contrary, the principal value to you of this training at the Business School will lie in the power that you will develop to analyze a situation, to formulate a program of action, and to carry that program into effect through the people in your organization or in your community. If in this joint educational venture we are successful in making you really tough-minded, you will not be looking for the easy answers. Business problems, as you are already aware, don't lend themselves unfailingly to one simple, right method of analysis which inevitably arrives at the one and only correct answer. If knowledge of a few formulae and ability to manipulate a slide rule were enough to produce the right administrative action, then you may be sure that the demand for really good executives would not so greatly exceed the supply. Business can hire plenty of average-grade technicians who can figure the right answers to the problems that lend themselves to exact routines and procedures. But business, by and large, does not pay a very high price for that kind of ability. What business does pay a premium for, and what the business community as well as the social community vitally needs, is qualities of judgment and leadership. You will find, I am sure, that you can't develop those qualities if you are looking for the easy answers. To oversimplify the world they live in is a favorite device of the tender-minded.

Finally, if we are successful in developing and strengthening these tough-minded qualities, you won't always try to play it safe. Playing it safe is a comfortable refuge of the tender-minded. But if you are really tough-minded, you will cultivate qualities of initiative and venturesomeness. You will not be afraid to act, even if you act on imperfect knowledge, for you will realize that all knowledge is imperfect and experimental rather than final. And you will not be afraid to take chances. It is a mistake to think that the proper use of Business School training is to enable you to obtain perfect security. You can never hope to make a perfect budget of income, expense, and profit. If you think you are doing so, you are probably playing it too safe. The essence of profit in a changing world is risk and uncertainty. Your objective should be, not the *avoidance of risk*, but the *intelligent management of risk*.

Today, more than ever, it is more—not less—risk-taking that American business vitally needs. So don't aim to use your Business School training to seek a stodgy, conservative safety, because, paradoxically, when all business tries to play it safe there is no safety for any business. Professional training for business administration is successful only if it produces a goodly number of men with a genius for risk-taking and a capacity for leadership.

You heard much a few years ago to the effect that the doors of opportunity arc rapidly being closed in this country and all over the world. I want to say to you as earnestly as I can that, if there are any doors of opportunity being closed in this country, they are not doors of the environment, they are doors of the human spirit. If you are tough-minded, you will use your Business School training to open those doors, not to close them. If we can keep those doors open in America, we can eventually get them open all over the world.

It would be a mistake to assume that the case method of teaching sprang full-panoplied from the brow of any single educator. Rather it was a product of many minds. One figure, however, was in the center of the various developments out of which grew the case method of business teaching. Melvin T. Copeland, protégé of Dean Gay, close friend of A. W. Shaw, director of the Harvard Bureau of Business Research when the organized collection of cases was first begun, and active collaborator with Dean Donham in the crusade to put the Harvard Business School on a case basis, is obviously the individual best qualified to narrate the story of the case method in its early beginnings. "Doc" Copeland has told this story specifically for this volume.

The Genesis of the Case Method in Business Instruction

MELVIN T. COPELAND

In the first catalogue of the Harvard Business School, issued in the spring of 1908 preparatory to the opening of the new School in September of that year, the following statement was published:

In the courses on Commercial Law, the case-system will be used. In the other courses an analogous method, emphasizing class-room discussion in connection with lectures and frequent reports on assigned topics,—what may be called the "problem method,"—will be introduced as far as practicable.

Edwin F. Gay, the first Dean of the School, was responsible for that decision. Since at that time I was assistant to Dean Gay in his course in Economic History in Harvard College, I had frequent contacts with him, and he often told me of some of his plans for the new School. The decision to have instruction "as far as practicable" take the form of classroom discussion of specific problems was prompted by the example of the Harvard Law School. The Law School, in fact, was by far the most serious competitor which the new Business School had to face. For some years numerous college graduates had been attending the Law School to prepare for business careers. The Law School training was highly esteemed in influential business circles, and that training was effectuated by the use of the case method of instruction. Hence, Dean Gay decided that instruction in the Business School should be patterned on the method used with such conspicuous success in the Law School.

The statement that instruction was to be by classroom discussion of problems was qualified by the phrase "as far as practicable" since there was uncertainty as to whether or not "problem" teaching mate-

25

rial would be available and also as to how far members of the Faculty
would be able and willing to carry on instruction by means of classroom discussion. A dean may decide on an objective, but the objective
is attained only when members of the faculty choose to implement it.

For twelve years after the Business School was established, Commercial Law was a required first-year course, and in that course the instruction was by means of discussion of selected law cases. Those cases
were taken from published court decisions, and they were utilized in the
Business School in the same way that cases were used in the Law School.

In subjects other than Commercial Law, no case material was
immediately available for teaching, and most members of the Faculty had been accustomed to lecturing rather than to leading classroom discussion. Dean Gay, however, held doggedly to his original objective, and in 1912 two steps were taken toward its further
implementation.

A. W. Shaw of Chicago, who published *System*, a magazine for businessmen, and also business books, was at Harvard during much of
the academic year 1910–11, and in the fall of 1911 he became a Member of the Administrative Board and Lecturer on Commercial Organization in the Business School. Mr. Shaw was an imaginative man,
prolific of new ideas, and he had observed business widely. He and
Dean Gay became close friends, their friendship, in fact, continuing so
long as Dean Gay lived. Mr. Shaw was instrumental in founding the
Harvard Bureau of Business Research in 1911. Between Mr. Shaw and
Dean Gay the idea of a new course to be required of all second-year
students in the School also was hatched. That course was to deal with
top-management problems, and it aimed also at integrating subjects
which the students had studied in the first-year program. The course
was called Business Policy. Mr. Shaw undertook to head up Business
Policy and to introduce into the course some of the results of his
observation of Professor Williston's handling of cases in the Law
School and of Professor Taussig's use of the discussion method in his
advanced course in Economic Theory in the Graduate School of Arts
and Sciences. The unique feature of Business Policy was the participation of about fifteen businessmen in the instruction. In several other
courses businessmen had been brought in as outside lecturers, but in
Business Policy each businessman who participated was to present to
the class a problem from his own desk. At the first meeting with the
class, he explained his problem to the students and answered such
questions as they raised, provided the questions could be answered.
At the next meeting of the class two days later, each student handed in
a written report embodying his analysis of the problem and his recom-

mended solution. At the third meeting of the week, the businessman discussed these reports with the class. On weeks when a businessman did not come in to present a problem, Mr. Shaw lectured to the class, and his lectures were published in 1916 in *An Approach to Business Problems*.[1]

The businessmen who participated in the instruction in Business Policy varied considerably in pedagogical ability, and their problems ranged from rather nebulous propositions to concrete administrative situations. Those problems were the first real cases, outside of the law cases, used in the Harvard Business School.

Although Mr. Shaw continued to participate actively in Business Policy for only a couple of years, the course was conducted on the basis described for six years, and after the end of World War I for another period of three years. Then a series of experiments with modified methods followed until 1930, when a new program of instruction in the course was started with written cases.

The second move which Dean Gay made toward his objective in 1912 was in connection with a first-year course, then entitled Commercial Organization and two years later renamed Marketing; and I was the guinea pig for the experiment. Since older members of the Faculty were not showing much inclination to supplant lectures with classroom discussions, the Dean decided to use a young instructor for experimentation, but he bided his time for a bit before his full intention became apparent. On the Monday evening when school opened in the fall of 1912, I had dinner with Dean Gay at the Faculty Club to discuss the various chores that had been assigned to me, and he then informed me that the course in Commercial Organization was so large that it was to be divided into two sections of about fifteen students each. Paul T. Cherington, who had been an instructor in the School since its opening, was to handle one section. I was to take the other. The first class meeting was to be at 9 o'clock on Wednesday morning. That was Dean Gay's initial step.

I, of course, conferred immediately with Mr. Cherington and obtained an outline of the course and the initial list of assigned readings. About ten days later, as I was coming from a meeting of the class, I met Dean Gay on the steps of Grays Hall in the Harvard Yard, where he had his office. He asked me how things were going, and since at the moment I was feeling optimistic I told him that I had found enough to talk about so far. "Humph," was Dean Gay's rejoinder, "that isn't the question. Have you found enough to keep the students talking?"

[1] A. W. Shaw, *An Approach to Business Problems* (Cambridge, Mass.: Harvard University Press, 1916).

This query was the next step. That question of Dean Gay's epitomizes the difference between lecturing and discussion.

From that day on, I did no more lecturing in Commercial Organization or in any other course. We had no case material and, in fact, little pertinent literature. We assigned readings in a variety of publications, and I attempted to carry on discussions which centered around those readings. It was hard going for both the instructor and the students, especially the students, but they took it as good sports.

The instructor, for his part, had learned immediately what a vast difference there is between lecturing and leading a classroom discussion. A lecturer can choose what topics he is to discuss and pass over any with which he is not familiar; but when a subject is open for discussion by the students, the instructor must expect to have many questions raised to which he has no answer, and he must, therefore, be prepared to admit humbly his ignorance.

In December, 1912, a book was published which Mr. Cherington had edited, entitled *Advertising as a Business Force*.[1] A substantial part of the book consisted of selected excerpts from articles in *Printers' Ink* and various other publications. Shortly after the book came out, Dean Gay proposed to Mr. Cherington and me that we should use this book as a basis for our classroom discussions. For my part, I again went along gladly and wholeheartedly with that suggestion. Such was the start of discussion, without cases, in Marketing.

When the class was divided into two sections, Dean Gay had stipulated that both sections should take the same midyear and final examinations. That was his means of compelling teamwork in instruction. These examinations typically included problems which were embryo cases. For example, in the final examination in the spring of 1913, one of the questions was the following:

4. The records of a certain department store, kept through several years, show that of ladies' gloves, sold at the following prices, only the lines selling at prices here indicated in italics have had any appreciable sale in the store:—

$0.75	*$1.50*	$2.75
0.85	1.65	*3.00*
1.00	1.75	3.25
1.15	*2.00*	3.50
1.25	2.25	3.75
1.35	*2.50*	*4.00*

(*a*) How would the store rearrange its stock plans as a result of these figures if it were the only store of its kind in the market?

[1] Garden City, N. Y.: Doubleday, Page & Company.

(*b*) How would these changes affect the buying methods of the store?

(*c*) Would your answers be the same if there were sharp competition in the market from other stores of equal strength and size?

The use of such case questions was actively encouraged by Dean Gay.

The nominal purpose for which I had been appointed an instructor in 1912 was to start a new course in Business Statistics, and in that course I also carried on the instruction through classroom discussion based on assigned readings and special problems which came to hand. Three years later I undertook to put together a book of readings on Business Statistics to serve as a basis for classroom discussion. That book[1] was published in 1917, but before it came out I had been called to Washington to serve on the staff of the Council of National Defense; and when I returned to the School in 1919, I was assigned to other teaching and administrative tasks, so that I never had an opportunity to use that book for teaching purposes.

Although he never visualized clearly a means of obtaining adequate case material for teaching, and though he had no funds available for any such purpose, Dean Gay was responsible for the incubation of the case method at the School. Dean Gay's interest in promoting this method of instruction, however, was limited to the Business School. He continued to give courses in Economic History in Harvard College and in the Graduate School of Arts and Sciences; and in those courses he lectured. In the Business School he was the chief administrative officer, and he took only a relatively small part in the classroom instruction.

In the spring of 1913 at the completion of the first year of classroom discussion, I had the good fortune to take a trip for a few days with Dean Gay and his young son to Jaffrey, New Hampshire. That was one of the rare occasions when Dean Gay took a holiday. He was enthusiastic about the "problem" method, and we frequently talked about it. As we were waiting for the train to take us back to Boston, I screwed up my courage to suggest to Dean Gay that he should use the problem method for his own courses in Economic History. His answer was a sharp and emphatic "No." I wanted to remark that he was assuming the questionable attitude that "My business is different"—an attitude that we were frequently encountering among business executives who were not disposed to encourage academic instruction in business administration. I did not make the remark, however, as I stood greatly in awe of Professor Gay, who was a learned scholar, a

[1] Melvin T. Copeland, ed., *Business Statistics* (Cambridge, Mass.: Harvard University Press, 1917).

forceful lecturer, and a kindly person, but who nevertheless had a brusque and positive manner which did not invite argument. Dean Gay continued persistently throughout his term of office to encourage me to keep on with the use of the problem method of instruction, but he never took his own medicine.

In 1919 Professor Gay resigned as Dean of the Business School, and Wallace B. Donham was appointed to take his place. Dean Donham was a graduate of the Harvard Law School, with extensive business experience. He was an enthusiastic believer in the case method of instruction, and he too decided to use me for experimentation.

A few days after he took office, Dean Donham called me in and asked me to give up certain other plans which I had in mind and to get out a case book in Marketing. Consequently, during that year I prepared cases as best I could, dictating them to the class day by day for subsequent discussion. There was no time for field research to obtain cases and no funds to finance any assistance. I put the cases together from various sources. One source was problems which had come to our attention in the Bureau of Business Research, of which I then was director, when we were gathering data on operating costs in various retail and wholesale trades. Another batch of problems consisted of those which had come to my attention during my wartime work in Washington. Still other problems had been gleaned from newspaper items, from business publications, and from other published sources, as, for example, the Federal Trade Commission's complaint against the steel companies for the use of basing point prices and the respondents' reply thereto. A few of the cases came from personal business acquaintances.

The cases were chosen to fit into a definite plan of instruction. They followed an outline which had been formulated during my teaching experience of the preceding years. Each case was expected to develop some point or points of basic significance in marketing administration.

The book in which those cases were published[1] came out in the summer of 1920; it furnished the basis for instruction in the Marketing course for the next three years. Some of the cases were long, some were short; some had much sharper focus than others; but each case involved a situation which called for an administrative decision, and, with all their deficiencies, those cases provided a far better basis for vigorous classroom discussion than we had previously had in Marketing.

[1] Melvin T. Copeland, *Marketing Problems* (Chicago: A. W. Shaw Company, 1920).

In December, 1920, a major new step was taken in the preparation of cases for instruction in business administration and toward the use of cases in courses other than Commercial Law and Marketing. At that time, as I have stated, I was director of the Bureau of Business Research at the School, an organization which had been established under Dean Gay in 1911 at the instigation of A. W. Shaw and for ten years had been carrying on studies of operating costs in various retail and wholesale businesses. In that research work, the Bureau had demonstrated an ability to obtain specific, detailed information from business concerns. It had acquired a growing reputation for dependability, since it handled all information confidentially without revealing the sources from which the information came. Only summarized results were published. Many businessmen outside the retail and wholesale fields where the cost studies had been carried on, such as manufacturers, bankers, and others, had taken an interest in the reports of the Bureau, so that it had a considerable number of business contacts as well as a reputation for dependability.

In December, 1920, Dean Donham asked me whether I thought we could collect cases for teaching through the existing organization of the Bureau of Business Research. He stated that he had $5,000 which had been given to the School by a businessman for whatever use the Dean deemed most important, and he proposed to apply it to the collection of cases for teaching. I enthusiastically welcomed Dean Donham's proposal, and the task was taken on. Here then, as a result of Dean Donham's vision and resourcefulness, we had the first opportunity to undertake the gathering of case material on a comprehensive and systematic plan.

The first subject in which Dean Donham proposed that the collection of cases should be undertaken was Industrial Management. The senior professor in that subject was not really in sympathy with the project, but he did not attempt to dissuade the Dean, and so the new venture was launched. At the time when the Dean made his proposal, there were two young men on the staff of the Bureau—Richard Lennihan and Clinton P. Biddle—and both went to work on the task of gathering cases. Mr. Lennihan had been one of my right-hand men when I was executive secretary of the Conservation Division of the War Industries Board in 1918, and in 1919 he had joined the staff of the Bureau. Mr. Biddle had become a member of the staff after graduating from the Business School in 1920. Not long afterward, another young graduate of the School, Donald K. David, joined our staff to begin the collection of cases in Retail Store Management.

During the first six months of 1921, enough progress was made to demonstrate that case material could be assembled by research men working in the field, and Dean Donham authorized the addition to the staff of a group of first-year students for the summer period to work as field men for the gathering of cases at first hand from business. The next year we began to employ more men for that work, and these were on a full year-round basis. The task was too difficult to be mastered by students in a three-month period.

Collection of cases necessarily involved a good deal of experimentation in learning how to find leads and sources for the information sought, how to persuade businessmen to open up their experiences to us, and how to present the cases, disguised as to their sources but still true to life in their essentials.

In this research the cases sought were not the rare, exceptional situations but rather the run-of-the-mine problems. No effort was made to obtain examples of either good or bad practice but rather to present typical problems faced by business administrators in their everyday operations. Commonly those problems were ones on which there were opportunities for differences of opinion. That quality made them particularly suitable for classroom discussion.

While the field work was carried on and the cases were written by research assistants, the success attained in procuring cases for any particular course depended largely upon the interest shown and the cooperation manifested by the member of the Faculty in charge of the course. To obtain the best results, it was essential for the Faculty member to provide the research assistant with a proposed outline of topics on which he desired cases and, further, for the Faculty member to suggest the sort of situations in which he surmised that such problems had arisen and to indicate the kind of information that should be included in each projected case, information bearing directly on the issue involved as well as background data. This procedure did not, of course, prevent the research assistant from bringing in cases on situations not in the outline when he found good ones.

After the research assistant returned from a field trip, he needed further assistance from the professor in evaluating what he had found and in deciding on the most effective form of presentation. It was incumbent on the professor also to read and edit first drafts of cases, and eventually to approve them in final form. All this research guidance, in addition to the task of preparation for classroom discussion, placed a heavy load on members of the Faculty—a load far heavier than the one ordinarily involved in the preparation and delivery of lectures.

Soon after it had been demonstrated that cases could be procured successfully by field research, Dean Donham began to take steps to stimulate the interest of more members of the Faculty in case research work and in the effective use of cases in the classroom. At frequent intervals over a period of a couple of years, the Dean held luncheon conferences, attended by selected groups of Faculty members and representatives of the research organization. At those conferences the problems of collecting and using cases were discussed. Some members of the Faculty welcomed enthusiastically the innovation which the Dean was sponsoring. The attitudes of other members of the Faculty ranged all the way from lukewarmness to covert hostility.

The Dean's ardent sponsorship of the case method received persuasive support from another quarter. As more and more courses were converted from lectures to class discussion, the students showed a strong preference for the case method, and their attitude soon became apparent to the instructors. This student attitude was a major factor in accelerating the use of cases in the classroom. Hence, within a period of about four years following 1920, a high proportion of the courses in the School were transformed from lecture courses to discussion courses.

In 1908 and even in 1920 no one visualized the magnitude of the task that was involved in attaining the objective of having instruction at the Harvard Business School conducted "as far as practicable" by the discussion of problems and cases. When the experiment of having cases collected by the research organization was started in 1920, Dean Donham had $5,000 in hand. Over the next twenty years he had to solicit gifts totaling upwards of $2,000,000 for that purpose alone. His unflagging interest in the objective, however, supported him in his crusade; and once started, the work never faltered.

During the period of more than thirty years of case collection at the Harvard Business School, cases have evolved in the direction of greater complexity, greater detail, and greater coverage, as contrasted with the relatively simple and somewhat sketchy case situations which were used in teaching in the early 1920's. There are still, however, very great differences among cases with respect to length and complexity, and there is still emphatically no such thing as a "typical case." To illustrate the diversity in present-day cases and to give the reader some tangible grasp of what cases are, it seems desirable at this point to reproduce several cases, together with comments by instructors showing the way in which these cases are, or may be, used. A majority of these cases are under fictitious names.

First, Harry L. Hansen presents the case of Florida Foods, Inc., which has several times been used as the introductory case in the first-year course in Marketing. Second, Robert W. Merry offers a considerably shorter case, the Hampton Manufacturing Company, in the general area of Production, showing that it is not necessary for a case to present a great deal of detail in order to afford opportunity for discussion of important questions. Third, Malcolm P. McNair describes the handling of the Conmay Company case, a hardy perennial which has appeared in more than one course in the Business School, with emphasis on the development of close and careful reasoning by students in a narrow situation. Fourth, John Lintner shows how a business-decision case can be used to further the understanding of broad national economic problems.

Some Selected Cases, with Notes on Their Use

I. A Case in Marketing   HARRY L. HANSEN

In an elementary course in Marketing, as in other basic courses to be taught by the case method, there is a very real problem as to what kind of case is best for introductory purposes. Individual students in the course may or may not have had any previous experience with the case method. Given these circumstances, some instructors hold that the content of the initial case makes little difference, that in the first meeting the instructor and the students are groping for a relationship and the important thing is the establishment of effective rapport.

Thus it would be entirely reasonable to begin with a relatively short and simple case emphasizing the importance of the consumer, for instance a one-page transcript of a conversation between a sales clerk and a customer in a retail store. By reading and studying the remarks of the two parties to the transaction, students would be led to perceive the importance of consumer attitudes to sellers and would begin to recognize that consumer attitudes and habits are at the base of any sound marketing program.

But there is no inherent reason why the initial case should not be a fairly substantial one which will afford some insight into possible approaches to effective analysis and at the same time serve to indicate the scope of the marketing function, that is, suggest the range of problems which furnish the content of the course. For a number of years a broad case of this sort has been used at the Harvard Business School to introduce the students to Marketing. Typical is the case of Florida Foods, Inc., reproduced below.

FLORIDA FOODS, INC.

Florida Foods, Inc., was organized in the spring of 1945 by the National Research Corporation for the purpose of producing and marketing orange and other citrus fruit juices in frozen concentrate and dry powdered form. Both the frozen concentrate and the dry powder were produced by a high-vacuum process developed by the National Research Corporation during World War II and first successfully used in the manufacture of blood plasma and penicillin. During the early part of 1945, the National Research Corporation constructed a pilot plant in Florida and produced orange juice powder of exceptionally high quality by the high-vacuum process. The NRC did not, however, wish to dissipate its research energy on business problems and therefore formed Florida Foods, Inc.[1] Because the product of the pilot plant was of exceptionally high quality and the Army Quartermaster Corps had displayed great interest in the powder, Florida Foods had obtained $2,590,000 through the sale of stock. Of this sum, $1,100,000 was set aside for the purchase of equipment and for construction of a plant in Plymouth, Florida, in the heart of one of the principal orange-producing districts, and the remainder was reserved for working capital. The tract selected for the plant was adjacent to the Seaboard Airline Railway and provided adequate space for expansion. The NRC granted Florida Foods, Inc., an exclusive license to use its process for 20 years. As compensation Florida Foods agreed to pay $2\frac{1}{2}$ % of its net sales of all citrus fruit products, either frozen or dehydrated, for 20 years.

It was expected that the plant would be completed by February, 1946, about the middle of the 1946 orange-picking season, and would have a daily input capacity of 20,000 gallons of fresh juice. Plans called for approximately 100 days of input of fresh juice, the period during which high-quality fruit was customarily available. The anticipated daily output capacity of frozen

[1] The name of the company subsequently was changed to Minute Maid Corp.—ED.

concentrate, an intermediate stage in the production of dry powder, was 5,000 gallons. The planned capacity rate of production for dry powder was about 5,500 pounds. This dry powder product would require an allocation of 1,250 of the 5,000 gallons of frozen concentrate. Of the remaining 3,750 gallons of frozen concentrate it was planned to sell 2,500 gallons and store 1,250 gallons for use in the manufacture of powder after the close of the picking season. Storage space for 215,000 gallons of frozen concentrate was planned, and it was expected that the powder would ultimately be produced on a year-round basis.

Because of the nature of the production process and the planned design of the manufacturing plant, the company was placed in a position where it could undertake simultaneously the marketing of both orange juice powder and frozen concentrate. It was, of course, possible for the company to devote all its efforts to the production and sale of the frozen concentrate, since all the fresh juice had to be processed into frozen concentrate before it could be dehydrated. The executives had considered this course of action shortly after the formation of the company but had discarded the idea largely because they believed the company's principal product advantage lay in the dehydrated product. The decision to develop the market for the powdered orange juice raised a number of complicated questions for the company with regard to both its production and its distribution, as, for example: (1) Should the company restrict its production to the dehydrated powder? (2) If both products should be produced, how should the company plan to balance the outputs without sufficient knowledge of the relative volume of demand? (3) Should greater emphasis be placed on developing the distribution of the powder or of the frozen concentrate? (4) If the demand for the frozen concentrate should average more than 2,500 gallons per day, ought the company to divert its efforts from the production of powder? (5) Should the company sell both products in the same markets, i.e., institutional and consumer?

During the first season at least, the company planned to secure its fresh juice by means of a pipeline from the juicing plant of the Plymouth Citrus Growers Association, which was adjacent to the Florida Foods plant. The company had signed a contract with the Association specifying that Florida Foods was to be supplied with its requirements of Grade A juice up to a maximum of 20,000 gallons per day. The price was to be the current weekly price charged by the Association for Grade A canned juice less canning charges. The Plymouth Citrus Growers Association was the principal packer of canned orange juice sold under the Crosse & Blackwell label. The president of Florida Foods, Inc., did not believe that the price of fresh orange juice would fall below 30 cents per gallon or go above 45 cents per gallon during the 1945–46 season. Since the Association had handled over 1,000,000 boxes of oranges, equivalent to 4,500,000 gallons of juice, during the 1944–45 season, company officials believed that an adequate supply of juice was assured. Estimates obtained by the company indicated that 80% of all oranges grown in the United States were ultimately consumed as juice, that the average consumption of fresh juice for each family was 10 gallons per year, and that the average consumption of canned juice was six-tenths of a gallon per year.

The frozen concentrate could be converted into a drink similar to that produced by adding water to the powder. One gallon of orange juice for consumer consumption could be made from one quart of concentrate. The product had to be maintained in frozen form prior to reconstitution. Company officials believed that it was more nearly comparable to juice obtained from fresh fruit than any other competing concentrate. One of the company's competitors had had a highly successful experience with the sale of frozen concentrate to a drug chain, which reconstituted and sold the product at its soda fountains. Although frozen orange juice concentrate for household consumer use was offered for sale in only a few test markets, growing consumer acceptance of frozen foods convinced company executives that they might be able to sell a considerable quantity of the frozen concentrate. They also expected, however, that since the technique for producing the powder was much more difficult there might well be more immediate competition in the marketing of the frozen concentrate than in the marketing of the powder.

Although the management did not have any actual cost figures from production experience, some tentative estimates were obtained from pilot plant experiments. These experiments suggested that the company could probably produce a quantity of powder sufficient to make about 18 ounces of juice for approximately 10 cents to 12 cents. This range of manufacturing cost depended on the cost of the fresh juice, which was expected to be between 40% and 60% of the total manufacturing cost. The cost of producing sufficient frozen concentrate to make 18 ounces of juice was estimated to be about 7 cents to 9 cents.

The executives for Florida Foods understood that a number of other companies were experimenting with equipment and processes for drying citrus juices to a powder. They believed, however, that the Florida Foods process was the only practicable one in existence which used a high-vacuum method, and they were confident that this process was superior to any other process. There were, of course, a variety of powders on the market containing some proportion of dried orange juice from which orange-flavored drinks could be made; but the management did not believe that such products were potentially competitive. The principal competition to the sale of the company's products was expected to come from fresh fruit and canned juice.

The dehydrated juice in powdered form had the characteristic odor and color of fresh juice. The process of reconstituting the powder was simple, merely requiring the addition of the proper quantity of powder to cold water. Approximately 1.1 pounds of powder was sufficient to make one gallon of juice of average solid content. It was necessary, however, when mixing to add the powder to the water rather than the water to the powder in order to prevent the formation of gelatinous lumps. In addition, the powder had to be measured with some care in order to obtain a mixture of proper strength. The company had made only informal taste tests, but these seemed to warrant the general conclusion that the product compared favorably with fresh juice in taste and appearance. Occasionally, testers had reacted against the product, arguing either that it was too sweet or that it contained no pulp. Although existing methods of measuring vitamin C, the principal vitamin present in orange juice, were in general unreliable, the president of the company was confident that, in so far as could be determined, the reconstituted product retained approximately 95% of the vitamin content of the fresh juice.

Apart from the convenience characteristic of the powder, the product had a number of other advantages from the consumer point of view. An unopened can would keep indefinitely without refrigeration. If the container was opened, it would keep several weeks in a mechanical refrigerator. Spoilage did occur rather rapidly, however, if an open can was exposed to moist air. The reconstituted juice would keep as well as fresh juice stored under the same conditions.

The president and the sales manager had given some thought to plans for packaging the powder for sale in the institutional and retail markets. The company planned to use a large moistureproof can for the institutional trade, but no decision had been made with respect to a package for home consumption. One suggestion was to pack the powder in moistureproof glasses similar to those used in packing cheese spreads. The glasses would be marked in such a way as to indicate the quantity of powder which had to be used in order to make a glassful of the mixture of the proper strength. It was suggested that these glasses should be attractively decorated in order that consumers might use them regularly for serving orange juice. The company was also considering several other types and sizes of containers. One type was a single-serving package similar to those which had been used by manufacturers of powdered coffee. The powdered juice could not, however, be packed in the usual envelope-type package, because when a considerable number of such packages were placed in a box for shipment the powder tended to harden into a solid mass, making the reconstitution process difficult. The company had also given some thought to using a family-size package and a week's-serving package.

With regard to the problem of selecting a brand name, no definite decision had been reached. The company did not want to select a "trick" name, for it was desirous of establishing the product in distributors' and consumers' minds as a staple. Some difficulties had already been experienced in this respect, for in a number of conversations with prospective distributors company officials had found that the trade seemed to consider the powder a specialty item. Several names such as "Three-Second Orange Powder" and "One-Step Orange Powder" had been suggested, but none of them appealed to the management. In connection with the problem of choosing a brand name, there was some question as to what the company could legally claim for its product, e.g., was it in fact fresh orange juice? Finally, company officials were giving some thought to the selection of a name which could be used on all the company's products, as, for example, the brand name "Del Monte" which the California Packing Corporation used on its canned goods.

The president of Florida Foods, Inc., believed that retailers would have to sell the dry or frozen concentrate necessary to yield 18 ounces of reconstituted orange juice at a retail price of about 17 cents to 21 cents. As an illustration of competitive prices during the first week of December, 1945, one of the largest grocery outlets in Boston was offering No. 2 cans (approximately 18 ounces) of California juice for 20 cents, No. 2 cans of Florida juice for 19 cents, and No. 5 cans (approximately 46 ounces) of Florida juice for 45 cents. Oranges of average size retailed in Boston at this time for 45 cents a dozen; a dozen of these oranges yielded about 32 ounces, or 1 quart, of juice. The average box of oranges contained 216 oranges and produced $4\frac{1}{2}$ gallons of juice. Other data secured by the company revealed that for the years 1942 through 1945 the average cost to the United States consumer of fresh whole orange juice was 1.4123 cents per ounce.

No detailed plans had been formulated for the distribution of the company's product. The management expected to enter the institutional market first by establishing its own salesforce to call on hospitals, airlines, and hotels. Almost simultaneously, however, it hoped to enter the consumer market. The company considered selling its products through so-called normal trade channels, i.e., brokers, wholesalers, and chain and independent retailers. The management recognized that pursuit of this course meant that the company would have to undertake a substantial promotional burden. Nevertheless, the sales manager was of the opinion that the company should institute its distribution through normal channels. In order to secure any promotional effort from the various types of outlets, the company would have to offer at least the standard trade discounts for specialty grocery products. The sales manager estimated these discounts at 2% to 6% of the broker's selling price to the wholesaler, 12% to 15% of the wholesale selling price for the wholesaler, and 24% to 25% of the retail selling price for the retailer.

Florida Foods, Inc., planned to sell its products f.o.b. plant with customers paying the freight. Transportation costs for both dry powder and frozen concentrate were less than for equivalent quantities of canned juice or fresh oranges.

What should Florida Foods' marketing program be?

At this stage in the course, and with a case of such dimensions, the instructor cannot expect the students to arrive at definitive conclusions as to the marketing program which the company should adopt. Rather he will direct the emphasis to seeing what the problem areas are and to formulating some rather general ideas as to what should be done.

Early in the class period, students see that the broad question as to "marketing program" needs to be given some such rephrasing as "What marketing problems are facing the company?" In other words, "Here is a manufacturer with a new product. What does he have to do to dispose of the product?" And discussion develops the thought that there are several distinguishable (though of course interrelated) problem areas, notably, merchandising, pricing, choice of distribution channels, and promotion.

The merchandising area is concerned with the product itself and its suitability for the market. Thus consideration needs to be given to the question how the frozen concentrate and the powder compare with fresh and canned orange juice and other citrus juices in taste, pulp content, appearance, and food value. There is some evidence in the case that the powder may be difficult to measure and mix. Furthermore, the reconstituted juice has no pulp, and some consumer prejudice may exist as a result of previous experience with inferior orange juice powders. It seems doubtful that the powder can compete in quality with the fresh juice. The frozen concentrate, on the other hand, when properly reconstituted is likely to compare favorably in quality with fresh juice.

A basic merchandising question in this case concerns the relative emphasis to be placed on the powder and the concentrate. From the case, it is apparent that initially the company executives regarded the frozen concentrate as of secondary importance. They believed that they had a unique manufacturing know-how with respect to the dehydrated product. Consumers were wary of dehydrated foods, however, while they were accepting frozen foods more and more readily. Ultimately the company found the demand for its frozen concentrate so strong that it abandoned production of the powder, which had never achieved much acceptance from consumers.

From appraising the product, students logically go on to consider potential markets and to point out that possible buyers include home consumers, institutions (restaurants, hotels, drug stores, hospitals, airlines, railroads, and schools), and perhaps the export market. For the frozen concentrate, the market will be limited to purchasers who possess freezing facilities. To institutional purchasers, price will presumably be important. The export market may be a promising one for the dehydrated product.

Some consideration may appropriately be given to the approximate size of the consumer market for orange juice, with a view, of course, to reaching some conclusion on the question whether Florida Foods might reasonably hope to capture a share of this market. Statistics in the case indicated that the average family consumes 10 gallons of fresh juice and 0.6 gallon of canned juice yearly. At an average price of 1.4123 cents per fluid ounce, 35,000,000 families spend over $630,000,000 yearly for fresh juice alone. Florida Foods is currently capable of producing 5,000 gallons of frozen concentrate daily, the equivalent of 22,000 pounds of orange powder. On the assumption that the plant operates 100 days a year, the annual capacity is 2,200,000 pounds of orange juice powder. Since 1.1 pounds of powder yield 1 gallon of reconstituted juice, 2.48 ounces of powder will be required to yield 18 fluid ounces of reconstituted juice. The theoretical capacity of the plant can be worked out as follows:

2,200,000 lb. powder = 35,200,000 oz.
   35,200,000 ÷ 2.48 = 14,200,000 packages (approx.), each yielding
18 fl. oz. reconstituted juice

At retail prices ranging from 17 to 21 cents per package, the company's sales at retail need to be roughly between $2,414,000 and $2,982,000 in order to dispose of output. Although the estimate of $630,000,000 for consumer expenditures for orange juice may seem high, the figures of $2,414,000 and $2,982,000 for sales of the company's output are only 0.38% and 0.47% of the $630,000,000 total. The assumption is not unreasonable, therefore, that Florida Foods can hope to market its product to consumers.

Next a question as to type and size of package is appropriate. For institutional buyers, the package undoubtedly will need to be large in comparison with the package for consumers. For consumers, should the package contain a week's supply, three or four servings, or a single serving? What instructions need to be printed on the package to overcome difficulties in measuring and mixing?

In the area of merchandising, price is important also. On the basis of the information in the case, some estimate should be undertaken of the price at which the company can afford to sell its products. First, attention needs to be given to the trade discounts which are customary. Then it is useful to set up a schedule showing, at a series of assumed retail prices, the sales revenue which will be available to the manufacturer after deduction of the discounts customarily granted to retailers, to wholesalers, and to brokers. Various combinations of assumptions are possible as to retail price, discount schedules, and production costs. Within the compass of whatever assumptions they regard as reasonable, however, the students ought to make some rough calculations along the following lines:

If it is assumed that maximum discounts are granted to retailers, to wholesalers, and to brokers, at unit retail prices of 30, 25, 21, and 17 cents the schedule of gross margins (to cover marketing expenses, general overhead, and profit) to the producer would be as follows:

(All figures in cents per unit)

Ultimate Retail Price	Price to Brokers*	Estimated Sales Revenue after Royalty Payments	Powder		Concentrate	
			Average Cost	Gross Margin	Average Cost	Gross Margin
30	18.0	17.5	11	6.5	8	9.5
25	14.9	14.5	11	3.5	8	6.5
21	12.6	12.3	11	1.3	8	4.3
17	10.2	9.9	11	—	8	1.9

* I.e., retail price less 25%, 15%, and 6%.

Assuming production balanced as described in the case, and a 25-cent retail price, total dollar gross margins would be as follows:

Product	Approx. Unit Sales	Unit Price to Brokers	Total Dollar Sales	Gross Margin per Unit	Total Gross Margin	
					Dollars	Approx. %
Powder.......	7,100,000*	14.9¢	$1,057,900	3.5¢	$248,500	23%
Frozen Concentrate.....	7,100,000	14.9	1,057,900	6.5	461,500	44
			$2,115,800		$710,000	34

* The equivalent of 14,200,000 packages of powder is 7,100,000 packages of powder and 7,100,000 cans of frozen concentrate.

The other angle of the pricing problem, i.e., determination of what price consumers will be willing to pay for the product, involves consideration of retail prices which are customary for competing fresh and canned juices and some judgment as to the comparative merits of the several products. If the frozen concentrate when reconstituted is strictly comparable to fresh juice, it may command a slightly higher price because of the factor of convenience in preparation and storage. If the price of fresh juice to consumers averages approximately 1.4 cents per fluid ounce, enough frozen concentrate to yield 18 ounces of juice might retail at 25 to 27 cents per can. A lower price will probably be necessary if consumers show preference for fresh juice. The low sales of canned juice in relation to fresh suggest that consumer preference for fresh juice is strong enough to outweigh the lower price of the canned juice.

When it comes to pricing the powder, if the reconstituted product is regarded as inferior to fresh orange juice and to the reconstituted frozen concentrate, the competition will be with canned juice in the 17- to 20-cents-per-can range.

In this Florida Foods case, the students' specific recommendations as to price depend to some extent on the calculations and the assumptions underlying them. Obviously several different assumptions are possible, and likewise several sets of resulting figures. At this stage in the course, the value of making any computations lies principally in driving home the importance of using to as good advantage as possible whatever figures are furnished in a case.

From the discussion thus far, students may be expected to have derived an understanding of the necessity for appraising both the product and the potential market, i.e., to recognize the importance of asking such questions as the following: Is the product properly related to the market? Who is going to buy it? Why? Just what does the market want? How well does the product fit the want? What modifications ought to be made? What price will the market pay? How does that price fit the costs? What are the desired sizes? What containers or packages should be used? Should the product be branded, or unbranded?

Turning from merchandising to choice of distribution channels, and still thinking of the specific problem of this specific manufacturer, students will perceive that in setting up any marketing program they need to consider such questions as the following: Who constitute the market? Where are they? If they are ultimate consumers, at what kind of stores do they buy? How often? In what quantities? Is it advisable to market this product through more than one type of retail outlet? Should an effort be made to have the product stocked by a majority of retailers? Should the manufacturer sell to retailers direct, or through wholesalers? If the latter, what kind of wholesalers? How many? Should still other intermediaries be used, such as manufacturers' agents or brokers?

Since the students have probably agreed that the market for the company's product is both domestic and foreign and that the domestic market includes both individual consumers and institutions, then the question arises as to where the company's initial marketing emphasis should be focused. The answer depends in the first instance on the company's conclusion as to the balance of production between the powder and the frozen concentrate. The frozen concentrate, at least, seems suitable for introduction to the consumer market. The powder appears to be better suited for commercial, institutional, military, and export markets, where refrigerating facilities may be limited and light weight is important.

If the frozen concentrate is to be marketed to consumers through retail grocery stores, use of wholesalers will be necessary to secure intensive coverage. The availability of cold-storage facilities in the wholesale trade will be an important consideration. The company will probably find itself limited to distribution through wholesalers specializing in frozen foods. If this should be the case, the problem of obtaining satisfactory retail distribution may be acute, since this is a relatively new branch of the food industry. Whether Florida Foods will need brokers instead of its own salesmen to reach wholesalers depends in part on cost and in part on buying habits of wholesalers in particular markets. The company's tentative choice of brokers seems logical, for the time being at least, in view of the high initial cost of a salesforce. Florida Foods will probably want to test its products in selected markets before attempting widespread distribution. Costs may also affect this pattern.

The possibility should be considered of selling through a large distributor such as Crosse & Blackwell. The advantages of using a large established distributive organization should be weighed against the disadvantages of introducing the new product under a distributor's brand, with the attendant possibility of losing control over pricing and promotional activities. Certainly unless Florida Foods can retain control over brand names such an arrangement should be a short-term one. The company ought to keep itself free to capitalize on unusual successes.

From their discussion of channels of distribution, students will gain some idea of the different kinds of intermediaries through whom goods move into the consumer market and the functions and costs which characterize each.

It is appropriate next to consider the problem of promotion. The manufacturer has a product presumed to be right for the market, and he has selected suitable channels of distribution. Now, how can consumers be induced to buy the product? What will make the retailers promote it? Shall the manufacturer advertise? What balance shall be sought between expenditures for advertising and for personal selling? What appeals shall the company use in its advertising? Shall sampling be undertaken in grocery stores?

For this product, advertising, sampling, and higher-than-normal discounts to distributors may all be suitable. Health, convenience, and price are the appeals which come to mind first as warranting stress in consumer advertising. The media which appear to need consideration are newspapers, magazines, and radio. Sampling may be important also in inducing customers to purchase this new product. To induce retailers to promote it, liberal discounts may be desirable. Private branding as a promotional device may be open to question.

In the area of promotion, however, as in the areas considered previously, it is possible during a single class session to do little more than glance at some of the questions which face Florida Foods, Inc., in marketing its product.

Placed in the introductory position, this case serves well to suggest the enormous range and scope of the marketing function. In succeeding class sessions, narrower problems usually will be discussed and more specific recommendations for action formulated.

II. A Case in Production   ROBERT W. MERRY

Within any given field of instruction, cases ordinarily are arranged according to a discernible plan. Thus for a course in Production the outline may be constructed in terms of a series of topics, such as foundry work, forging, casting, machining, metal forming; it may be developed according to levels of management activity, such as problems of the foreman, the superintendent, the production staff, the vice president for manufacturing; it may be organized according to different industries, such as metals, wood, plastics, electronics, textiles; or it may be arranged according to types of activities, such as methods work, training, time study, wage administration, plant layout, production planning. In spite of the seeming differences in these plans of instruction, a single case may fit several of them equally well. The extent of flexibility in use is dependent only on the limits of substance of the case and the limits of its users' imagination. An illustrative case will help to demonstrate this flexibility.

HAMPTON MANUFACTURING COMPANY

As a result of a shortage of approximately 90 shaftings, Department B of the Hampton Manufacturing Company showed a low percentage of delivery promises kept. Department B was regularly supplied with shaftings by Department A, which machined them from shafting stock kept in the general stores building. To enable Department B to proceed with its orders requiring shaftings, more large shafting stock had to be purchased immediately and a premium of approximately $6,000 had to be paid for quick delivery.

An assistant to the production manager, who had been assigned to investigate the situation, had found that the foreman in charge of machining shaftings in Department A had made heavy withdrawals of shafting stock from the general stores building and had machined a large quantity of small shaftings. These were on hand in Department A, but there were no large shaftings available for forwarding to Department B. This condition had come about because the foreman of Department A had totaled the shafting requirements for several weeks ahead in order to keep his costs as low as possible and at the same time permit his men to make their normal earnings on piece rates which had been set on larger lots than were then coming through the factory. On his own initiative he had withdrawn the necessary stock and ordered the machining through in these large lots. Hence the machined shaftings available were shorter than those currently needed in Department B, and since the stock had been cut up it could not be used for the larger apparatus.

The foreman in Department B had been given a copy of the schedule and orders for the shaftings to be machined in Department A. The foreman of Department A, on the other hand, had not received copies of the schedule for Department B and had therefore assumed that Department B was following the work. Since the two departments were located at some distance from each other, in different buildings, the production chasers of Department B had not followed successfully the machining of shaftings which was being done in Department A. The production chasers were further hampered because they were not well acquainted with the personnel in Department A.

To prevent a recurrence of this situation, the assistant to the production manager who had made the investigation conferred with the foremen of the two departments concerned. Three remedial proposals were discussed at this meeting. The first was to issue orders to the foremen to manufacture strictly according to schedule so that a shortage of material would be prevented. Merely to issue these orders, however, seemed insufficient, since no check would be made on whether they were being carried out.

The second proposal was to revise piece rates and base them on smaller lots, thus removing the temptation from the foreman to maintain the normal earnings of the workers by long runs and large lots. This plan seemed inadvisable, however, both because the decline in orders for stock machines was believed to be temporary and also because considerable expense would be incurred in revising the rates.

The third proposal was to change the paper work routine so that Department A would receive copies of Department B's schedules and would assume responsibility for machining Department B's shaftings. Under this system there would be less lag in production, and the production chasers in Department A would take over the work which the Department B chasers had failed to do successfully. If the piecework earnings for the shorter runs did not meet the guaranteed day rate, Department B could be charged with the difference.

A first reading of the Hampton Manufacturing Company case reveals the initial source of difficulty. Smaller lots were coming through the plant because of depressed sales for stock machines, a condition expected to be temporary. Both the foremen mentioned were affected by this circumstance. The foreman of Department A observed the shorter runs and thought about their effect on his department in terms of increased unit costs of production and of decreased earnings for his employees. He saw a way to keep his costs low and to maintain the earnings level of his men, and he acted accordingly.

The foreman of Department B took no special action to meet the new situation. In fact, he had not been checking on the Department A schedule (as he should have done, since that schedule was provided him), nor had he been checking up on his expediters (as he should have done, in view of the changing character of production orders). The evidence available seems to indicate that, apart from being somewhat insensitive to new conditions, he was not even ordinarily competent in supervising his own men.

Clearly control over production in the plant at this time was faulty. The usual routines would have afforded control had they been followed. But, had they been followed, unit production costs in Department A would have risen and employee earnings there would have fallen. The foreman of Department A perceived the problem and took steps which he considered appropriate to meet it. Properly, a solution should have rested on a balancing of factors within the department against pertinent factors outside the department. And unless the company's foremen had been trained to consider the interrelationship of departments such balancing was the task of higher supervision. In this particular situation, however, higher supervision seems to have been unaware of the problem. It had apparently not provided any means of keeping itself informed.

As a result of the breakdown in supervision, the drop in sales of stock machines created an unforeseen abnormal situation in the plant. The actions of plant personnel to adjust to this situation delayed deliveries beyond promised dates. Such delayed deliveries were likely to lead to a still further drop in sales. The sales department might well look upon meeting delivery dates as a prime objective, and this objective probably should, in turn, become a major manufacturing goal.

None of the suggested measures appears to offer a lasting solution. To manufacture strictly according to schedule would solve none of Department A's problems and would tend to restrain the foreman from exercising initiative. Revision of piece rates strikes nearer the heart of the problem. Such a plan would remedy the immediate difficulty, but it must be borne in mind that the executives believed the current condition to be only temporary. Nevertheless, a varying piece rate by groups of lot sizes could conceivably work, although it might be somewhat cumbersome. The proposal that the foreman of Department A be given the responsibility for producing for Department B's schedule has merit in terms of the apparent capacities of the two foremen but does not provide for meeting future unusual conditions. Furthermore, any move of this sort should conform to the established practices of the company with regard to departmental relationships. The existence of a single problem affecting two specific departments is not sufficient to warrant altering an entire company program. The question whether responsibility for checking output rests with a primary department or a later department needs to be examined in the light of effects elsewhere.

Capacity to handle the unusual is one of the outstanding requirements of a good foreman. To deal with the exceptional, foremen need to know how their actions will affect the company beyond their own departments. Furthermore, to do their own jobs well even within their departments, they need to understand what their responsibilities are for meeting output schedules, holding down costs, maintaining worker satisfaction, and the like. The problem that has arisen in this situation is by no means unusual, nor is it particularly difficult. The basic weakness lies, not in any system, but in the inadequacy of the foremen. One of the foremen appears to be incompetent within his own department in the aspects that are described. The other foreman appears to be doing an excellent job internally, but to be lacking in the broader company view often necessary for the best decisions. This line of analysis leads to the conclusion that the most needed action arising out of this experience is good foreman training, aimed to develop the foremen's grasp both of the problems wholly within their departments and also of the problems that extend beyond their departments.

This analysis of the case situation suggests a wide range of opportunities for using the case in an instructional plan. The case would fit into an examination of factory problems in machining as compared with other metal working processes, into a section on foremen among levels of management activity, or into a topic on metals among different industries. In a course organized according to activities, it would fit into a section on production control.

Instead of fitting the case into a particular preconceived spot in a course, it is possible to draw from the case itself the kinds of situations inherent in it. The broadest subject inherent in the case appears to be that of *production control:* how should the production activities be planned so as to avoid a recurrence of this problem? Further examination of the case leads to recognition of the general problem of *supervision* and the need for *foreman training*. Study of the source of the difficulty described and of the effect of the actions taken directs attention to the *relationship between sales and production, between the sales department and the operating manufacturing departments*. The importance of the problem is clear because of the ultimate effect, the failure to meet promised delivery dates. The case could be used suitably, therefore, in a topic concerned with *meeting delivery promises*. Such a topic might be a part of a larger section on *manufacturing objectives*. Penetrative thinking about the nature of the *allocation of cost* could even be obtained through discussion of where to charge the $6,000 premium and whether to charge Department B with any deficiency encountered by Department A if piecework earnings fall short of the guaranteed day rate.

The case presented here is fairly simple, quite brief, and easily understood. Yet it offers the wide variety of uses indicated above. Many cases will present a far greater choice of use than this one. The imaginative capacity of the instructor may suggest a large number of possibilities. Yet in every instance the case will teach largely whatever is in it. Discussion will range over most of the considerations inherent in the case, for the student learns about each topic always amidst many other related considerations. But the emphasis to be given any particular aspect will be dictated by the position in the outline. Although in each successive case within a topic other considerations vary and the details of the situation are different, the topic itself remains constant. This constancy of topic in a continually varied environment provides the emphasis that leads to a growing and dynamic understanding of the topic.

III. A Case in Control   MALCOLM P. McNAIR

Although in many business situations it is necessary for administrators to make decisions on the basis of incomplete evidence and on the basis of weighing intangible or indefinite factors, nevertheless the executive will encounter from time to time specific problems, or parts of problems, which lend themselves to close logical or mathematical analysis. The power to develop such a close logical analysis (together with the capacity to distinguish among situations in which such analysis is or is not appropriate) is an important tool of the business administrator. One of the areas where this kind of analysis is important is the behavior of costs. The basic concept that in a given situation some costs are fixed while others are variable in relation to output is a reasonably simple one. To apply this concept in a particular situation, recognizing that the fixed or variable character of costs is related to time as well as to magnitude of changes in the output rate, and to understand that for decision-making purposes the concepts of fixed and variable costs must be geared to the particular proposal under consideration—such analysis, if the student is to master it, requires intensive training by means of a series of differing case situations, all revolving around the concept of fixed and variable costs. At various times one of the cases used in such a series has been that of the Conmay Company. This case was originally written for the course in Public Utility Management; subsequently it was used for a number of years in the course in Business Economics; more recently it has appeared in the course in Control.

CONMAY COMPANY

The Conmay Company furnished local transportation for Hampton, Ohio, an industrial city with a population of about 100,000. The company's system, with 70 miles of track, used 9,300,000 kilowatt-hours of electricity annually. This was generated in the company's plant at a total annual cost of about $179,000. In 1922, the company was beginning to lose patronage because of the growing ownership of automobiles. The general manager, with a view to lowering expenses, suggested that the cost of power might be reduced by scrapping the power plant and purchasing energy from the station of the Hampton Power Company, which was less than a mile away.

The Hampton Power Company offered to enter into a cost-plus contract on terms which are described below. The general manager of the Conmay Company then undertook to determine the highest price at which the Conmay Company could afford to purchase its power.

On the basis of a coal cost of $6 a gross ton, a Conmay Company engineer computed the cost of power at the company's plant to be as shown in Exhibit 1.

The output of the Hampton Power Company's station, which supplied the city of Hampton and several neighboring communities, was about twice that of the Conmay Company. The generating equipment of the Hampton Power Company was ample to supply the Conmay Company's power needs, and was believed to be as reliable as that of the railway company. The average age of the Conmay Company's generators was 20 years.

The Conmay Company's load would increase the Hampton Power Company's output 50% and would lower its unit cost of production even if an additional generator had to be installed. The Hampton Power Company offered to take the Conmay Company's load at switchboard cost plus 20% for overhead and profit. Switchboard cost was defined as the actual average

EXHIBIT 1

COMPUTED COST OF GENERATING ELECTRICITY IN THE CONMAY COMPANY'S PLANT, BASED ON AN ANNUAL DIRECT-CURRENT OUTPUT OF 9,300,000 KILOWATT-HOURS WITH COAL AT $6 PER GROSS TON

	Cents per Kilowatt-Hour
Total costs, other than fuel..	0.570
Fuel cost, coal at $6 per gross ton...................................	0.724*
Total operating cost..	1.294
Fixed charges on plant, $58,915 annually.............................	0.633
Total cost per kilowatt-hour..	1.927
Approximate total annual cost, 9,300,000 kilowatt-hours...............	$179,200

* Based on an estimated average use of 2.7 pounds of coal per kilowatt-hour.

EXHIBIT 2

ESTIMATED COST OF ELECTRICITY TO THE CONMAY COMPANY IF PURCHASED FROM THE HAMPTON POWER COMPANY ON PROPOSED COST-PLUS BASIS

	Cents per Kilowatt-Hour
Contract cost:	
Switchboard cost other than fuel for 20,000,000 kilowatt-hours output, alternating current..	0.574
Switchboard cost other than fuel with output increased to 30,000,000 kilowatt-hours...	0.383
Fuel cost, coal at $6 per gross ton...............................	0.509*
Total switchboard costs...	0.892
Plus 20% for overhead and profit.............................	0.178
Total charge per kilowatt-hour by Hampton Power Company.......	1.070
Additional cost to Conmay Company:	
Margin against estimated loss of 10% in converting to direct current...	0.119
Substation operating expenses, estimated at $5,000 annually.........	0.054
Fixed charges on new substation, 12% on investment of $110,000....	0.142†
Total cost to Conmay Company...................................	1.385
Estimated annual cost, 9,300,000 kilowatt-hours....................	$128,800

* Based on an estimated average use of 1.91 pounds of coal per kilowatt-hour.
† Includes depreciation, taxes, insurance.

production cost for the total load at the Hampton Power Company's switchboard. The operating expense accounts to be included were specified. The proposed contract was to be for 20 years, subject to cancellation after 10 years.

If the Conmay Company accepted this offer and closed its own plant, its entire power requirements would be transmitted from the Hampton station through duplicate underground cables to a new substation which the Conmay Company would have to build. At that station, the electricity would be transformed from alternating current to direct current. The estimated cost of the substation was $110,000.

An estimate of the cost of power under the proposed contract was prepared by the Conmay Company's engineering department from data furnished by the Hampton Power Company, supplemented by estimates of the additional costs to be assumed by the Conmay Company. This estimate is summarized in Exhibit 2.

The book value of the Conmay Company's generating station less depreciation was $370,644, and the scrap value was estimated at $57,500. Annual taxes on this plant were $6,000, and insurance costs were $717; the remainder of the $58,915 annual fixed charges was depreciation on the plant.

What was the highest price at which it would have been profitable for the Conmay Company to purchase its power?

What price per kilowatt-hour should the Conmay Company have suggested in its counteroffer?

The student should recognize at the outset that this case represents an intermediate stage in the negotiations between the Conmay Company and the Hampton Power Company. Conmay evidently has approached Hampton and has been quoted the price of 1.070 cents per kilowatt-hour shown in Exhibit 2 of the case. Conmay must now decide whether to accept the figure of 1.070 cents or whether to propose some other figure as a counteroffer. It is needful to remember that the cost to Conmay if it buys this power from Hampton consists of two parts: (1) the amount paid to Hampton and (2) the costs of the additional facilities required.

An appropriate method of analysis is to begin by determining the limits of the bargaining range, in other words by calculating both the maximum amount which Conmay can afford to pay and also the minimum amount which Hampton can afford to take. The figure finally agreed on if the deal is made presumably will be somewhere between these two points. Hence after the mathematical calculations have been made it will be necessary to consider briefly the relative bargaining position of the two companies in order to determine what sort of counterproposal Conmay might make.

The following reasoning and calculations apply to the determination of the maximum amount which Conmay can afford to pay.

Conmay now has a plant which presumably is in a condition to run for some years. The fixed charges on this plant will continue in any event and therefore do not need to be considered at this point. The total operating cost (Exhibit 1) is 1.294 cents per kilowatt-hour, or a total of $120,342 on 9,300,000 kilowatt-hours. Against this figure is to be considered the total new cost of power if Conmay buys from Hampton on the basis of Hampton's offer, which cost, as shown in Exhibit 2, will be approximately 1.385 cents per kilowatt-hour, or $128,800 for 9,300,000 kilowatt-hours. Therefore Hampton's offer as it stands obviously is disadvantageous.

The highest price which Conmay can pay is represented by the difference between the costs which it can get rid of if it buys from Hampton and the new costs which it will incur. The cost which Conmay can escape is 1.294 cents per kilowatt-hour. The new cost which it will incur is roughly 0.315 cent per kilowatt-hour (the sum of the three items of additional cost shown in Exhibit 2). On this basis a figure of 0.979 cent per kilowatt-hour appears to be the top price Conmay can pay. This calculation needs some refinements, however. In the first place, no interest has been included on the investment in the new substation. If interest is assumed at a rate of 5% on an average investment of $55,000, the interest expense is $2,750, or 0.030 cent per kilowatt-hour. This cost may be included as follows:

	Cents per Kilowatt-Hour
Substation operating expenses..................	0.054
Fixed charges on substation...................	0.142
Interest on investment in substation...........	0.030
	0.226

This last figure covers all additional costs except the conversion loss. For purposes of a meticulous calculation, the conversion loss should be figured not on Hampton's cost but on Conmay's. If the loss is 10% of the current purchased, it is obviously 11.1% of the current received, i.e., 11.1% of the cost to Conmay of the 9,300,000 kilowatt-hours. Since this full cost to Conmay of the 9,300,000 kilowatt-hours proposed to be purchased from Hampton is the figure which it is desired to ascertain, the following equation will serve:

$$x = 1.294 - 0.226 - 0.111x$$
$$1.111x = 1.068$$
$$x = 0.961$$

This figure of 0.961 cent per kilowatt-hour then may be taken as the top price which Conmay can pay, on the assumption that it keeps its existing plant.

But this assumption is not the only one possible. By scrapping its existing plant, Conmay might rid itself of certain expenses, specifically taxes and insurance on the plant, which together now amount to $6,717, or 0.072 cent per kilowatt-hour. Also by scrapping the plant Conmay can obtain the scrap value of the plant of $57,500. In other words, the company will avoid the cost of having this much money tied up in the plant. Thus on the assumption that the plant is scrapped, taxes and insurance and interest on scrap value may be included in the computation of cost which will no longer be incurred. Then the total cost which Conmay can escape appears as follows:

	Cents per Kilowatt-Hour
Operating cost	1.294
Taxes and insurance	0.072
Interest on scrap value	0.031
	1.397

Again, however, it is necessary to make the adjustment with respect to conversion loss; and if an equation similar to the one above is used the result is as follows:

$$x = 1.397 - 0.226 - 0.111x$$
$$1.111x = 1.171$$
$$x = 1.055$$

This figure of 1.055 cents per kilowatt-hour is the highest figure which Conmay possibly can afford to pay, and is, therefore, the top of the bargaining range.

Here it may be noted in passing that the two calculations for interest, i.e., interest on investment in a new substation and interest on the scrap value of the plant, have such similar results that for rough practical purposes they might be assumed to cancel. Therefore a student would not be subject to criticism if at this stage of the discussion he offered a calculation as follows:

	Cents per Kilowatt-Hour
Operating cost	1.294
Taxes and insurance	0.072
	1.366

$$x = 1.366 - 0.196 - 0.111x$$
$$1.111x = 1.170$$
$$x = 1.053$$

But whether the calculation is made on the more meticulous basis which yields the figure of 1.055 cents per kilowatt-hour or whether it is made on the rougher basis which yields the figure of 1.053 cents per kilowatt-hour, it is still clear that Conmay, even if it scraps its plant, cannot afford to pay the figure of 1.070 cents per kilowatt-hour asked by Hampton (Exhibit 2).

When the class discussion has been brought along to this point, the student should recognize that there are still further considerations which may have a bearing on the figure that Conmay can afford to pay Hampton. In the various calculations offered, the tacit assumption has been present that Conmay's plant is in reasonably good condition and will not require any capital expenditures for some time to come. If this assumption is not valid and if Conmay can forecast capital outlays that will be necessary within a foreseeable period to keep its plant in good condition, then interest and amortization in connection with these outlays obviously will be variable costs which the company could avoid if it made the deal with Hampton. If Conmay can see such outlays ahead, then the total of its escapable costs is of course larger than the foregoing calculations have indicated, and hence the annual amount it can afford to pay Hampton is correspondingly higher. Conceivably the future outlook with reference to the condition of Conmay's plant may be such that Conmay can afford to pay the price of 1.070 demanded by Hampton.

With one end of the bargaining range determined, the students need next to turn their attention to the calculation of the other end, i.e., the minimum price which Hampton can afford to take.

What additional costs does Hampton incur by increasing its output from 20,000,000 to 30,000,000 kilowatt-hours? If Hampton can get a price which will just cover these additional costs, it will be as well off as at present. On the basis of the figures given in Exhibit 2, Hampton's true increment costs appear to be primarily the fuel costs of 0.509 cent per kilowatt-hour. Obviously the 20% for overhead and profit, amounting to 0.178 cent per kilowatt-hour, is not an increment cost. Apparently the same is true of the switchboard cost other than fuel since this cost amounts to 0.574 cent per kilowatt-hour for a 20,000,000 kilowatt-hour output and to 0.383 cent per kilowatt-hour for a 30,000,000 kilowatt-hour output, roughly the same dollar cost in each instance. Incidentally, it may be noted that the 30,000,000 kilowatt-hour figure obviously has been rounded off, since Hampton would need to deliver 10,333,333 kilowatt-hours in order to give Conmay 9,300,000 kilowatt-hours on a direct current basis. Apparently, therefore, any amount which Hampton can persuade Conmay to pay in excess of the 0.509-cent average cost will be virtually profit to Hampton. Even if the 20% for overhead and profit is left out and if Conmay should pay the total switchboard cost of 0.892 cent per kilowatt-hour, apparently Hampton would stand to make a profit on the deal of

0.383 × 10,333,333, or $39,577. This calculation, of course, assumes no lowering in the rates to Hampton's other customers.

Therefore a figure of approximately 0.51 cent per kilowatt-hour (or slightly more) is established as the minimum price which Hampton can afford to take. Hence the bargaining range lies between this figure and the figure of 1.055 cents per kilowatt-hour which represents the maximum that Conmay can pay. In the light of this reasoning, what sort of offer should Conmay now make? At this point in the discussion of the case it is appropriate to speculate with reference to the relative bargaining position of the two companies.

There are presumably some elements of strength in Conmay's position. In the first place, Conmay has an existing plant which apparently will be serviceable for some time to come. Consequently Conmay is not under the necessity of making a disadvantageous bargain. Furthermore, it does not appear from the statement of the case that anyone else is bidding for the additional power which Hampton has to offer. Against these points of possible strength there are some weaknesses in Conmay's position, the chief of which is that the street railway business obviously is a declining business, and hence Conmay on principle presumably is loath to make additional capital expenditures to maintain its plant. This weakness in Conmay's bargaining position may be serious if there is any evidence that Conmay's plant will require some replacement in the relatively near future.

As regards the Hampton Company, its strengths are Conmay's weaknesses, and vice versa.

In the negotiations much will depend on the level of fuel prices. If the existing price is on the high side of its range over previous years, Hampton cannot make so strong an argument as it can if the fuel price is on the low side of the range. Apart from this important factor of fuel prices Conmay can of course argue that on a fixed-price basis Hampton will stand to gain from any technological improvements in the electrical generating industry. On the other hand, Hampton can come back with the very plausible contention that over the period of time for which the contract continues there will actually be some new variable costs other than fuel; there will be a greater load on its generators, replacements will be required sooner, and actually the company may have to make outlays for stand-by equipment for use in the event of a breakdown.

After discussing all these various pros and cons in the bargaining situation of the two companies and relating them to the calculations which have gone before, students should be expected to come up with a specific counterproposal for Conmay to offer. One plausible proposal might be an offer to pay fuel costs of 0.509 cent per kilowatt-hour plus half the switchboard costs other than fuel, or a total of 0.70 cent per kilowatt-hour. In addition Conmay might offer to sell its existing plant to Hampton for the latter to use as stand-by equipment. On this basis Conmay might get a little better realization than by scrapping the plant, and at the same time Hampton might be saved the cost of putting in additional equipment for stand-by capacity. Such a deal might shift the bargaining range up a little for Conmay and down a little for Hampton.

IV. A Broad Economics Case   JOHN LINTNER

In the second half of their first year, students at the Harvard Business School are required to take a course in Business Responsibilities in the American Society. The purpose of the course is to develop familiarity with the broad economic, political, and social environment within which business decisions are made and the business process takes place. The cases used involve consideration of the effect of such environmental factors on the shaping of business decisions, and recognition of the impact of such business decisions on the economy itself. The course is organized under two broad headings, Business Competition and Economic Stability. Under the first of these headings the cases currently used concern such problems as unfair trade practices, bigness and monopoly power, restraints of trade, patent policy, price agreements, open price reporting systems, resale price maintenance, price discrimination, and geographic pricing systems. In the area of Economic Stability the cases concern the relationships to business conditions of inventory policies, plant expansion decisions, wage rates and escalator clauses, price policies, and the size and use of profits; inflation and deflation; government credit restrictions and other measures for economic stabilization in a defense economy; and fiscal and monetary policies and other programs intended to promote and maintain high levels of income and employment in peacetime. In this part of the course a typical case is the following one of the Dempsey Shoe Company:

DEMPSEY SHOE COMPANY

Late in May, 1936, the purchasing committee of the Dempsey Shoe Company, an Illinois corporation engaged in the manufacture of men's shoes, met to determine the company's leather buying policies for the ensuing season. The purchasing committee was composed of the president of the company; the controller, who was also sole-leather buyer; and the upper-leather buyer. At this meeting the committee considered the extent to which the company should make forward commitments on sole and upper leathers and the desirability of borrowing through note brokers for the purpose of increasing raw-material inventories.

ESTIMATING REQUIREMENTS

Prior to each shoe season the controller prepared an operating budget. The preparation of the budget began with independent estimates of prospective sales submitted by the president, the sales manager, and the manager in charge of the stock department and inventory. The president and the sales manager based their estimates, which were total figures only, on general business conditions, opinions advanced by the retail trade, and their own knowledge of conditions in the shoe market. The manager in charge of the stock department and inventory estimated total sales for each of the company's 200 styles of shoes, basing his figures on past sales records and salesmen's reports of their anticipated volume. From these three independent estimates a final forecast of total sales was prepared, and the estimate by styles was readjusted to this new figure. Using this final sales forecast as a basis, the controller worked out a production plan for each style and an estimate of manufacturing expense by months. He then used the production plan as a basis for estimating the company's upper-leather and sole-leather requirements for the period, for each kind of leather used. A comparison of these requirements with the company's stocks of leather was next made in order to determine the quantity of each kind of leather which should be purchased during the season to cover production needs. The purchasing committee then tentatively decided at what times this leather should be purchased.

As another step in the budgetary procedure, the estimated sales, collections of receivables, and total costs of doing business were used in preparing a monthly cash budget. This gave the company a basis for estimating its cash position at the end of each month of the period and enabled it to plan its bank loans in advance. All the figures entering into the budgets were provisional and subject to modification at any time. Thus, if conditions warranted, the purchasing committee on the basis of revised estimates might reconsider its recommendations and change the dates and amounts of purchase.

PURCHASING PROCEDURE

The Dempsey Shoe Company used only two grades of sole leather, both of which were of high quality since it was the company's policy to manufacture only better-grade shoes. Each grade was purchased in five "irons" or weights. About 80% of the company's sole-leather requirements was purchased in the form of cut soles while the remaining 20% was purchased in the form of whole stock, which was cut by the company to its own requirements.

The company's requirements of upper leather were much more varied than those of sole leather. In the manufacture of the 200 styles of shoes in its line, the company used approximately 50 kinds and colors of upper leather in 150 grades and weights. For purposes of forward purchasing, however, only about 13 kinds of upper leather were important enough to follow closely. The remainder were purchased as required to replenish stocks of finished shoes or to fill orders already received.

Upper leather was purchased in the form of tanned whole hides and skins and was cut by the company. Prior to making contracts for purchase, the company cut up samples submitted by individual tanners. When the results of the cutting were satisfactory, the company offered the vendors certain prices per square foot for the lots from which the samples had been taken. If, after negotiation, mutually satisfactory prices were agreed upon, the company made the purchases.

It was not necessary for the Dempsey Shoe Company to maintain large stocks of leather at all times in order to insure continuity of supply, since substantial stocks of leather in all standard grades were ordinarily available from tanners for immediate delivery. Any standard leathers could be obtained in 10 or 12 days from the tanneries and in two days from tanners' warehouses located within a few miles of the factory. Delivery from warehouses, however, was disadvantageous because an additional freight charge was levied on such merchandise. Purchases from warehouse stocks were therefore made only when absolutely necessary and then confined to small quantities sufficient merely to cover production requirements until shipment could be made direct from the tanneries. Even when temporary shortages of standard grades developed, as happened occasionally, and the company found itself unable to obtain its full requirements in advance, arrangements were easily made with suppliers for fill-in shipments in quantities sufficient to allow the maintenance of production schedules. Thus, as a general rule, the company could expect to be protected against shortages of raw materials even when it purchased on a hand-to-mouth basis.

PURCHASING POLICY, 1929–1932

In 1929, purchases of leather for stock styles were confined to immediate production requirements, and leather for nonstock styles was purchased only as orders were received. This procedure was followed partly because the company's records lacked some of the information needed to guide a careful forward buying program and partly because the prices of raw materials were falling. The officers in charge of purchasing for the company had not given much attention to the available statistics on the hide and leather situation when estimating probable price trends, and had based their recommendation for purchases primarily on hunches and personal contacts with the market.

In 1930, a new controller, Mr. Reynolds, was hired by the company. He had formerly been employed as the sole-leather buyer for one of the largest shoe manufacturing concerns in the United States. Within two years after

EXHIBIT 1

DEMPSEY SHOE COMPANY.

Balance Sheets, as of December 31, 1929–1935

	1929	1930	1931	1932	1933	1934	1935
Assets							
Cash	$ 790,014	$ 190,232	$ 150,400	$ 170,152	$ 157,318	$ 155,460	$ 252,535
Marketable Securities	—	517,462	707,168	628,344	155,804	105,937	113,743
Accounts and Notes Receivable	1,996,828	1,781,862	1,017,215	838,794	1,405,763	1,125,110	1,340,297
Inventory	990,904	853,249	966,553	699,421	948,282	1,211,623	1,537,512
Total Current	$3,777,746	$3,342,805	$2,841,336	$2,336,711	$2,667,167	$2,598,130	$3,244,087
Plant, Equipment, etc. (less deprec.)	164,094	158,858	202,159	185,144	119,905	163,878	149,908
Investments	10,398	3,652	3,290	3,292	5,006	3,292	3,052
Deferred Charges	64,812	51,834	56,809	30,382	28,540	55,914	41,292
Total	$4,017,050	$3,557,149	$3,103,594	$2,555,529	$2,820,618	$2,821,214	$3,438,339
Liabilities							
Notes Payable	$ 1,200	$ 1,200	$ 180,000	$ 65,000	$ 125,000	$ 125,000	$ 500,000
Accounts Payable	22,430	72,238	80,130	26,065	61,343	86,138	105,195
Accruals	65,706	57,192	46,769	17,941	47,381	75,393	112,304
Reserve for Taxes and Dividends	176,946	149,532	82,123	—	36,408	23,321	48,040
Total Current	$ 266,282	$ 280,162	$ 389,022	$ 109,006	$ 270,132	$ 309,852	$ 765,539
Other Reserves	480,349	266,712	121,158	71,696	140,285	93,461	105,098
Preferred Stock	1,039,900	731,400	375,100	97,400	—	—	—
Common Stock	1,352,400	1,352,400	1,352,400	1,352,400	1,352,400	1,352,400	1,352,400
Surplus	878,119	926,475	865,914	925,027	1,057,801	1,065,501	1,215,302
Total	$4,017,050	$3,557,149	$3,103,594	$2,555,529	$2,820,618	$2,821,214	$3,438,339
Net Sales (12 months ending 12/31)	$7,327,040	$6,608,571	$5,271,123	$3,641,846	$3,925,976	$4,454,783	$4,976,342

Mr. Reynolds had assumed the duties of controller for the Dempsey Shoe Company, he had set up a control system for estimating sales of shoes by individual styles, salesmen, and outlets and for estimating production of shoes by individual styles, for six-month periods, from January to June and from July to December. From these figures the company's future raw-material requirements by kinds of leather were determined, and the buying executives of the company were able to base their purchasing policy on these estimates of future needs.

FORWARD BUYING, 1933

Prices of hides and leather dropped steadily from 1929 until February, 1933. As a result, the hand-to-mouth policy followed by the company during this period afforded protection against heavy losses from a decline in value of a sizable raw-material inventory. In March, 1933, however, the members of the purchasing committee believed that prices, which then were at the lowest level in over 30 years, could not go much lower, and that any increase in general business activity would bring a general commodity price advance, in which hide and leather prices would participate.

After 1929, the company had had its cash balances considerably augmented by reduction of accounts receivable and inventory; and, although it had retired approximately $1,000,000 worth of 7% preferred stock with the cash so received, it still had in February, 1933, about $800,000 in cash and securities, primarily railroad bonds of low yield. Company executives believed that in the future it would probably be better to have these funds invested in commodities than to have them in bonds or lying idle in banks where they would draw no interest. In anticipation of an early upward turn in the business cycle and of a moderate advance in leather prices, the purchasing committee voted in March, 1933, the immediate purchase of enough staple leather to cover the company's requirements for shoe production until the end of the year. Thereafter prices advanced rapidly, and the leather used by the company cost much less than would have been the case if a hand-to-mouth policy had been followed throughout 1933. Special kinds of leather required for highly-styled shoes continued to be purchased only as needed to fill orders already received.

Since the company's forward purchases of leather were for definitely scheduled production, with no intention of subsequent sale for a speculative profit, the company did not consider its forward buying in 1933 to have been speculation. The purchase had been arranged to protect the company against loss in the event of a price advance rather than to allow the company to make a greatly increased profit in 1933. (Except in periods of declining demand, the gross margin between factory prices and leather costs on a unit basis amounted to approximately 50% of selling prices.) Advances in the price of shoes customarily lagged behind advances in leather prices because intense competition forced shoe manufacturers to postpone advances in the prices of their finished products until stocks of raw materials bought at lower prices were exhausted. Those companies which failed to anticipate raw-material price advances and were caught with depleted inventories of hides and leathers were forced to absorb losses or reductions in profit in the periods following the beginning of an advance in leather prices.

PURCHASING POLICY, 1934–1935

The success of its forward buying venture in 1933 encouraged the company to continue the policy whenever the purchasing committee believed that price advances were likely. Between 1933 and 1936, the company did not resume its hand-to-mouth buying policy. On no occasion after 1933, however, did the company purchase more than enough leather to cover its budgeted requirements for the ensuing production season, that is, for six or seven months. The company attempted, so far as possible, to make forward purchases during the dull periods between production seasons, either in July and August or in February and March. The policy of purchasing ahead only the kinds of leather called for by the production plan was maintained, and the company did not at any time purchase leathers for resale.

When the purchasing committee believed that prices were about to weaken, stocks of leather were allowed to decline to as low as two or three months' supply. The company made no attempt, however, during periods of falling leather prices, to hedge its physical inventories by sale of hides futures on Commodity Exchange, Inc. The purchasing executives of the company believed that hedging by this method was impractical for several reasons. In the first place, they believed that trading in hides on the commodity exchange was controlled by large tanners, who could artificially influence prices by withdrawing temporarily from the hide market or by putting large lots up for sale. Furthermore, hide and leather prices were not closely correlated, and a rise or fall in the price of the hides did not necessarily mean a corresponding change in the price of leather.

By 1935, the company executives were strongly of the belief that substantial sums should be kept invested in raw-material inventories, and, lacking surplus funds of its own, the company borrowed heavily from note brokers in order to maintain inventories at desired levels.

DISCUSSION OF FORWARD BUYING, MAY, 1936

In May, 1936, prior to the beginning of shoe production for the spring, 1937, selling season, the company had on hand and on order nearly 450,000 pairs of outsoles, or approximately six months' supply. It also had on hand more than 500,000 square feet of upper leather, or between three and four months' supply. When the forecast of expected leather requirements (Exhibits 2 and 3) was prepared in May, 1936, therefore, it was apparent that the stocks of sole leather on hand were nearly sufficient to meet the season's requirements, and that the company, unless it changed its policy of purchasing only leather required in the ensuing season, would not be in the market for

EXHIBIT 2

DEMPSEY SHOE COMPANY

Outsoles in Sight (Pairs), May 20, 1936

Grade	On Hand	On Order	Total in Sight	Expected Requirements May 20 to Dec. 21, 1936	Recommended Immediate Purchases
10 F	25,640	0	25,640	40,596	
9 F	15,420	2,540	17,960	35,762	
8½F	14,000	0	14,000	6,365	
8 F	13,500	0	13,500	32,482	
7½F	1,830	0	1,830	7,494	
10 #1	90,500	27,860	118,360	136,146	
9 #1	20,000	97,360	117,360	163,904	60,000*
8½#1	50,540	41,400	91,940	86,330	
8 #1	21,880	6,260	28,140	19,808	
7½#1	8,920	0	8,920	11,720	
Total	262,230	175,420	437,650	540,607	60,000

* To be delivered July–September, 1936.

a great deal of sole leather before December. Substantial purchases of upper leather could be made, however, without departure from policy.

When the purchasing committee met to discuss its leather buying program for the remainder of 1936, Mr. Reynolds declared to the other members of the purchasing committee that he did not expect the sole-leather market to move upward at least until the fall. This belief, he said, was based on examination of all available statistics and on conversations with tanners' representatives. He stated that, while there was a shortage of that age of cattle that best supplied the heavy high-quality sole leathers used by the Dempsey Shoe Company, and while there was a tendency on the part of German and French buyers to purchase large quantities of South American sole leather to replenish their stocks against the possibility of war, the bullish influence of these factors on prices was neutralized by the usual fall-season withdrawal of American manufacturers from the sole-leather market.

Mr. Reynolds pointed out that, with but one exception, the company ought not to plan to add to its stocks of sole leathers, at least until September. The exception was No. 1 grade, 9-iron sole, the price of which seemed temporarily to have weakened as a result of overstocking by tanners and subsequent pressure to market these stocks. This type of sole was currently priced in the market at 37 cents a pair. A tanner from whom the Dempsey Shoe Company customarily purchased this grade of sole had quoted a price of 35½ cents a pair, or 1½ cents below the existing market price. Mr. Reynolds believed that the offer resulted from a temporary glut and that it would be withdrawn before active trading in sole leather began again in the fall. He

EXHIBIT 3

DEMPSEY SHOE COMPANY

Upper-Leather Requirements (Square Feet), May 12–December 31, 1936
(Based on Sales Estimates)

Kind of Leather	Expected Requirements, 5/12–12/31/36	On Hand or on Order, 5/12/36	Required to Purchase, 5/12–12/31/36	Recommended Immediate Purchases*
Black Russia.........	453,720	207,951	245,769	180,000
Color 79 Russia.......	138,252	52,236	86,016	36,000
Imported Box Calf....	116,310	61,521	54,789	36,000
Color 144 Homespun..	43,230	30,900	12,330	10,800
Color 55 Russia.......	42,066	21,150	20,916	15,000
Black Tweed Grain....	42,030	24,237	17,793	15,000
Brown Shaggy†.......	40,680	12,936	27,744	22,500
Black Kid............	30,720	15,450	15,270	—
Grey Shaggy†........	28,500	11,100	17,400	12,000
Black Kangaroo.......	19,740	8,850	10,890	8,400
Color 88 Shetland.....	17,574	9,510	8,064	3,600
Brown Tweed Grain...	13,890	5,250	8,640	8,400
Sand Shaggy†........	12,840	6,510	6,330	3,600
Other Types..........	130,560	79,492	51,068	Order as needed to cover orders received
Totals.............	1,130,112	547,093	583,019	351,300

* For delivery over the period May through September, 1936.
† For high style, nonstaple numbers.

recommended that the company purchase 60,000 pairs of soles of this type immediately in order to take advantage of the temporary price concession. Such a purchase would bring the company's sole-leather inventory to more than 90% of requirements for the next seven months. The other members of the purchasing committee agreed with Mr. Reynolds that this was a wise move and authorized the immediate purchase of the suggested quantity, to be delivered in equal installments in July, August, and September.

The buyer of upper leather reported to the purchasing committee that the price structure in the upper-leather market was somewhat stronger than in the sole-leather market and that the customary between-season weakness had not developed. His impressions of the price situation were based on personal visits to the hide and leather market and on conversations with representatives of tanners and shoe manufacturers. He did not follow current statistics closely since he did not believe that they reflected actual conditions well enough to justify dependence on them; he preferred to base his recommendations on what he termed hunches. It was his opinion that prices would not

EXHIBIT 4

AVERAGE WHOLESALE PRICES: OAK SOLE LEATHER AND CHROME CALF LEATHER

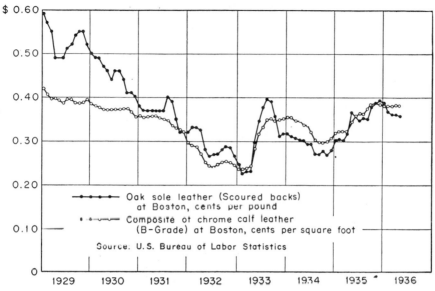

EXHIBIT 5

MANUFACTURING INVENTORIES AND SALES, 1929–1940
(Dollar figures in millions)

	Leather and Leather Products			Total Manufacturing		
	Dec. 31 Inventories	Sales	Inventory-Sales Ratios	Dec. 31 Inventories	Sales	Inventory-Sales Ratios
1929	$452	$1,863	25.4%	$13,917	$75,165	18.1%
1930	400	1,486	28.7	12,258	61,141	21.4
1931	314	1,187	30.1	9,856	45,820	24.1
1932	229	899	30.2	7,944	31,987	27.8
1933	281	1,058	24.1	8,846	35,639	23.6
1934	274	1,197	23.2	9,468	46,370	19.7
1935	310	1,348	21.7	9,870	53,962	17.9
1936	336	1,485	21.8	11,551	64,377	16.6
1937	345	1,544	22.1	12,980	70,483	17.4
1938	289	1,308	24.2	11,545	57,410	21.3
1939	310	1,435	20.9	12,547	65,699	18.3
1940	316	1,499	20.9	14,021	75,784	17.5

Source: Moses Abramovitz, *Inventories and Business Cycles* (New York: National Bureau of Economic Research, Inc., 1950), Table 107, p. 563, Table 113, p. 568, and Table 114, p. 569.

EXHIBIT 6

NET CHANGE IN NONFARM BUSINESS INVENTORIES, 1929–1950

(Millions of dollars)

Industrial Groups	1929	1930	1931	1932	1933	1934	1935	1936	1937	1938	1939
Manufacturing											
Change in book value	598	-1,553	-2,239	-1,846	828	598	381	1,586	1,340	-1,268	713
Inventory valuation adjustment	313	2,300	1,645	691	-1,406	-462	-168	-491	4	637	-499
Net Change	911	747	-594	-1,155	-578	136	213	1,095	1,344	-631	214
Wholesale Trade											
Change in book value	-74	-527	-832	-358	268	226	9	487	70	-403	236
Inventory valuation adjustment	105	581	419	183	-357	-160	-8	-201	140	205	-159
Net Change	31	54	-413	-175	-89	66	1	286	210	-198	77
Retail Trade											
Change in book value	87	-1,390	-1,148	-1,136	223	-16	394	831	209	-490	312
Inventory valuation adjustment	173	857	771	383	-708	-31	-81	-128	-145	303	-194
Net Change	260	-533	-377	-753	-485	-47	313	703	64	-187	118
All Other											
Change in book value	589	-579	-475	-601	1	44	-80	69	205	-136	-37
Inventory valuation adjustment	23	277	190	85	-197	-26	-20	-38	-59	39	-28
Net Change	612	-302	-285	-516	-196	18	-100	31	146	-97	-65
Total Nonfarm Inventories											
Change in book value	1,200	-4,049	-4,694	-3,941	1,320	852	704	2,973	1,824	-2,297	1,224
Inventory valuation adjustment	614	4,015	3,025	1,342	-2,668	-679	-277	-858	-60	1,184	-880
Net Change	1,814	-34	-1,669	-2,599	-1,343	173	427	2,115	1,764	-1,113	344

Industrial Groups	1940	1941	1942	1943	1944	1945	1946	1947	1948	1949	1950
Manufacturing											
Change in book value	1,363	4,053	2,323	826	−593	−1,122	6,160	4,417	2,746	−3,032	4,574
Inventory valuation adjustment	−89	−1,732	−771	−579	−221	−435	−3,192	−3,852	−1,532	1,311	−3,214
Net Change	1,274	2,321	1,552	247	−814	−1,557	2,968	565	1,214	−1,721	1,360
Wholesale Trade											
Change in book value	157	794	−316	−128	293	646	2,073	1,067	725	−579	1,531
Inventory valuation adjustment	5	−626	−272	−161	−29	−104	−1,236	−1,088	58	531	−1,236
Net Change	162	168	−588	−289	264	542	837	−21	783	−48	295
Retail Trade											
Change in book value	656	1,309	234	−185	269	382	4,133	2,305	2,337	−1,294	3,647
Inventory valuation adjustment	−81	−808	−506	−151	−78	−94	−2,190	−1,707	−587	706	−1,756
Net Change	575	501	−272	−336	191	288	1,943	598	1,750	−588	1,891
All Other											
Change in book value	59	521	91	−88	124	173	980	923	355	−357	512
Inventory valuation adjustment	−35	−95	−27	−36	−29	−44	−394	−657	−385	221	−472
Net Change	24	426	64	−124	95	129	586	266	−30	−136	40
Total Nonfarm Inventories											
Change in book value	2,235	6,677	2,332	425	93	79	13,346	8,712	6,163	−5,262	10,264
Inventory valuation adjustment	−200	−3,261	−1,576	−927	−357	−677	−7,012	−7,304	−2,446	2,769	−6,678
Net Change	2,035	3,416	756	−502	−264	−598	6,334	1,408	3,717	−2,493	3,586

Source: National Income Supplement to the *Survey of Current Business*, 1951 ed., Table 33, p. 200.

drop as the dull season advanced but would increase prior to the resumption of large-scale purchasing in the fall. He recommended that the company immediately purchase about 350,000 square feet of various kinds of upper leathers and thus bring its inventories of upper leather to approximately 900,000 square feet. If this was done, approximately 80% of the company's upper-leather requirements until the end of the year would be covered. Mr. Reynolds and the president agreed with the upper-leather buyer that no price weakness in upper leathers was probable, and that it would be wise to increase stocks in anticipation of price advances. They therefore voted to purchase upper leathers in the recommended quantities.

The carrying-out of these recommendations would result in increasing the sole-leather and upper-leather inventories from approximately $350,000 to approximately $500,000. The company's bank loans in May, 1936, had been reduced to about $300,000 from the December, 1935, level of $500,000. The financial budget of the company indicated that they would be reduced to approximately $100,000 by July, when the bulk of deliveries on the new purchases would begin. The company would have no difficulty in borrowing at a rate of 1¼% such funds as were needed to pay for the new inventory as it was delivered. Mr. Reynolds, the controller, reported that he was constantly besieged by note brokers seeking to lend the company money and that the company could borrow substantially in excess of $500,000 if it desired to do so.

Exhibits 4, 5, and 6 provide pertinent data on the general economic environment in which the Dempsey Shoe Company's buying policies were determined.

Exhibit 4 sets forth in graphic form the monthly average wholesale prices for the period 1929 through May, 1936, of Oak Sole Leather, a representative grade of sole leather, and a composite price of B grades of Chrome Calf Leather, a representative type of upper leather.

Exhibit 5 sets forth data for the entire Leather and Leather Goods Industry, which includes not only shoe manufacturers but also tanners and other manufacturers of leather products, and for Total Manufacturing Business. The table includes data on inventories, sales, and inventory/sales ratios as of the end of the years 1929–1940, inclusive.

Exhibit 6 sets forth estimated data for all business units in the economy, other than farms, for all manufacturing, for all wholesaling, and for all retailing businesses. The table includes data for each year, 1929 through 1950, on the changes in book value of inventories, the inventory valuation adjustment, and the net changes of inventories (after the valuation adjustment).

In using this case in class we frequently begin by asking a student whether he agrees with Dempsey's leather-buying and inventory policies. Many students will support these policies on the grounds that they have been profitable for the company and that the risks involved, especially since Mr. Reynolds joined the management in 1930, have

been prudently acceptable. They will emphasize the substantial bene-
fits that Dempsey has obtained from its system of budgeting and control. They will point out that this system has made it possible for a
much broader range of information on market conditions and price
trends to be used effectively in forming judgments on procurement policy in the light of sales prospects and changing financial and inventory
positions. These developments under Mr. Reynolds's direction have
increased Dempsey's profits and contributed to the strength of its position generally. In particular, they made possible a longer inventory
position during the upswing to mid-1936 than would otherwise have
been held.

Some students, however, may question these policies on the grounds
that they involve considerable speculation on price movements and
that such speculation is not the proper business of a shoe manufacturing concern. Others will accept the company's view that it was not
speculating, since it merely covered anticipated production requirements for varying periods up to nine months in advance and did not
undertake to buy any leather for resale. Discussion, however, will
bring out the fact that following 1933 management made a definite
move to increase inventories relative both to current sales and to
anticipated production schedules because it expected investments in
inventory to be considerably more profitable than holdings of bonds or
idle cash. Although the company bought no leather for resale as
leather, it clearly was making investments in leather for resale after
fabrication into shoes.

The purpose of such class discussion is not to quibble over the semantic question of where legitimate forward buying leaves off and
outright inventory speculation begins. Rather it is to develop a distinction between the normal operating margin derived by the company from its manufacturing operations as such and the essentially
investment (or capital) profits and losses realized by the company
from its investment in inventory. This distinction helps to clarify
the analysis of Dempsey's policies, particularly with reference to the
effects of changes in inventory position when raw material prices are
fluctuating.

From the figures in Exhibit 5 and from the inventory-sales ratios
for Dempsey which can be derived from Exhibit 1, it appears that an
elapsed time of three months between the purchase of leather and the
sale of finished shoes is generally representative of the facts for most
shoe manufacturers. If this lead time is accepted and if the statement
in the case is likewise accepted that the factory price of finished shoes
is roughly twice the cost of the leather used in the shoes, then it is use-

ful for the class, first, to calculate the operating margin under assumed conditions of stable prices, of rising prices, and of falling prices and, next, to work out figures on the assumption that when prices are rising the Dempsey Company buys its leather five or six months in advance of sales while competing companies adhere to their established three months' lead time and that when prices are falling Dempsey reduces its lead time to between one and two months while competing companies continue on the three months' basis.

Elementary though they are, these calculations serve to demonstrate the relationship of material costs to operating margins under conditions of marked price movement. The assumptions are highly artificial, however, since in actual practice, when prices are declining and markets are weak, price shading will reduce the normal operating margin. In these circumstances all companies will be affected; but the company with lower-than-typical coverage of production schedules and prospective sales will gain an advantage over other companies. And in times of rising prices, companies with a longer-than-average inventory position will have the advantage.[1]

At this point in the discussion, students may suggest that Dempsey might simply hold its prices while other companies increase theirs on the basis of rising leather prices and the runoff of low-cost inventory. If this suggestion were followed, Dempsey would secure additional profits, but as a result of greater increases in volume, not as a result of any change in the margin between its inventory costs and its selling prices. Actually, in these circumstances, Dempsey would probably not keep its prices down unless it anticipated that by doing so it would achieve substantially increased sales volume, and then only if it had unused capacity to satisfy the additional orders.

Some students are also likely to suggest that, if Dempsey refrained from increasing prices when other shoe firms with a shorter inventory position were attempting to increase theirs in line with rising leather costs, the other firms might be unable to increase their prices and might be caught in a margin squeeze. Even under these conditions,

---

[1] At some stage mention needs to be made of the relationship between inventory profits and losses and the "inventory valuation adjustment" used in preparation of the national income accounts. (This adjustment is described in an appendix to a technical note on the National Income Accounts assigned earlier in the course.) In some classes with a strong background and interest in accounting there may also be some discussion of last-in-first-out (LIFO) as against first-in-first-out (FIFO) inventory accounting procedures. Similarly some time may be spent on discussion of hedging operations and the conditions under which they become possible and desirable. In any event detailed exploration of these matters is left for more advanced courses.

although Dempsey was forgoing the higher profits that might be available in the short run, it would gain substantial advantages, if not in immediately higher profits, as is most likely, then at least in financial strength and competitive position.

During the discussion of the situation prevailing in a period of advancing leather prices, students who have supported Dempsey's buying policies may be queried as to whether they do so on the basis of any particular characteristics of the shoe industry. They may point out that the case indicates that there will usually be no general price increase on shoes until old inventories have been worked off by most companies. Discussion naturally leads to some consideration of the results of Dempsey's policies under various relationships between leather and shoe prices. There may also be some discussion of whether competition works in a similar manner in other industries with which the students are familiar and whether buying policies comparable to Dempsey's would be profitable and desirable for companies in these other industries.

After some such analysis as the foregoing, it is possible to consider intelligently what the decision on buying policy should have been in May, 1936. Here the pertinent factors include a detailed appraisal of the company's financial position, the market prospects for the sale of shoes, and the prospective price trends for different types of leathers, as well as the company's current inventory position. The possibility of getting more explicit information to supplement the upper-leather buyer's hunches may be explored, and some analysis undertaken of the extent to which the company's position may become exposed and weak in the event of a downturn in the market.

Following this discussion the Dempsey Company's past leather-buying and inventory policies may be reviewed with particular reference to their effect on price movements in the leather market. Some students will note that Dempsey increased its leather purchases in 1933, when demand and prices for leather were at low levels, and will argue that the added orders bolstered leather prices when they were depressed. Similarly, they will observe that Dempsey cut back its purchases in 1929 and 1930, when leather prices were high, thereby damping inflation in these prices. These students may draw the conclusion that Dempsey's buying policies thus tended to even out demand and prices in the leather market. Others, however, may point out that Dempsey did not start buying at a time when leather prices were still falling, and did not cut back its purchases at a time when leather prices were rising—which it would have had to do in order to even out fluctuations in prices. These students may logically go on to argue that Dempsey's augmented purchases at a time when prices were rising simply gave a speculative fillip to a price movement that was already on the up trend, and that, conversely, Dempsey's cutting back of purchases after prices had begun to fall simply had the effect of depressing the price structure still further. In both situations, therefore, it could be held that Dempsey's buying policies intensified rather than diminished the fluctuations in leather prices.

At this point it is helpful to urge the students to put some figures on their ideas. In 1932 Dempsey's sales averaged $300,000 per month. With a 50% margin on sales price to cover all value added (including operating profit) and with a two months' inventory coverage, the leather costs of inventory would be $300,000, and leather purchases would average about $150,000 per month so long as sales remained at this level. If sales increased by 10% to a level of $330,000 per month, leather purchases to service these sales would also increase by 10% to $165,000 per month. But such purchases would no more than maintain physical inventory at the old level. In order to restore inventories to as much as two months' coverage of sales, Dempsey would have to step up its leather purchases by an additional $30,000. Furthermore, if Dempsey had not anticipated the increase in its sales, the physical volume of its inventory would be reduced, and this deficiency also would have to be made good by still further orders in the leather market. In short, *even though Dempsey merely sought to maintain* its previously existing inventory-sales coverage, the increase in its demand for leather would be considerably greater than the percentage increase in its shoe sales.

It is possible by developing the figures for two or three more "rounds" to show that if in any period sales simply held their higher level and did not increase further there would be an actual *decline* in leather purchases.[1] Sometimes also an additional stage is introduced to show how the already magnified effect of any change in final sales at one level upon purchases by that level from the next, even though the purchases were merely to maintain inventory-sales ratios, would once again be magnified or "accelerated" when purchases were made by this second level from *its* suppliers. Such calculations are likely to be of especial interest to students who have had experience in machine tool and other highly volatile industries that depend on a derived demand.

Dempsey, however, not only maintained its two months' coverage of production schedules in 1933 but increased its purchases still fur-

---

[1] There would also be a decline in leather purchases if the absolute amount of the increases in shoe sales declined.

ther in order to lengthen its inventory position. The added orders for this purpose were several times as large as those required merely to maintain a given inventory position as sales increased. For instance, in the situation just assumed, in order to raise its inventory coverage from two to four months' sales, Dempsey would have to buy $330,000 more leather; and to move from two to six months' coverage it would have to make additional purchases of $660,000 in the leather market —the equivalent of four months' regular buying (on an average monthly basis) at the higher rate required by the higher level of final shoe sales.

When the increased buying required to lengthen an inventory position is added to the already magnified increase in raw material demand needed merely to hold a given coverage of sales as final sales are increasing, the impact on the materials markets can be very great indeed. And this is precisely what Dempsey's policies involved. Conversely, the class may develop figures to show that any decrease in Dempsey's sales would be reflected in a much greater reduction in its leather buying even if it maintained the level of its inventory in relation to sales. Any shortening of its inventory position in a period of declining sales volume would seriously compound the drying up of demand in the materials markets. For instance, with sales running at $600,000 per month, as they were during 1929, leather purchases would amount to an average of $300,000 per month. A four months' inventory position would represent a leather cost value of inventory of $1,200,000. If sales were to decline by 10% to a level of $540,000 per month, leather purchases required to service the lower level of sales would also decline by 10% to a level of $270,000. But continuance of purchases even at this reduced level would mean that the initial volume of inventory was physically maintained, although four months' coverage of sales at the new level would require inventories of only $1,080,000. A reduction of 10% in final sales consequently would mean that Dempsey could cut its inventory purchases by $120,000 in addition to the reductions in buying needed on a continuous (average) basis to service the lower level of sales. Thus, even if Dempsey maintained its inventory at the same ratio to sales, the percentage decline in its leather buying for a substantial period would be considerably greater than the percentage decline in its sales. If Dempsey reduced its inventory coverage from four months to two months, the required level of its inventory would fall from $1,200,000 to $540,000. In this situation a 10% decline in sales coupled with a shortening of its inventory position from four months to two months would mean that Dempsey could be out of the leather market entirely for a period of about 2½ months or that alternatively it could cut back its leather buying by 50% for a period of well over half a year.

Here it is pertinent to consider what would be the effect on general levels of prices, production, and income if Dempsey's purchase and inventory policies were followed by all business firms. In the discussion of this issue students are led to trace out the resulting changes in the national income accounts and in the balance sheets of the monetary system (with which they are already familiar). A relatively few entries in the national income account will suffice to show that changes in final levels of sales will have a magnified effect on levels of income, production, and prices, even if inventory-sales ratios are no more than maintained. This is true because production schedules and buying orders will be stepped up to meet the increase in final sales and also to provide the additional inventory needed to match the higher level of sales. Both the increases in production and the increases in purchases to cover future production will have a *magnified* effect on general levels of production and income since they will add to the income of individuals and other firms in the economy and will thus lead to further increases in purchases and sales, which in turn will result in still further increases in income, and so on. The students will also note that Dempsey's policies during the period 1933–1936 involved the activation of substantial idle bank balances in the early part of the period and a substantial increase in bank loans (and hence in the public's money supply) toward the latter part of the period. And of course the respending of these funds by others similarly led to still further increases in sales and income, just as in the years between 1929 and 1933 reductions in inventory led to cumulative reductions in income and production with concomitant repayment of bank loans and consequent reductions in the money supply and general spending.

The data in Exhibit 6, appended to the case as part of the general economic background, are useful in showing just how large and important the changes in inventory have been on several occasions in the last two decades. In 1937, for instance, business firms added 1.8 billion dollars to inventories, while in 1938 production fell short of sales by 1.1 billion dollars. This nearly 3 billion dollar drop in production accounted for almost half the entire decline in the gross national product between the two years. Similarly, between 1948 and 1949, the drop in business firms' investment in inventory totaled nearly 6¼ billion dollars, actually considerably more than the decline in outlays on plant and equipment and on residential housing or in the total national product.

Toward the close of discussion of the Dempsey case, the students are led to argue the question whether business firms, in framing their inventory policies, should take into account these possible broader effects of their actions. Do such broad effects define an area of responsibility for business management, such as Dempsey's? Can executives reasonably be expected to weigh the broad impact of their decisions and as a result to refrain from taking the action that might be most profitable and desirable in terms of the interests of the firm itself, of its stockholders, and frequently of its employees as well? Does it matter whether other firms are accepting such broader responsibility, if it is a responsibility, at the same time? Is this something that only large firms need consider? And even in the case of a large firm whose shift in action might be great enough by itself to have some traceable effects, what inventory policy for that firm would contribute the most to stabilizing business conditions?

Ordinarily the discussion is not carried to the point where there are clear and generally accepted "answers" or judgments regarding these broad questions of responsibility. Similar questions are raised again, notably in a case on investment in a new plant, and also in a case where the immediate issue is maintenance of production in the face of a declining demand in order to support incomes in a community where the firm is a large employer. Also the Full Employment Acts of 1945 and 1946, and a policy statement on Economic Stabilization issued by the Committee for Economic Development, are discussed later in the course to raise such related issues as the following: if individual business firms do not properly have any major responsibility with respect to stabilizing business conditions, and/or if, at best, they can individually do little to discharge such responsibilities as they have in this regard, what then should their position be on public policies designed to contribute to these goals?

Those who are in the best position to testify as to the immediate impact of the case method are the students who have taken courses under this program. With a view to eliciting testimony of this kind the planners of this volume at the time when the project was first conceived invited young research assistants and instructors in the School, all of them recent graduates, to submit papers on the case method in a competition for two prizes, one offered at the research assistant level, the other at the instructor level. Substantial excerpts from four of these papers, reflecting particularly the reactions of the authors as students under the case system, are presented in the following pages. The first of these papers is by Donald R. Schoen and Philip A. Sprague, the second by W. Waller Carson, Jr., the third by Powell Niland, and the fourth by Albert H. Dunn, III.

The Case Method as Seen by Recent Graduates

I. What Is the Case Method?

DONALD R. SCHOEN AND PHILIP A. SPRAGUE

A research assistant at the Harvard Business School often finds himself speculating about the significance of his activities in collecting and writing the cases which form the working tools of the School's educational process. This speculation is characterized by his posing to himself such questions as the following: "Precisely what is the case method?" "What is the nature of the learning process under the case method?"

This paper is an attempt by two research assistants to answer these questions. Throughout we are trying, on the basis of our recent experience as students and our current status as apprentice members of the Faculty, to place the emphasis on the question which can be simply stated but not so simply answered, "What's really going on at the Harvard Business School?"

THE CASE METHOD—IS THERE ONE?

Just what is it that we so knowingly refer to as "the case method"? In a broad sense we can define it by contrast with the so-called lecture method. Instead of textbooks, the case method uses descriptions of specific business situations. Instead of giving lectures, the teacher under the case method leads a discussion of these business situations.

On closer examination, however, we find that this definition doesn't really tell us much. We can understand what this method is only by looking at a few instances of what goes on in the classroom.

Here is a class, for instance, in which the instructor is trying to sharpen the students' insights in the field of Human Relations. The assigned case seems to be more a dramatic narrative than a business problem. It tells simply, and partly through the use of dialogue, the story of a young girl who, as the result of many circumstances, has lost her job and ended up in the hospital. The instructor starts the class hour by asking one of the students the question "What interests you in this case, Mr. Jones?" From then on, the discussion appears to be directed entirely by the class. The casual observer will probably be puzzled by the apparent lack of participation by the instructor; his main function seems to be to fill the blackboard with a variety of student comments. Yet the intentness with which the students are taking part makes it clear that something important is happening.

Should we conclude, then, that good case-teaching involves the use of simple cases, that the instructor must inject himself only rarely into the discussion, that the purpose of the class hour is to offer a series of unintegrated ideas with the integrating process to be carried on by the student?

If we do, what then do we think of a concurrent experience in a class in the Control course? The case furnishes only the material necessary to answer the specific question "Should the Conmay Company scrap its power plant and buy electricity from the local public utility?" The instructor quite obviously has worked out beforehand a "correct" solution, and the hour is spent drawing from members of the class the many variables involved in reaching such a solution. To be sure, there is considerable emphasis placed by both students and instructor on the imponderables which complicate a purely mathematical solution. Clearly, though, the discussion is being led by the instructor toward a predetermined end.

Is this the way cases ideally are taught? Can we decide which of our two instances thus far is the better use of the case method?

Let us look at still another class, this time in Business Policy. Here the case is written with a broader scope. We have a complete story of the Allenby Chemical Company from 1920 to the present. Personal relationships, production techniques, balance sheets, methods of distribution—all the many variables of the business situation in which the company finds itself are written up in the case. The instructor starts the hour by asking, "Mr. Smith, you are president of Allenby. As of January, 1948, what are you most worried about?" As in our first instance, the instructor lets the class carry the ball at the outset. Gradually, however, some agreement as to major issues and significant problems emerges, and at the end of the hour the teacher is consciously trying to permit only such discussion as will help sharpen that agreement.

Is this combination of nondirective and directive approaches "the case method"? Is it the broad case which is characteristic?

Obviously the answer is that each of these instructors is following *a* case method of instruction, but none of them *the* case method. It seems important to us to recognize explicitly in this discussion that a wide variety of techniques are being used and can be used. These techniques change from course to course as a result of (1) variations in course objectives, (2) differences in personalities and abilities of individual teachers, and (3) differences in the data with which courses must be concerned. Even within a single course, teaching methods will vary over a period of time as the class progresses or as the particular emphasis changes.

The final form of the cases in a course and of the instruction itself depends on all three factors. Cases may be written so that the student is faced with a decision to make; or they may simply recount what happened, what was decided, what the president thought, and so on. They may focus on a particular aspect of a large situation or be concerned with the whole situation. The teacher may lead the discussion or let the class lead it; he may try to work toward a "school solution" or point up the many solutions that can be arrived at. All these variations will be made in accordance with the instructor's evaluation of what he wishes to present, of what he hopes to achieve, and of himself.

Granted, then, that there is no one case method, that it means, and is, many things to many people, what are the similarities, the points in common, which all teaching at the Harvard Business School has; what are the common denominators of Faculty and Staff activity? We feel that there are at least three:

(1) A focus on experience. Since the School has as its primary purpose the training of men for positions of actual business responsibility, all its activities stem from, and are beamed at, the problems of current business. Its materials in large part are derived from actual experiences in business or government. Its Faculty is composed almost entirely of men who would fit quite easily into responsible administrative positions. Its ability to attract men for graduate work depends, in the last analysis, on its capacity to maintain in the business community a feeling that such work pays off.

Because of all these facts and because emphasis is on providing the student with the typical rather than the atypical situation, courses are forced to reflect "what is real" rather than one man's conception of "what ought to be," as determined in the relative insulation of an academic institution.

(2) An accent on the particular rather than the general. On the assumption that the businessman's primary forte should be decision-making rather than theory-construction, and that skill in making decisions comes from practice, emphasis is placed on the case situation as such rather than on compiling theories from a number of cases. The differences between, rather than the similarities of, a number of cases are continually stressed in order to ensure that students will solve problems in terms of these specific situations.

(3) A focus on the student's "having an experience." This is to say that individual courses and the curriculum as a whole are designed not simply to convey knowledge but to require the student to assimilate useful ways of thinking and the data they demand in a meaningful (to him) manner. The thesis that learning is solely an intellectual process is not accepted; instead considerable attention is given to stimulating both the emotional and the intellectual reactions of the student.

THE CASE METHOD—ITS IMPACT ON THE STUDENT

Just as there is no one way of teaching by the case method, so there is no one way of learning from it; students learn in different ways and in different degrees. Again it is possible, however, to distinguish a pattern, or common thread, which we have chosen to describe in four stages: an initial reaction of frustration, an arousal of curiosity, a development of insight, and a final achievement of administrative power.

The frustration is a very natural first reaction on the part of a student who finds himself in the classroom with a completely strange set of tools, a new approach, a different emphasis from that which he has faced before. The comforting certainties of mathematical analysis, the facts of English history, the development of political theory, have been replaced by shifting sets of data, often incomplete, on the basis of which the student is being asked to make decisions.

Although the areas of first-year study seem to cover the whole range of business activity—Finance, Production, Administrative Practices,

Marketing, Control, Public Relationships and Responsibilities[1]—the characteristic emphasis is continually placed on specific situations and experiences.

Instead of beginning with a textbook on principles of marketing, the student is given a pedestrian description of how the Ward Machine Company put a mechanical shaver on the market. Instead of a book on Human Behavior, he is given a transcript of a conversation between a foreman and a worker.

The initial atmosphere of the classroom does little to restore a feeling of certainty. The behavior of the professor is strangely disconcerting. There is an absence of professorial dicta, a surprising lack of "answers" and "cold dope" which the student can record in his notebook; rather he is asked what *he* thinks, what *he* would do, what problems *he* feels are important.

Similarly he finds that today's problems cannot necessarily be solved by yesterday's solutions. Every time he feels that he has arrived at generalizations or principles which will apply in all cases, he is confronted with a new set of variables which will not yield to such analysis. The plea that he has insufficient evidence or data on which to make a decision is more or less ignored; he is told to do the best he can with what is available.

He finds that the variations and ramifications of blueprint reading, of debits and credits, of common stocks, of markups and markdowns, are not dwelt on, as such, but seem to come up as a part of a case or a group of cases. Just when the hairsplitting stage is reached in a discussion of the Cost of Living Index or the Dow-Jones averages, the instructor shifts the emphasis to "What would you say to the boss?"

The student is not allowed to use his favorite phrase, "other things being equal"; he cannot "ignore for the moment" the marketing aspects of a production case. Broad as his study areas are, they won't stay put. In a Finance class he may find that the decision whether the XYZ Corporation should seek additional funds through equity financing or through a short-term bank loan hinges on his appraisal of the future market for the company's new Widget; similarly, half the classroom hour in Production may be spent in discussing the human relations problems involved in changing the work flow in the ABC Company's plant.

These restrictions and limitations occasion pit-of-the-stomach reac-

[1] This is the list of course titles as it stood in 1948–49. Variations in phrasing occur from year to year.—ED.

tions which can hardly be termed academic. The student learns quickly that there is much he does not know, that short-cut solutions and theoretical shadowboxing will not clarify issues or unravel real problems.

In this setting, his natural curiosity not only is stimulated but works toward constructive ends. He sees and "feels" the need of finding out how others have solved their problems and what methods they have used. He not only accepts but asks for an exposition of the techniques, such as double entry bookkeeping, nondirective interviewing, and statistical sampling, which executives before him have found to be effective tools. Data, methods, techniques, analytical approaches, and so on, are absorbed by him in a realistic context, not as unrelated material to be returned to the instructor, orally or in writing, at a later date.

At some point, from continued emphasis on group as well as individual activity and from his written reports on cases as much as from his oral classwork, the student achieves insight into his personal makeup. As he airs his views, feelings, reactions, attitudes, and prejudices and sees them reinforced or rejected by thinking individuals around him, he has an opportunity to re-evaluate and reappraise his own character and personality. Preconceived notions and handed-down attitudes examined in an atmosphere of reality and with a focus on effectiveness can be seen for what they are.

Intellectually, too, he begins to realize that there are a variety of ways of looking at business problems. In his second year especially, when he has further opportunities to learn and use specific skills and methods of approach to the more particular problems of, say, accounting or advertising, he begins not only to understand that realistic situations are manageable but also to discriminate between various means of managing them.

Finally, as the student gets more practice in approaching and solving problems, as he learns the vocabulary and the methods of marketing, production, finance, and so on, as he achieves a knowledge of his abilities and shortcomings, he begins to sense a power and facility in dealing with the manifold variables of a modern business situation. This is not to say that he is an expert administrator; rather, perhaps, that he knows he is not. He has, though, composure in the midst of complexity, and he is confident that skillful thinking and activity, in terms of particular situations rather than in terms of principles learned by rote, can lead to successful handling of the problems he faces during his administrative career.

II. Development of a Student under the Case Method

W. WALLER CARSON, JR.

It is the purpose of this paper to describe the case method of instruction and to trace the reaction and development of a student by examining the author's own recent experience as a student at the Harvard Business School. With this examination as a basis, the unique values and limitations of the case system are discussed.

Perhaps the most striking experience of the student confronted with the case method for the first time is the discovery that the preparation of most assignments differs from any in his previous school or college training. I found that I was not held responsible in a retentive way for a given body of facts or propositions upon which subsequent work would depend. The primary responsibility in preparing for each class session was for a common-sense analysis of the relationships involved in a printed description of a situation in a business concern. Such a description, called a "case," seemed most often to be written from the point of view of one person within the company's organization. Typically, it included a statement of the nature of the industry and perhaps some background information about the company's operations and organization, along with such quantitative and other factual information as might be available to the individuals chiefly involved, *whether or not pertinent.* The inclusion of irrelevant information in the cases was an important device to force us to think about selection of information in making our analysis. The case frequently dealt with a situation in which some decision seemed called for or had just been made. Sometimes the situation as described was such that the responsible executive was not aware of an impending decision or problem. But generally the more subtle cases, in which we students were required to decide whether or not an issue was immediately present, were left for later in the program. In our early assignments a few leading questions were appended to the cases to help direct us to the significant areas of the situation and guide us in preparation for class discussion. Later in the program, as we gained proficiency in analyzing cases, specific questions were omitted, and we were forced to seek our own means to get into the heart of the problem.

From the first assignment, we felt an intense interest in the cases, both because of the uniqueness and freshness of the material itself and because of the competitive spirit prevailing among us. My own preparation for a class generally consisted of careful reading, some experimental figure work to discover the relationships inherent in any financial data which might be presented, and some thought about the significance and solution of what seemed the most important problems.

During the first few weeks, case problems constituted the leading topic of conversation among my classmates out of class. It soon became apparent that discussion of a case in a small group was a valuable preclass activity. Even with careful individual preparation, we almost always discovered that other members of the discussion group had found different problems and emphasized different aspects of a particular case, disagreeing over their relative importance. And in the classroom itself, too frequently for our peace of mind, the discussion centered upon still other combinations of problems within the same case, some of them unrecognized in our preparation.

At the beginning of the program there was a widespread feeling that we were not making progress. What were we learning? There seemed but little increase in our usable knowledge. The discussion of a case assigned today did not seem to build upon conclusions we collectively reached yesterday. We felt that many issues involved in particular cases were not resolved and not fully understood as we went on to our next assignment. From time to time our instructors assured us that we were not expected to be able to resolve all phases of each case so early in the program. The result was that many questions were in our minds concerning what we were trying to learn from these cases. Interest in the daily work was actually stimulated. Later, as we gained power in discussing problems, fewer issues remained unresolved.

From time to time, in studying particular cases, many of us were handicapped by lack of knowledge of specific institutions or business practices, such as the organization of certain markets or financial institutions. Our needs were ultimately met in a number of different ways, through discussion with colleagues, some of whom might have greater knowledge of the particular area, or through the instructor's answers to student questions in class, or occasionally through collateral reading. Although this lack of specific knowledge seemed to slow our progress, the study of the case material created the need for seeking these specific pieces of information and showed us why they were worth acquiring. The result was greater rapidity of increase in our knowledge than we realized. The raising of natural questions in the mind of the student is a very significant characteristic of the case method. The need for searching analysis and for knowledge of business institutions and practices is made real, and the possible uses are repeatedly demonstrated.

Gradually, as we progressed in our program, we felt greater confidence and ease in approaching a new case, reading it, analyzing it for problems, and considering possible solutions. The difficulties of terminology[1] became fewer as our familiarity with the conventions of business increased. We achieved a widening acquaintance with the range of business problems. Through repeated analysis and discussion of fresh cases and exposure to an increasingly greater variety of problems in many kinds of companies, we gradually seemed better able to discern and weigh the factors bearing on one issue. We were becoming more proficient in a conceptual kind of reasoning, balancing nonquantitative and highly intangible factors with the results of cost, quantity, price, rate, and profit analysis to arrive at a decision.

With advancing maturity in our point of view, we were discovering that frequently either of opposing alternatives was tenable, depending in some instances upon matters of interpretation but more often upon varying individual judgments concerning the relative emphasis to be given the various significant factors. We found it fruitful to approach these problems by using common sense rather than precedent as the test of alternatives, by seeking full understanding of the essential facts rather than projecting our own opinions or prejudices as though they were the facts. We began to gain a realization of the complicated nature of these situations, in which human personality, motivation, and group behavior were essential determinants. We began to feel out and understand our own reactions toward these situations.

From the first, we had been presented with management problems in which the complex interrelationships of production, marketing, finance, and human relations were all present. Gradually we felt a growing power to analyze and understand them. But, as our initial confusion diminished, it was replaced by an increasingly skeptical attitude. We began to be highly critical of all decisions and all possible lines of action. Our instructors, at the same time, began to bring special pressure on us in the matter of taking action after we had achieved understanding of a situation through critical analysis. We learned that action had to be taken in many instances even in the face of limited information and that absence of action must be a considered decision, not made by default. It is significant to note that the case method was stirring up an extraordinary amount of activity in our minds. In our skeptical and critical attitude, we were asking important questions concerning the feasibility of the actions under consideration.

---

[1] The case method avoids academic arguments over terminology by accepting the terms used by the principals in the particular case. At the same time the students are made aware of the differences in the use of terms.

As we were pressed to make decisions and to recommend action, we demanded more data. We were critical of the cases as too limited to convey the experience and intimate knowledge of business possessed by the participants in a situation and inadequate to convey impressions of the personalities involved. All these developments were highly effective in maintaining our rapid rate of learning.

But in some respects we seemed to be stretching the case medium to its limit. Under the pressure to be decisive, to be willing to commit ourselves and take a stand, there was a tendency to make assumptions rather easily in order to supplement the material gathered for us in case form. There was a general understanding, mistaken or not, that all the information needed and used to reach a decision was to be found within the confines of the printed pages of the case. In short, many of us were becoming increasingly conditioned to an essentially artificial kind of relationship with business situations. We knew them primarily through the medium of our case material and were content to treat cases as complete statements of knowable reality. Our techniques of reading and analyzing cases became highly stylized. Much of the freshness of the printed case as a medium was gone. Out-of-class discussion was more and more confined to those cases on which we were to complete written assignments.

In our earlier contact with the case method, we had seemed to be coming closer to the realities of business. Now that we felt that we had achieved a degree of mastery in comprehension and analysis of case materials, our interest tended to level off, and the thoroughness and eagerness with which we had formerly prepared each case declined. The greatest further advance toward understanding business problems came in collecting our own information in the execution of assignments requiring research in the published sources normally available to businessmen, and in assignments to study particular companies or industries wherein much information was obtained by interviews with operating personnel.

The rapidity with which we arrived at these successive attitudes varied from man to man, depending on individual aptitudes and maturity. For most of us the skeptical stage was reached sometime in the second year of our two-year graduate program.

From the foregoing description of the author's experience it is apparent that the case method stimulates an unusually high degree of mental exertion on the part of the student. The case method is essentially a discussion method. Confronted with cases as a medium of learning, the student experiences a gradual growth in the maturity of his point of view, but the path is not smooth. His mental reactions run successively from great interest and natural curiosity to confusion and some degree of frustration, and then to various degrees of skepticism. In the long run, progress seems to be rapid. The student grows in analytical ability and in power to discriminate among relationships of different kinds. As this development takes place, the cases which he is assigned for study should increase in length and complexity.

A major problem that confronts the student in each case is the extent to which he can derive generalizations of greater usefulness than mere solution of the current problem. He comes into contact with views ranging from outright denial of the possibility of deriving any valid generalizations to a belief that the generalizations to be abstracted from cases are one of the most valuable features of the case system. Here a utilitarian point of view is of value. One of the student's important jobs in the case method is to distinguish between areas where generalization is feasible and areas where it is dangerous, i.e., to determine when a generalization seems to have sufficient validity to be useful. The student needs to recognize that the dangers of too broad generalization can be minimized by his being alert to factors which differentiate one situation from another and which thus narrow the scope for truly useful generalization.

The case method, then, has unique values for business education. It develops analytical ability in a practical way by presenting the student with realistic business problems. It leads to maturity, a broad point of view, and an understanding of the intrinsic nature of business by presenting a wide range of cases involving highly complex problems. By interesting the student, raising questions in his mind, and requiring a great deal of mental activity on his part, the case method enables the student to make progress with noteworthy speed.

While the positive values of this method outweigh the limitations, it is well to recognize the latter. Although the case method has realism, it is by no means identical with reality. The case writer has made a selection of the facts for the student, who gains little practice in seeking and recognizing pertinent facts and relationships in the continuum of daily detail that makes up the life of people in business. The medium, the printed page, is restricting and incapable of conveying many subtle but important overtones of human personality and conduct. Finally, the student faces a given problem for a relatively short time and without operating responsibility. In the actual situation, of course, operating personnel must live with their problems. In these respects, the case method lacks some realism, but it seems to convey more of the essential nature of business administrative problems than any other method.

III. The Values and Limitations of the Case Method

POWELL NILAND

My knowledge of the case method has come from my contact with it as a student and, more recently, as a research assistant; I do not have any considerable acquaintance with its use outside the field of business administration or in ways other than those employed at the Harvard Business School. My experience to date, however, has caused me to become an enthusiastic advocate of the case method for teaching business administration. At the same time, I believe that the lecture method can make a smaller but essential contribution.

The case method has unique characteristics which make it highly effective in training the student to cope with situations which confront an individual business. First of all, the case material is interesting to the student. It is real, it is lifelike, and it deals primarily with concrete and specific questions—Should the production manager recommend to the board that the Ajax Company erect a new factory building?—rather than with generalities and abstractions—What are the general advantages and disadvantages of a single-storied versus a multistoried building for production purposes?

Realism is enhanced further by the student's being cast in the role of the administrator rather than in the role of an outsider studying the performance of an administrator. For example, in a case presenting the situation which confronts a production manager, the student takes the position of the production executive and decides what, if anything, should be done and how any recommendations are to be accomplished. Thus because the raw material of instruction is concrete, specific, and personal, it is more easily visualized by the student.

Not only can the student visualize the subject matter of the course, but cases have the appeal of a "story," a human interest appeal. Most people are interested in learning what other people do, how they do it, and whether they succeed or fail. This applies particularly with reference to business; witness the popular appeal of Horatio Alger's "from rags to riches" series and the wide reading of biographies of leading administrators.

A second characteristic which makes the case system effective in the teaching of business administration is that it provides experience in performing essential parts of the administrative task. The student studies by partaking of the administrative process. The importance of this fact lies in the nature of the administrative process. My analysis of that process is to regard it as consisting of (1) skill in making decisions and, after objectives and means have been decided, (2) skill in achieving the objective by working through people. A division of the process into two parts is artificial since they are mutually interacting, but the concept is useful for discussion. A skill is developed largely by doing, rather than by assimilating through verbal means what another has learned. One cannot learn to play tennis by reading a book or listening to a lecture; even watching others in action is not enough. One must actually *play* to learn. Others may help, but *doing* is all-important. Since, in my opinion, administration is a skill, it can be learned only through *doing*.

Furthermore, the case system puts the student in the *habit* of making decisions. Typically, he prepares a case for each day's class in a course, and for two or three different courses each day. The frequency with which he has to do this accustoms him to the decision-making process, including the exercise of his analytical and critical thinking and the exercise of his imagination. Thus he not only exercises his capacities daily and develops his skill but also develops self-confidence and willingness to accept responsibility. All this takes place within a framework of time limitations, a characteristic of an administrator's job. Time limitations apply not only to the total amount of time which may be allotted to preparation of one case as compared with another but also to the time which may be allotted to the different elements of each case. The student soon perceives the necessity of deciding upon the important factors in a situation and, in analysis and planning, of spending most of his time and effort on the more important elements and a minimum on the less important. This, of course, is developing "judgment."

Administration is a group process, and under the case method the students get some "feel" for the importance of the group. In class the students themselves play a major part in analysis of the case situation and planning of action. Outside the classroom the students discuss cases with one another in preparation for the class periods; indeed, it is quite customary for even the lunch hour conversations to be filled with discussions of cases! At the Harvard Business School, assignment of a series of written reports on specific cases is an integral part of the case system; group discussion of the report cases is not merely permitted, but prescribed. Thus the student becomes accustomed to participating in a group undertaking. The individual, nevertheless, is responsible for his own solution, and his analysis and program of action cannot rely merely on the fact that a majority of the group agree with it.

Another important characteristic of the case method is that it forces the student to think analytically and constructively. The use of the case method generates pressure on the student to think. This result is accomplished in several ways. First, the student is put in the position of the administrator and asked, "What should be done to accomplish this objective?" The method appeals to the student's desire to be an administrator by allowing him to act like one. Secondly, the case presents a challenge. The case approach has an element of the competitive spirit that most sports have, with the challenge being presented by the problem rather than by human opponents. Thirdly, the case system gives the student a sense of participation that is lacking (or present to a much smaller degree) in the lecture method. The individuals in the class *contribute* toward the solution rather than *receive* the solution from the instructor. After a relatively short time under the case method, it is significant that the students become vocally dissatisfied when the instructor takes up most of a class period reciting *his* ideas instead of developing theirs! And, finally, the discussions both within and without the classroom result in critical examination of one another's ideas, and this pulling and hauling of ideas refines each student's thinking. It is well known that talking over our problems with someone else stimulates us and helps us to clarify our thinking.

Although I feel that the case system is primarily important in developing skill, it also provides for the student's acquiring interrelated factual knowledge. The student not only accumulates facts but learns how to utilize them in solving an administrative problem. For instance, the student acquires knowledge not merely of the general functions of advertising but of the varying effectiveness achieved by advertising in a series of specific situations in which the results are modified by the difference in products, the difference in types of customers, and the difference in promotional programs. Or, in considering the problems of a tannery, the student in his analysis and planning must relate the situation of the individual tannery to the whole leather industry. To this end he must familiarize himself with certain essential background material. Later he may study another firm in the same industry and observe the individual differences between firms and the somewhat different relationships of each to the industry. Similarly, realistic preparation of cases demands that the student accumulate some knowledge of general economic conditions and that he consider their influence on the individual firm's situation.

As a result of thorough analysis of many cases, derived from different departments of a business, from different industries, from different stages in the distribution process, from different types of organizations

— in short, cases in a large variety of economic settings—the student accumulates a considerable store of factual knowledge with perspective and with an awareness of the interrelationships involved. This mastering of facts in relationship to one another is important because a business executive acts in an individualized situation and must know what effect, if any, action in one department will have on other phases of the business.

The case method develops in the student a facility for effective utilization of all the factual knowledge at his command. A critical attitude is engendered which results in the student's becoming able to select from his general store of knowledge those facts and theories which can be useful and learning how to apply them to the particular situation at hand. It also trains the student to evaluate the possible impact of economic developments, and thus facilitates adjustment to change.

Thus far, I have presented the merits of the case method, as I see them, from the standpoint of the student. The case method, however, has its disadvantages. First, progress in developing administrative skills is slow, and student and teacher alike feel thwarted, especially in the early months, when the student first comes into contact with the case method and is seeking to comprehend his changed position and responsibilities under the case method of instruction.

Secondly, the case method as applied to instruction in business administration assumes a basic knowledge of facts as well as a maturity— a readiness for acceptance of responsibility—that, if the results are to be realistic, puts a lower limit to the youthfulness of the student. I am referring not necessarily to chronological age nor merely to an intelligence quotient but also to biological development and to the combination of characteristics that we term "personality." Deeper analysis and the precise determination of the minimum requirements, however, I leave for others more competent than myself.

Perhaps this second limitation of the case method is related to another: that there sometimes results an overemphasis on positive decisions, decisions to take action where action may not be justified or to force a solution where none is feasible. For instance, there may be an unwillingness to admit defeat in a business situation and to liquidate the business. Negative decisions, however, are important in business administration. As Chester I. Barnard so succinctly phrases it, "The fine art of executive decision consists in not deciding questions that are not now pertinent, in not deciding prematurely, in not making decisions that cannot be made effective, and in not making decisions that others should make."[1]

Occasionally a student offers a completely unrealistic, farfetched analysis of a case situation, perhaps as a result of his being so intent on achieving a solution, any solution. This behavior too may stem from overemphasis, in the case method, upon positive decisions. Nevertheless it is the opposite difficulty which is likely to prove more serious, namely, the underlying human tendency to procrastinate, resulting from the desire to avoid making positive decisions. Thus it seems necessary that the emphasis in the case method should continue to be directed to the decision-making process.

A more important limitation of the case method is that it oversimplifies the business situation. Recognition of a problem is simplified because the areas to be searched are limited by the case itself, a condition not typical of business. Furthermore, the factors involved and much of the information needed for analysis and planning have been incorporated in the case by the case writer; whereas in the business situation, deciding what information is required and getting it (if it is available with an appropriate expenditure of effort) are an important part of the task of the administrator. At least a partially offsetting gain, however, is that this short cut gives the student time to consider a great many more problems than would otherwise be possible. By the time a graduate has reached an administrative post, he is likely to have absorbed many factual details and much background material that he can call upon to help him in a given business situation.

Another important limitation of the case method is that it cannot synthesize the whole administrative process. After analysis is completed and plans have been laid, there is the actual carrying-out process, the daily supervision of details on a face-to-face level, and the checking up on results, in preparation for which the case method can be of limited help. Here too the knowledge that comes from actual performance is required, and the case method is less effective than for other phases of the administrative process. But group discussions and, in some courses, a project in the form of a report compiled, organized, and written by a group of four or five students give at least the beginnings of practice.

Being the work of human beings, the case method, of course, is not infallible. In the selection and presentation of cases there are errors of

[1] Chester I. Barnard, *The Functions of the Executive* (Cambridge, Mass.: Harvard University Press, 1938), p. 194.

interpretation by the instructor; in the collection of case material there are errors of commission or omission by the instructor and the research assistant. That the case method always will be short of perfection on this score, however, only limits and hardly destroys its usefulness; and on balance I believe it is unequalled as a method of developing administrative skill in handling problems arising within an individual business.

But training in ability to cope only with typical individual business situations is not enough to produce the well-rounded business administrators whom our present-day society, and undoubtedly our future society, demands. As President Conant pointed out in his foreword to *Education for Business Responsibility*, "Such men must understand not only the practical working of business organization but also the economic and social climate in which business operates."

Granted the need for broad economic and social knowledge on the part of the business administrator, then is the case method the best means to use for this type of training? Broad economic and social knowledge may be conveyed as a by-product of analysis of cases presenting individual business situations, but the process is a piecemeal one, and the student's knowledge may exhibit frequent and wide gaps. To attempt to convey broad economic and social knowledge systematically through a series of special cases, however, has the disadvantage not only of artificiality but also of slowness. Thus it seems to me that some use of the lecture approach, together with class discussions and outside reading, is appropriate in equipping the embryo administrator to cope with extra-individual-company situations. Even in these areas, however, I believe that, with due regard to appropriateness and time pressure, supplementing the lecture approach with a few cases can make the educational process even more effective.

IV. Basic Characteristics of the Case Method

ALBERT H. DUNN, III

The case method is a complex method of instruction, which stubbornly refuses to stand still to be photographed. Perhaps, however, its character can be illuminated by consideration of the significant questions "Who should study under the case method?" and "What should be studied under the case method?"

WHO SHOULD STUDY UNDER THE CASE METHOD?

Some students derive great benefit from case method study, while others adjust themselves to it poorly or not at all. The basic equipment which the case method student should possess is not dissimilar to that needed by the lecture student. They both must be intelligent, curious, industrious, and retentive and must have an acceptable ethical code. But the student who would prosper under the case method must have other endowments, which are not requisite to success under the lecture system of instruction. He must be capable of happy adjustment to a truly democratic process, and he must possess a tough yet flexible mind. Without these two qualities he misses much that the case method offers, and is liable to suffer mental anguish to no purpose. Under the lecture method of instruction, neither the acceptance of truly democratic methods nor a tough and flexible mind is requisite. On the contrary, a facile memory and a willingness to accept authority are often the winning factors when the grades are distributed to a lecture class.

The mind that can adjust easily to a democratic learning process has a number of distinguishing qualities, not the least of which is willingness to accept risk. The risk element is present in several forms under the case method, and the student who is to profit from case instruction must be prepared to take these chances.

By placing its emphasis on free discussion of the case material in class, instead of on authoritative exposition of the material by the instructor, the case method involves the student in the risk of uncertain progress. At no time during the learning process can he look into his mirror and tell himself with certainty, "I know this and this, but I haven't yet learned this. I have progressed thus far from yesterday and so far from a month ago." This risk of uncertain progress appears to loom considerably larger under the democracy of the case method than under the authority of the lecture method.

In undertaking any formal educational process, the student is forgoing the experience, income, and accompanying social advantage which he might acquire if he were working. But under the case method, the student must be willing to accept this risk plus that of his uncertain progress. If he cannot readily condition himself to accept this double risk, he either wastes his time in fruitless worry or leaves school.

The student under the case method must develop the art of floundering gracefully in this uncertainty. He must ultimately come to enjoy or at least to live at truce with uncertainty, or the case method will be unbearable for him. Not all students are emotionally constituted to accept this floundering and uncertainty. The psychology of some men drives them to seek surety and to shun doubt. Such men, in my observation, seldom make outstandingly successful case method students.

The mind that will grow under a democratic learning process is willing to participate actively in its own training. Lacking this quality, the student is passive and loses much of the value of the case method because he does not personalize what he is learning by participation in the learning process. He becomes the poor possessor of secondhand ideas and techniques.

Without class discussion the case method is sterile. The student must be willing to state his analysis and conclusions and to defend them in a critical atmosphere. In addition, he must be prepared to expose his conclusions to rebuttal, knowing that he lacks complete knowledge of the situation. This requirement adds to the difficulty of participation and demands a special kind of courage. The student must be willing to go as far as the facts of the case will lead and then to go on into the unknown, guided only by the *direction* of the preceding reasoning. Moreover, he must do this in the public atmosphere of the classroom.

Willingness to accept the risk of uncertain progress, willingness to set aside reticence in defending their logic, and courage to go a step beyond the facts are the qualities which the case method requires of its students.

The successful case method student must possess an unusually strong and resilient mind. Without such equipment it is difficult for him to learn from the *situations* upon which the case method is based. Rather he will tend to seek infallible principles instead of welcoming multiform situations.

He must be strong enough to accept the fact that no one can, or will, give him a definitive answer to his problem. The problem posed by a case is not a circuitous means to a predetermined end but a tough business puzzle to which both instructor and student must bring all their skill and insight, all their logic and analytical ability. No one can give them an answer to this puzzle, since it has no "answer" in the sense that a difficult physics problem has a solution. The case method student must be flexible enough to accept the "gray" answer and to set aside his natural predilection for blacks and whites. The variables in the field of business administration more often than not preclude a Q.E.D. answer to business problems. It is the student's task to steer the variables toward a reasonable course of administrative action, which is not, however, an answer in the scientific sense.

Under the case method, not only must a student forgo reliance on an instructor's authority, but he must be eager to develop his own conclusions. He is forced to sink or swim on his own power. He does not have the support of a large body of opinion and recommendation offered by his scholastic superiors. He will be judged by the quality of his own reasoning, the presentation of his analysis, and the depth of his insight.

Perhaps the most important of all the qualities required of the case student is a willingness to act and to accept the responsibility for action. This responsibility is difficult under the case method because here, as in business, the student must take action without all the data which he desires as a basis for his decision. He must accept the responsibility for action even when he feels that under ideal conditions he would have more time to ponder and more extensive data with which to work.

This responsibility-for-action requirement of the case method is perhaps its principal distinguishing characteristic. The lecture technique for the most part does not have action as its goal but seeks to implant knowledge or instill appreciation. The case method student must be able to learn the techniques of *reasoned action*. It might even be fair to say that he must not be unduly reflective or unsure of himself lest he neglect action for introspection and self-doubt.

WHAT SHOULD BE STUDIED UNDER THE CASE METHOD?

The case method is not widely used in advanced education for reasons of its cost, the paucity of skilled case instructors, and the long-standing precedent of the lecture method. In some fields, also, the alliance between the material to be studied and the case method will always be an unnatural one. Therefore, some commentary is appropriate on those areas in which the case method functions effectively and those areas in which it functions poorly.

As mentioned earlier, the case method is a most satisfactory means of developing the student's ability to act in situations which combine personalities with fact. It does this by schooling him to inquire and to analyze. Conversely, when the objective of learning is *appreciation* or *knowledge* for its own sweet sake the case method falters.

In business administration, action, in the context of people and data, is paramount. Hence in the teaching of business administration few principles can be forged which will guide the student infallibly to a proper business decision. The only "principle" of any use is the development of the student's ability to reason his way through a maze and arrive at a conclusion for action. It is this sort of reasoning for action which the case method fosters so well in the student of business administration.

Under the case method, a student quickly learns the semantics, i.e., the meanings of language in his field, not as definitions by rote but as the sense and feeling for shades of varied meaning among terms commonly in use. No amount of textbook application can give him this knowledge so thoroughly as does the case method. He learns, for instance, that profits are different things to different people (and governments!) or that burden and variable costs take on in almost every instance special significances from particular situations.

This absorption of semantics is not an educational end of the case method but a by-product of the student's case work. It develops as his attention is focused on the problems of his cases until, almost unconsciously, he comes to understand and interpret a language which was mumbo jumbo to him a few months earlier.

One of the most significant things the case method can give to a receptive student is variously called "business intuition," "insight," or "judgment." This quality is partly the result of the student's cultivation of his ability to analyze, partly the result of his mastery of the semantics of business, but in other ways it is more than the simple sum of these two things. It is the "feel" for a business situation, the ability to ask the right questions of a business problem, a reasoned hunch as to the proper course of action. All this can be summed up in the propensity of the case-trained student to land on his feet in a business situation.

On the other side of the argument, there is doubt whether the case method is the best way to teach methodology such as accounting, statistics, or the operation of machine tools. The arbitrary imposition of a case framework on the transmission of *fact* from instructor to student is highly artificial, and students may become resentful and impatient. There is a traditional form for balance sheets; there is only one way to strike a median; and the turret lathe has a standard nomenclature. Information of this kind is poorly transmitted in case form, since that form implies the existence of a problem, such as whether the reserve for depreciation should appear on the liability side or the asset side of a balance sheet.

Certainly, once the basic facts or methods have been expounded, then case instruction comes into play in exploring the limitations, the use, and the application of the data or methods. That is to say, the student learns little from a case problem as to where the depreciation reserve belongs on the financial statement, but he learns much from coping with problems of depreciation reserve policy under varying sets of circumstances.

CONCLUSION

In conclusion it is interesting to speculate on a possible connection between the increasing use of the case method in education and the far-reaching changes in our scientific and social environment that have taken place since the turn of the century. In the areas of administration, notably business and public administration, the impact of change upsets the supposed "principles" (other than the moral principles) of yesterday and replaces them with what may be termed "currently useful generalizations." Thus, as the world has become more and more complex and as, under the impact of science, one seeming certainty after another has given way to doubt, it has become more and more necessary to teach the *action* arts from the simulation of experience rather than from abstract principle.

When cases and case discussions rather than textbooks and lectures constitute the major vehicle of teaching, what is the part which the instructor should play in the classroom? On this question there are perhaps almost as many opinions as there are case instructors. In the following paper, Kenneth R. Andrews offers one concept of the instructor's role.

The Role of the Instructor in the Case Method

KENNETH R. ANDREWS

I

Everything said in any symposium dedicated to the "case method" of teaching administration raises questions about the role of the instructor. What is his job?

At first glance his duties seem less onerous than those of a lecturer in the main stream of educational tradition. Students seem to do all the thinking, most of the talking, and make for themselves the relevant discoveries. If they originate the ideas, organize the discussion, and establish their own rate of progress, their instructor need not prepare lectures, prescribe texts, serve up precepts in palatable form, or test for regurgitation of fact and principle. If the end is not knowledge, the instructor need not know all.

In actuality, however, the direction of free discussion toward specific goals increases the demands made upon the instructor. Active student participation in the learning process serves no purpose unless class discussions are emotionally satisfying, intellectually productive, and occasionally profound enough to provide prejudice-shattering encounters with the facts of life. The instructor is responsible, therefore, for the value of the talk he presides over. He hopes the talk will broaden judgment and affect behavior.

Case teaching, in short, like case learning, calls for more skill than knowledge. The instructor provides the impromptu services which any group discussion requires. He keeps the proceedings orderly. He should be able to ask questions which invite advance in group thinking and at the same time reveal the relevance of the talk that has gone before. He needs the ability to weave together the threads of individual contributions into a pattern which not only he but his class can perceive. He needs the sense of timing which tells him that a discussion is not moving fast enough to make good use of available time or is racing away from the comprehension of half the class. He knows what to do on such occasions. He exercises control over an essentially "undirected" activity, but at the same time he keeps out of the way, lest he prevent his class from making discoveries new also to him. Since unpredictable developments always distinguish real learning, he examines his class rather than his subject. His workshop is not the study but the classroom. He is the architect of a constantly complicating social structure, for a poorly integrated group cannot provide for itself much educational experience. He must himself be a student.

Now, as if the skills which case teaching particularly demands were not enough, the case instructor ideally exercises as well the intellectual and social skills of preceptorial teaching, without the advantages of preparing in advance how and when he will exercise them. The most important condition of all learning is the interest of the learner. In case teaching, the instructor not only catches the interest of his students, he keeps them interested in each other, in the case before them, and in the aims of the course. His own share of the pedagogical virtues —inspiration, humor, approachability, enthusiasm, articulateness— must be as substantial as any sophomore spellbinder's, and his skill in drawing upon them must be adequate to situations he cannot predict.

In the face of these large requirements (placed side by side with the limiting fact that faculty members must be recruited from the human race), I think it is fortunate that the skills demanded are not beyond the range of skills which can be learned. The case method is itself an ample vehicle for the training of instructors. It appears to be as efficient in finally producing qualified professors as in preparing students to learn from experience. Despite the truth that, as in the case method of *learning* administration, no hard and fast rules exist to regulate the pedagogy, I think it still possible to inquire into the instructor's function and how he can play his difficult role with passable effectiveness.

The ideal conduct cited here may seem and may be an unrealistic celebration of unattainable skills. Part of the vitality of the case method, however, is the restlessness of aspiration it stirs among those who learn and teach. The goals are as important as the performance, which may fall short of them. If no one person can exercise continually the skills I consider desirable, he at least acquires a sense of direction from seeing ahead of him the course he wants to follow.

At the outset, description of the role of the instructor cannot be a quest for technique. There are many "case methods"; the multiplicity is traceable to differences among successful teachers and to the variety of case materials. No teacher qualified by the communicable enthusiasm demanded by his profession is barred from developing his own gifts. No static procedure should stereotype his approach to his classes.

To fill the gap left by the elimination of technique, the instructor addresses himself to the combination of case, class, and subject he is teaching. He formulates teaching practices to accommodate the variables in the classroom situation before him. He subordinates his personal aspirations and convictions to his observations of classroom reality. Students learn that successful treatment of a case consists most often of examining the case situation as primarily a configuration of fact and feeling which must be dealt with *as such* rather than as an example of an inductively attainable generalization. When the instructor adopts toward his students and his subject the same orientation, he is ready to lead a case discussion and remain free himself in exercising his leadership. To the man who is looking at the territory, ways to cross it become clear and classroom progress becomes measurable.

Within the latitude thus available, two general activities need additional attention. It seems to me tentatively true that in the way most natural to him the instructor must work consciously first to build and protect a cooperative, informal relationship between himself and his students. The second task common to all varieties of case instruction is the stimulation of discussion toward course and school objectives. Common to both these creative aspects of the instructor's role is the paradoxical problem of control. The instructor must keep discussion free and yet direct its course toward productive ends. As an instructor, he finds himself cast as a student. Now, as a nonauthoritarian leader, he discovers he must be an administrator as well.

II

Successful application of the case method of instruction to the classroom presumes a relationship between student and instructor and among students which is quite different from that prevailing under more traditional forms of instruction. Students now are not sitting at a professor's feet; they find themselves forced to stand on their own. The instructor cannot be a lawgiver or an oracle. He establishes himself— preferably without saying so—as a fellow student and proves by behavior that he means it. He makes himself available as an equal when his students are conditioned to expect him to assert himself their superior. His students, initially confused by both method and instructor, come eventually to know that his participation will provide all the help they need.

In preceptorial teaching, the instructor appears as an authority. Students, he hopes, listen to him. In quiz-sessions or discussion periods, he often probes into or patronizes their ignorance, exposes their fallacies, reveals their deficient preparation. He exhorts faster and faster absorption and use of what he has found to be worth learning. He sits in judgment over the acquisition of communicable wisdom. No matter how brilliant and kindly, he stands in relation to his students as a critic. In case teaching, such a relationship, especially when complicated by the initial confusion attending the method, is never fully productive. Undistorted communication and mutual understanding in the classroom, as everywhere, are possible only when adverse criticism is not explicitly or implicitly involved and when self-consciousness, emulation, and anxieties of all sorts can be laid aside.

Confusion and insecurity will never be replaced by independence and tough-mindedness in the classroom until a case has been laid open by discussion and has yielded up gain to its students. That in turn will not happen while confusion clouds the search. The instructor can break out of this circle by giving his first attention to an atmosphere not of disapproval but of informal friendliness that will permit students to grope their way to competence.

The instructor can listen with an intentness that should not be concealed to everything that is said, with the demonstrated purpose of understanding, not criticizing, its relevance and importance. He can best teach respect for student views by exhibiting it himself. He can help people say what they are stumbling over. He can, with questions that show his interest (not his brilliance), help a man make his point clear or clarify his thinking until it is expressible. The instructor can demonstrate that he will not with approval or disapproval fence in the discussion or insist that the same formal approach be taken to every case. If initially he extends the same interest to all things said without trying to label them as important or trivial, his class will recognize that as individuals they can voice an incomplete idea or an unconventional conclusion without encountering derision. They may gradually feel free to fight their way publicly through ignorance, perplexity, and loose thinking without fear of being pilloried for the effort. After a few weeks of practice, students and instructor may be members of a productive group, capable of self-propulsion toward mastery of the subject. The problem of the instructor-student relationship sometimes vanishes before a startled recognition of what a group of intelligent students can accomplish without detailed dependence upon professorial authority and knowledge.

If permitted to do so, then, a new class can move beyond the banes of case discussion (collective monologue, irrelevancy, boredom, timidity, triviality, individual and group introversion) into productive discourse. Retrogression in the face of new cases full of essentially unsolvable problems is always possible. As time goes on, the instructor, better known now to his students and they to him, can take steps more directive than permissive to preserve the relationships once achieved.

When, as will happen, the student throws up his hands and asks the instructor to provide answers to the questions implicit in the case, the instructor may return to the student or to the class the responsibility for doing the work of the class. He will ask the student to present his own thinking first. If he wishes eventually to offer some answers, he may do so after the class has wrestled with the case, for then his answers will not have taken the place of the thinking of the class. However he handles the students' desire that he solve the problems in the case, he will not capitulate to the request for aid and comfort unless he wishes to abandon the case method for something less painful and less effective.

In addition to disclaiming the role of authority which his students wish him to assume, the instructor may have to deal with more violent disruption. Like all social units, a class is susceptible to the volatile reactions of the individuals who comprise it. Occasionally the instructor, weary perhaps at having to play so many parts, will find himself cast briefly as group therapist. If he notices that the discussion is listless and disjointed, as eventually he will, he would do well to identify rather than ignore the block. If he asks what is going on, he will at once test the strength of his relation to the class. If that strength is adequate and if his class knows he will not misuse the information, he will get an answer, or perhaps a hundred different answers. He may then find himself in the middle of an outpouring of feelings clustered around the grading system, the work load, the complexity of recent cases, the confusion of working out a cogent attack on intangible problems—around the resurgent insecurities of genuine learning.

On a hot spring afternoon, for example, a hundred men talking about a case on administrative reorganization of a railroad grew more and more listless. The number of participants dwindled to the handful who will always talk. What they had to say threw little light on the problem of introducing change among personnel who had for years been habituated to behavior no longer acceptable to higher management. The physical restlessness, the shuffling of paper, and the collapse of interest afflicted the instructor, who was getting bored himself, so sharply that he asked, "What's gone wrong with the discussion today?"

The inattention vanished with a snap. A total silence, induced by the shock with which graduate students will usually greet implied criticism of their performance, lasted for a minute. Then one man stuck up his hand to answer that the Production exam they had just had was enough to queer any discussion of somebody else's human problems. Here he was interrupted by a man who complained both about the ventilation of the room and about the inadequacy of the information in the case. He was followed at length by a dozen other students and topics. The instructor did not hear all they said because he was considering with some concern what one visitor from the United States Military Academy and two others from civilian colleges (who were investigating the merits of the case method) were thinking about.

Finally one student announced that he had reached the point of knowing what certain people were going to say and wished he could hear some voices less often and others more. The whole class applauded. A relatively calm discussion of the problem of student participation followed, ending in agreement that the problem could be solved by students who had been holding their peace. At the end of it the instructor called a recess. For ten minutes he was assured by various members of the class that the restlessness was resentment against some of the more eager volunteers. When the class reconvened, the discussion went better—and well beyond the final bell. Students volunteered who usually spoke only when spoken to. The visitors observed that the outburst was "interesting," but they looked a little as if they thought the procedure undignified.

Dignity aside, the surest method of dealing with such an outburst is for the instructor to suppress his own defensive reactions and to refrain from combatting student emotion with faculty logic. As feeling spends itself and the class behavior itself becomes a case for analysis and action, the class will sometimes recognize its need for adjustment to reality. If some action should be taken by the instructor, he can take it, referring difficulties that do not fall under his jurisdiction to others. In any case, the instructor's role is first to detect and then to allow the free expression of any feelings that congest the premises and impede the progress of his course. If he does not, he will lose control of the climatic conditions under which a class can work effectively.

Group therapy can easily take so much time that course objectives are prejudiced. A class might, if invited to do so, prefer spilling feelings to grappling with case problems. The instructor can avoid this possibility without restricting freedom of discussion by assuming always that the case is the object of primary interest and by recalling attention to it by question or comment. He will seldom have to stop to lift the lid if everyday discussions are free rather than repressive and if arbitrary limitations on procedure do not bottle up considerations relevant from the student's point of view. The everyday humor, informality, and freedom of a temperate classroom climate will not often breed thunderstorms, unless the instructor seems to be hoping for rain.

Creating a classroom environment that will permit achievement of important discussions and preserving it against regression are not difficult. If permitted to do so, the class will provide the structure necessary for coherent group thinking and develop a code of its own to regulate participation, to provide for progress, and to direct activity toward the greatest usefulness to the participants. If the instructor allows unity to emerge on its own terms, he is well started. If he refrains from the seven pedagogical sins of condescension, sarcasm, personal cross-examination, discourtesy, self-approval, self-consciousness, and talkativeness, he can hope for the best without worrying about the techniques whereby it can be achieved.

III

Maintenance of group good health and the formation of supple working relationships between students and instructor are only means to serve educational ends. It is instructive, of course, for the members of a class to learn by experience how to listen to each other and how to make themselves understood; but in a class, as in a more permanent organization, the purpose for which the participants are gathered together must not be lost sight of. The instructor, while he preserves the essential environmental conditions, guides the discussions toward the objectives of his course and ensures that they serve as new experience for each of the participants, including himself.

If the establishment of classroom relationships is a social skill, the direction of class discussion is primarily intellectual. This leadership must be flexibly responsive to the situation in order that the understanding which the student reaches shall be his own, not his instructor's. The shifting situation unfolding in the classroom must be subjected to running analysis. And as the instructor looks ahead, his leadership is that of the explorer of new territory. It is not the instructor's highest function to lead tourists over a path worn smooth by previous trips. Each time it is taught, if it is taught well, the case is made by group analysis a situation somehow different from what it was in last year's classes. Different approaches to its handling are called for. Different derivations, some more useful than others, will be made by different students. Without knowing in detail what each of his students is thinking at any moment, the instructor must make sure that personal decisions are finally made and that the group has accomplished whatever it began.

As the leader in the logical development of the case discussion, the instructor uses three tools of infinite flexibility which can promote the productivity of case discussion without taking from students the responsibility for doing their own work. He may (1) ask questions, (2) restate and rethread what is said, and (3) voice his own opinions and draw upon his own knowledge of fact. The attainment of skill in combining these three activities can challenge the instructor's capacity all through his career.

For centuries, under all systems of instruction, successive generations of teachers have been asking questions. The interrogation most effective for the stimulation of case discussion derives from this great tradition, but some questions of hallowed respectability can be eliminated at once. The questions which are prepared the night before to plunge straight to the heart of the case's knottiest congestion will either fall on deaf ears or wrench the class's conversation out of its natural shape. Questions which seem to call attention to an individual student's immaturity or obvious error will freeze their victims and silence the witnesses of an unfair contest. Questions designed only to establish the amount of preparation the student has devoted to the case introduce disciplinary considerations which blight more effective incentives to hard work. Questions which display the instructor's virtuosity meet the fate they deserve; he has to answer them himself.

The questions the instructor finds most useful are phrased on the spot to serve their directional purpose. Depending on the stage of the discussion and the appropriateness of their context, they can be broad questions designed to open the discussion but not to predetermine its course or questions serving to clarify what an individual has said ("Do you mean that . . . ?") or to invite expansion ("Do you have more to say about . . . ?"). In subjective areas questions should identify opinions that have been stated as facts, re-establish the tentativeness of bald statements about what *is* rather than what *may be*, and qualify dogmatism in any form ("Do you think that true in all such cases?" "How does that apply to the situation described in this case?").

As a discussion takes shape, questions that more pointedly invite forward motion toward understanding the basic issues of the case, that keep attention on issues as already defined, or that objectively inquire into the premises upon which a facile conclusion rests become possible because they arise naturally out of the requirements for acceleration which an interested class will respond to as time grows short. The questions drawing upon all the skill an instructor can muster are those

which serve to suggest, when they are thought about, connections between individual contributions made by students or connections between cases as they accumulate toward the unity dictated by course
objectives. It is chiefly in the perception of a continuity linking separate situations that many students come to learn from case experience.
("Is your point related to Mr. Y's?" "Does your observation apply also
to yesterday's case?" "What does that have to do with the bigger questions of . . . that we have been looking at?")

The most directive questions are those which sometimes an instructor finds himself asking when a class has passed beyond the point
where under its own power it can cope with the case. When the
issues have been examined and decision is imminent but not easy,
questions from the instructor can serve to restrict unintentional eva-
sions, unproductive repetition, and the backward wash of the discussion as it beats against the toughness of the problem. Here he must ask
for what he and his students do not yet know—*how* this objective can
be reached, that problem solved, this countereffect guarded against.
Often these questions can be as insistent as earlier questions were nondirective, for by this time they are reminders of what the whole class
wants to know. So long as the class continues to wrestle with the problem, then questions are effective. If the answer is not forthcoming, the
instructor should not begin to plant ideas or fish for specific materials.
The case left unfinished is often more productive of further progress
next time than one polished off by the instructor as the closing bell
strikes.

Questioning comes so naturally to pedagogues that as a tool of the
case method it can easily be overused. Ordinarily in a free-flowing discussion questions can be infrequent. If the questions come casually and
naturally as responses to what has been said (rather than pop out of the
instructor's mental file of "points not covered yet"), not only will they
be understood and quickly responded to but they will be inconspicuous
aids to the discussion, serving to advance but not to force the discussion. The good case analysis is not a series of questions by instructor
and answers by the students. When students follow each other without
interference by the instructor, his role as questioner is thereafter to
keep himself and everybody else informed about what is going on and
where they are going. One of the best classes I have ever attended was
opened by the instructor's asking, "Mr. X, will you begin?" No other
questions were necessary that day.

The question is the invitation to further thought, the reminder that
discussion must get somewhere, the lever for control of the intellectual product of group intelligence. Restatement, the second major

activity of many instructors, is the means by which the progress prompted by the question is marked, clarified, and made usable.

A free-flowing discussion, moving fast, winding back upon itself, eddying about semantic snags, is extraordinarily hard to follow. The remarks made by the individual students are almost all impromptu; they usually last less than half a minute. They are often incompletely thought out and are always imperfectly expressed. A man sometimes seems to change his mind in the middle of a sentence. The instructor can slow the current and clear its course by pausing frequently to re-phrase very briefly in his own words what has been said. Less often he may summarize the entire discussion to date.

The principal function of restatement is to translate individual remarks into a common language for purposes of clarification. As each student comments, he speaks in his own language and from his own understanding of himself and of the case. The instructor's contribution is to make sure that the substance, clarified by restatement, forms part of the visible accretion. As he verifies what has been said, he gives the student an opportunity to correct or extend the new version of his remarks.

If restatement is to be constructively directive, it must not distort the student's comment by either minimizing its implicit content or exaggerating it. The instructor must not jump to conclusions about what the student means to say, must make no substantive additions, and must not suggest by the spirit of his impromptu condensation that he agrees or disagrees with the observations. He may point up the idea; he may turn it in his hand so that all the facets are visible. The student himself may be surprised by seeing his idea thus illuminated; but he should not often feel that *he did not say that* and that his meaning has been distorted. If, as sometimes happens, distortion does occur, or if the student's thinking advances, as it should, as he hears the paraphrase, he must be able to correct or expand the record without rebuff from the instructor.

To restate what has been said, in order to assist understanding without making students permanently dependent on such assistance is a delicate task, but not an extraordinarily difficult one. If the instructor listens intently to what is said and if he tries to understand before he tries to evaluate, he will understand it. Useful restatement requires only willingness to listen and concentration upon what is said. The astonishing results which this willingness and concentration produce when applied to an apparently innocuous comment will do more than exhortation can to persuade a class toward the same efforts in understanding each other's point of view, skill, and experience.

The recognition which restatement permits in student and class can also be achieved by a periodical summary of class discussions. This sort of performance by the instructor can indirectly point the way to further progress by marking and underscoring that already achieved. It should not be a regular occurrence. Most of the time the student must summarize for himself, just as he must decide for himself what he has learned. No one else can tell him. Sometimes, however, a restatement of the major themes of a particularly complex discussion will retrieve for further thinking important issues which might otherwise elude attention. Such occasions give the instructor opportunity to identify ideas with the names of the students who proposed them first. Casual recognition of the sources of important individual contributions is a means to acknowledge to those responsible the debt of the group and to imply that within the structure of group performance it is individual capacity for original thinking and cooperative behavior that a school of administration exists to foster.

The third instrumentality for control of discussions and achievement of course objectives, statement by the instructor of his own objectives and of his own knowledge of fact, is much more heavy-handed than the question and the restatement. If the instructor announces his own views early, he may shut off the opinions of students who disagree or encourage unduly those who share his sentiments. If he draws heavily on his own experience, he may bore the inattentive or reduce to silence those who feel they cannot speak with such authority. If he lectures at length, he may exceed the capacity for useful absorption. Under the case method the role of the instructor is so heavily weighted toward leadership as a participant rather than toward authoritative direction that there are those who hold that an instructor should never project his own opinions and information into the deliberations of his students.

It seems to me unnatural to proscribe this activity, so long as it is participation and is not (however well-intentioned) a kind of overlordship. When the essential relationhip between student and class has been successfully formed and tested, then the instructor can speak as a participant and will usually be listened to as such. He need not fear that his remarks will be interpreted as quotations from tablets of stone if the students know how he intends them. He can circumvent the dangers of being misunderstood, which always vitiate one-way communication, by waiting to speak until his questions have stimulated answers which have been examined from all sides and until mutual understanding of the major threads of the discussion has been verified by restatement. Then, knowing his students and knowing the route whereby they have reached the farthest destination of which they are currently capable, he can contribute his ideas to the common pool. And he should, if his ideas seem likely to stimulate further progress into subsequent cases.

The most enthusiastic supporters of the case method recognize that, after all, there is a limit to the altitude to which a class can lift itself by its own bootstraps. If questioning fails to clear the way, the instructor can speak to regenerate the self-propulsive power of the class or to clarify a difficulty surmountable only with technical knowledge. "Lecturettes" may begin or end a class hour or appear at any point when progress in discussion is balked by lack of information. Since the resumption of discussion will provide a test of how well the instructor was understood and since he speaks his piece only when his class has need of it, is ready for it, and can make use of it, he has an enormous advantage over the full-time lecturer. The flexibility of the case method, then, is such that it will accommodate some of the practices of preceptorial teaching, so long as the instructor's orientation permits recognition of the classroom situation as the guide to action.

The instructor who is curious about the case method may well take alarm at such dissections as this. In the absence of abundant classroom transcripts to provide illustrative material, he may still wonder *how* questions may be asked, opinions restated, and personal knowledge and opinion presented to meet the requirements of classroom climate and to approach the objectives which the case method envisions. The answer to the *how* question resides in the class performance. Close attention to what is going on before the platform will provide after the first five minutes of the first case discussion more questions than can possibly be asked, more ideas than can be examined through recapitulation, and material for more professorial comment than a man can express in a week. The problem of controlling a discussion will cease to be difficult when the capacity of students for free discussion is released; techniques for playing the instructor's role become unnecessary. With the knowledge of his subject and with sufficient nimbleness of mind to qualify him for any rostrum, his hand on the reins can be light. He derives his teaching practices from the class, not from any less useful source.

However his judgment prompts him to behave in the classroom, the instructor plays a multiple role. He is student, listener, and analyst. He is questioner, paraphraser, and minuteman lecturer. He plays these parts without costume changes, and he never steals the show from the rest of the cast.

In the conducting of any formal educational enterprise, there are details of size of class, length and nature of assignments, intensity of questioning, use of call lists, grading of classroom performance, and so on, to which some attention must be given. Under the case method, the importance attached to these quasi-mechanical factors will vary considerably, depending on the nature of the material, the maturity of the students, and the preference of the instructor for nondirective discussion or for closely controlled analysis and discussion. The following observations set forth views on these matters expressed by various members of the Business School Faculty in the course of a survey conducted shortly after World War II. They are summarized from material prepared by Robert W. Merry for inclusion in a memorandum to the Committee on Educational Policy from the Subcommittee on Instruction Methods, then under the chairmanship of Professor Harry R. Tosdal.

Use of Case Material in the Classroom

ROBERT W. MERRY

With respect to the practical aspects of conducting a class under the case method, we propose to discuss the following topics: size of class, assignments, discussion of cases in the classroom, sustaining interest, call lists, grading, and encouragement of volunteering.

SIZE OF CLASS

There is apparently a widespread impression that the case method works most effectively with small classes. This impression is not, however, confirmed by experience. At the Harvard Business School, over a period of years classes have, in fact, ranged from six or eight students to more than 100; and the consensus seems to be that numbers from forty or fifty to eighty are the most satisfactory. When the class is too large, the group may be somewhat unmanageable. The success of the case method depends to a marked degree, of course, on the development of active discussion. In a very large class, it may well be impossible to give an opportunity to everyone who wishes to speak; and when students are repeatedly denied the chance to contribute, their interest diminishes. Furthermore, when the class is large and more students volunteer than can be heard, nonvolunteers cannot easily be drawn into the discussion. The initially reticent stay reticent. In a very large class also, the instructor has difficulty in getting to know the students, and the students to know one another, with the result that a too formal atmosphere prevails well into the year. In a class of more moderate size these disadvantages are not present.

At the other end of the scale is the class which is too small. Here also it may be difficult to secure active discussion, but for a somewhat different reason. Experience seems to indicate that at least ten or twelve outstanding students are necessary to ensure a lively and fruitful discussion. In a small class, that many outstanding students may not be registered. Or, if they are, on a given day preparation may have been skimped because of a heavy work load elsewhere, and the good students who are present and prepared may not be sufficiently numerous to carry the discussion forward.

ASSIGNMENTS

The usual assignment for outside preparation is one case per class per course, although this practice is by no means universal. In a course where the cases typically are long and complicated, a single case may be assigned for two or three class periods. (Here it should be remarked parenthetically that discussion on the second day and on the third proceeds more satisfactorily if the assignment for the day has suggested angles requiring careful further preparation.) In other courses several cases may be assigned for a single meeting. And there are many possible procedures between the two extremes. Several short cases may be taken up one after another. One case may be discussed in detail, the others in the group being assigned for background. Or a number of cases may be assigned but the discussion limited to specific aspects, indicated in advance. Or a full case may be accompanied by a series of short sketchy situations that provide variants to the conditions of the principal case.

There is no uniformity in the method of giving assignments. Most frequently the assignment for the following meeting is given orally in class. Occasionally, though rarely, there is a standing assignment to read one or two cases beyond the case under discussion. Sometimes mimeographed assignment sheets are distributed at the beginning of the term or at intervals throughout the term; when these are used, the assignment made in class is likely to be very brief. Regardless of the procedure in making an assignment, however, the instructor may find it helpful to comment on the position which the case occupies in the scheme of the course, to clarify the relationship among cases, and to call particular attention to significant aspects for special study. Occasionally also he may want to set the scene, as it were, especially with reference to the timing of the case. In assigning a problem which faced executives in 1946 or 1947, for instance, he may want to remind the class that at this time the country was just emerging from a period of merchandise shortages, that price controls were just being lifted, and so on. Especially with cases dating back a number of years some setting of the stage helps to hold the students' preparation at a realistic, practical level. In connection with old cases also it often happens that a roughly similar situation exists currently, as, for instance, the anticipatory price rise following the beginning of the Korean war in 1950 in comparison with the price rise of 1940–41. Where there is such a parallel, discussion is likely to be the most spirited when it is focused on the recurrent aspects of the problem.

On the desirability of furnishing a detailed course outline, opinion differs. Some instructors believe that a detailed outline helps the students to grasp the concept of the course and the particular area of study at any time, that it serves as a guide to give meaning to current discussions by showing their relation to the subject as a whole. Other instructors have had the experience that students tend to confine their examination of the case to the restricted area indicated in the outline and may overlook much of the value of the case for areas beyond the special field.

Where the case material includes figures, the instructor may find it desirable, in commenting on the assignment, to offer fairly specific guidance. Sometimes figures are presented in a case primarily for background; at other times they are critical to the questions at issue. The two situations may be difficult for students to distinguish, and the instructor may need to indicate that a few, or many, calculations will be necessary for an intelligent understanding of the case.

WRITTEN ASSIGNMENTS FOR CLASS

Normally, student preparation consists principally of thoughtful reading of the case, probably with underlining of the text and the making of marginal notations. Where mathematical calculations are pertinent, some notes on these will ordinarily be brought into class. Occasionally also the student will have jotted down a rough outline of factors bearing on the principal issues and some tentatively formulated conclusions. In a few courses, at certain stages periodic written assignments form a regular part of course work. At a point where calculations or procedures are important, for instance, the preparation of a page or two of written notes may be asked for. Or in connection with an advertising problem the students may be required to draft copy or submit a suggested layout.

A form of written assignment which is of marked value is the preparation of a brief summary or a list of "currently useful generalizations" based on a group of cases having a common theme. Such an assignment encourages the students to undertake a process of periodic consolidation and appraisal which otherwise they are likely to postpone under the pressure of day-to-day work.

Sometimes an instructor endeavors to sharpen preparation by asking the students to bring to class a brief written analysis of an assigned case. This analysis will serve primarily as an aid to discussion; the instructor may or may not collect and read the papers. Some instructors like to give such an assignment because then the preparation of that particular case is more careful and thorough than would normally be obtained. But the device should be used sparingly because it is likely to take a disproportionate amount of time away from the students' preparation for other courses. The students cannot prepare a number of acceptable written papers each day, give the necessary attention to the succession of longer assignments always pending, and still keep their academic engagements. Ordinarily, with their notes to refresh their memory of the case and of the thinking which accompanied their preparation, the students come to class sufficiently equipped to make an intelligent contribution to the class development of the case. Except in unusual circumstances, the written analysis of cases for daily classroom discussion does not produce results commensurate with the effort expended by the students.

DISCUSSION OF CASES IN THE CLASSROOM

In the classroom there are many ways by which the instructor can open the discussion. Some instructors habitually start with the question "What is the issue?" and from there go on to "What are the pertinent facts?" Others start with "What are the facts?" Others begin by asking, "What action should be taken?" And still others simply ask, "What about this case?"

In printed or mimeographed cases, questions, which may be either specific or general, frequently appear at the end. One instructor may choose to begin with these, because presumably the students will have read and thought about them and will thus be prepared to discuss the particular aspects to which they are directed. Another instructor may prefer to disregard the printed questions and to approach the case from a wholly different angle. Students may be called on to criticize action already taken by the company, or to plan a future course of action, or both. Under the case system, discussion commonly proceeds by breaking down the given situation and examining critically each of the parts. In this atmosphere there is a very real danger that students may develop a hypercritical or negative attitude, concentrate on pointing out at what stages something was done badly or arguing why some proposed course of action should not be undertaken, and carry their analysis and recommendations no further. In such situations, the instructor may need to make a conscious effort to direct the students' thinking into affirmative, constructive channels, to instill some feeling for the importance of positive action: "These are the circumstances; this, broadly, is the thing we are aiming to achieve; how can we accomplish it?" Here frequently it may be salutary to ask a student to imagine himself in the shoes of the responsible executive: "Mr. Jones, you are the sales manager. Never mind all the negative factors. Tell us how you would deal with this situation constructively."

Where a student is given a free hand in analyzing and discussing a case, he needs time to demonstrate his thinking; and the number of participants in the discussion in the class hour will sometimes be no more than five or six. On the other hand, if the instructor chooses to call on a succession of students for one or two points apiece, as many as thirty to forty-five students may be drawn into the discussion. The choice of procedures depends on the personal preference of the instructor, the nature of the material, the size of the class, and the maturity and experience of the students.

Under the case method the objective is to arrive at a decision, ordinarily a decision as to action to be taken. The selection of method by which to reach the objective is, of course, the province of the instructor. He may call upon the student to state his decision and then to develop his reasoning and defend his position. Or he may concentrate on securing analytical development for a large part of the period, with the class formulating a decision after the discussion has proceeded for some time. Several students in turn may state their individual conclusions and advance relevant arguments. And then, after the discussion has gone on for a while and it is fairly clear that the consensus is in a particular direction, the instructor may ask one of the students to pull together and summarize what has been said, or the instructor himself may choose to phrase the summary. Where there is manifest agreement, it may save time for him to do the job, especially if the discussion is at an intermediate stage and the summary is largely transitional. When it comes to the final decision on action to be recommended, sometimes a class vote is taken. It must be borne in mind, however, that often no single decision is reached by the end of the class period, the case being left for further thought.

It sometimes happens that the decision of the company is not reported in the case but is known to the instructor. If there is clearly no breach of confidence involved, the instructor may choose to pass the information along to the class, with or without comment on the outcome.

SUSTAINING INTEREST

From time to time class interest needs to be built up or sustained. Often a change of pace may be helpful. The instructor can modify his line of questioning, illustrate from his own experience, or turn to a new aspect—for instance, examination of the available statistical material. Expressions of opinion by the instructor should be given sparingly lest students, even those accustomed to the case method, fall into the habit of expecting "the answer" regularly to be furnished to them. Humor and a sense of showmanship are useful in case teaching, as in lecturing. Demonstrations, samples of products under discussion, motion pictures—all have their place. The blackboard is useful, not alone for figures and diagrams, but also for listing pros and cons as they develop, for indicating areas of discussion, for clarifying an involved outline, or merely for introducing some animation.

The quality of the discussion may be affected to a certain degree by such an apparently irrelevant detail as whether the instructor sits or stands. The instructor may choose to sit at the desk, where he can glance at his notes, because he feels that there he has better control over the discussion. From behind a desk, however, it may be difficult to keep the class discussion moving at a lively pace. Some instructors feel that they can secure a more spirited discussion by carrying on the class from a position in front of the desk. Once the discussion is well under way, however, with the students arguing among themselves, he may beneficially retire to the fairly inconspicuous position behind the desk.

In some courses, swing-over charts help to keep the class interest high. When the case involves relations between people and the material for discussion consists of dialogue, successive utterances may be printed on large cards stacked at the front of the classroom. One remark at a time is discussed, with possible rejoinders, before the card is swung over and the actual response is shown, to be discussed in its turn.

Role playing is another device which is effective in stimulating and maintaining interest. Students are assigned to represent designated persons in the case, the objective being to personalize the case for the students, to make them feel the reality of the situation, and to lead them to give thought to the personalities and relationships which are concerned. When roles are assigned in advance, preparation may be expected to be excellent on the part of the individuals selected, but superficial among the rest of the class. When the class is divided in advance into groups from each of which it is announced that one student will be selected for a specified role, general preparation is good, provided the groups are small enough so that each student has a reasonable chance of being the one selected. When the assignment is in vague and indefinite terms, however, merely indicating that at the next meeting some students will be asked to play roles, the results are not very satisfactory. Nor is sustained role playing successful when introduced without advance notice; it is a task for which more than ordinarily intensive preparation is required.

Somewhat akin to role playing is the device of turning the development of a case over to a team of two or three students. The assignment is given well in advance, and in their preparation the members of the team make a thoroughgoing analysis. For purposes of class presentation they divide the areas of discussion among themselves in whatever way they judge to be the most effective; and during the class hour they may expect to be interrupted frequently by questions or comments from the floor. Sometimes students who stand in some traditional awe of their instructors are willing to argue more vigorously with their own contemporaries.

CALL LISTS

As an aid to stimulating wider discussion a call list may be useful. It furnishes the instructor with a ready name when no one volunteers; it may be used to call the instructor's attention to the peculiar experience or special background of certain students in the area of the current case, so that these students may be given an opportunity to contribute their special knowledge to the discussion; and over a period of time it assures full participation by the class, since it normally will include the names of at least some students who have not spoken recently.

Active discussion, with widespread participation, thrives best in an informal atmosphere. A very important contributing factor is the ability of the instructor to call the members of the class by name. The instructor, therefore, will be well advised to memorize his class at an early point in the year. The means by which he acquires this command of names, of course, depends on the bent of his own social skills. Important among the aids are photographs, seating plans, and call lists, particularly when used in conjunction with one another.

GRADING

Practice in grading class discussion varies widely. Few instructors actually write down grades while the class is going on. To do so diverts their attention from the discussion while they assess each student's contribution. The pace of discussion is retarded, and the grade, hurriedly set, may not represent a considered judgment. From the students' standpoint, furthermore, the consciousness that discussion is being graded interferes seriously with free participation.

Many instructors never grade class discussion at all but depend on accumulated impressions, so that by the end of the term they are able to put down an appraisal for each of a majority of the men in the class. Obviously this plan is well adapted to a small class but not so well adapted to a large class.

An intermediate procedure, considerably used, is for the instructor as soon as possible after class to sit down with the classroom seating plan before him and call to mind the students who contributed appreciably to the discussion during the hour, making some notation in appraisal of each performance. For an instructor who uses this procedure, the call list or some part of it can be made up to include students for whom no impression has recently been recorded. In a class where a few students have been doing most of the talking while a large majority have sat silent, the instructor may choose to limit participation, for at least a part of the hour, to students who have not contributed to the discussion for several meetings past. He may announce flatly that he does not want to hear from anybody who has spoken during the last two or three meetings.

When the students look upon the class period as a forum for working out joint analyses of the case material, the discussion is more vigorous than when they regard it as primarily an occasion for assigning grades. The instructor will, nevertheless, find that from time to time he needs to press the students to think more deeply, to master the facts of the case, to formulate issues, to separate important facts from unimportant ones, to reason logically, to proceed from premise to conclusion, and to weigh opposing considerations. If a student's preparation has been superficial or if he is relying on personal hunches or timely interjection of catch phrases, it is possible to indicate to him that there are many things in the case which he has not seen, that more careful preparation would have shown them to him. The manner in which this is done is of some importance. Bearing down with questions as to facts, mathematical calculations, or the reasoning behind a particular conclusion can achieve the desired result without antagonizing either the student himself or the other members of the class.

The instructor, if he encounters inadequate preparation, needs to make some diagnosis of the difficulty. A second-year student may be sufficiently familiar with the vocabulary of the subject and sufficiently glib to try skating along on the class discussion without having prepared the case himself. A first-year student, on the other hand, may give a superficial analysis because he genuinely does not know how to go about analyzing the case situation and is not sufficiently trained in imagination to suggest other approaches. It is this student, particularly, who will benefit from close questioning ferreting out clues overlooked or lines of attack which might profitably have been pursued.

ENCOURAGEMENT OF VOLUNTEERING

Lively discussion is dependent on alert voluntary participation by the class. If the instructor takes to stating his own opinion as to what is correct without paying sufficient attention to the students' views and without leading the students along the path of his reasoning, discouragement of volunteering definitely will occur. Such discouragement will appear also when the instructor seems to be "looking for the answer" and calls on one student after another for a statement of conclusions without giving any of them an opportunity to develop his reasoning. More often than not, of course, there is no one "right answer," and the substance of the decision is likely to be less important than the exercise of decision-making. Along with the decision there needs to go some appreciation of the problems of carrying out the decision and in case of a negative decision—not to accept this offer, not to buy that piece of equipment—some suggestion of a feasible counterproposal.

When the discussion is not running in the direction which the instructor thinks is important for understanding, his best procedure is to listen to what the students are saying. They may be developing something significant which the instructor himself has not thought of, or they may have run into a road block which interferes with their progress. In this latter event, the instructor will either abandon the particular line of questioning or develop some new questions designed to remove the difficulty. If the students have failed to grasp the significance of certain things in the case and so have not seen the issue which the instructor is trying to emphasize, it may be desirable to say frankly, "Let's back off and make a fresh start" or "Let's approach this problem for a moment from a completely different direction." The students need to be stimulated to arrive at a decision for themselves.

If the students are carrying on a vigorous discussion among themselves and advancing the development of the case, the instructor does not need to cap each contribution with an appraising comment, as if he were dealing with a high school student's recitation: "Well done, Jones." He should recognize that students like to feel that their efforts have not gone unnoticed; but he may well find that his most effective comment is one which carries the class a step ahead: "Does the point of view which you have expressed, Jones, then lead to this position . . .?"

Occasionally, for the purpose of achieving reasonable coverage, particularly if the period is drawing to a close, volunteering may have to be curtailed, and then the instructor needs to be careful to accomplish such curtailment without discouraging the practice of volunteering.

Students' questions likewise present the problem of how much class time can justifiably be given over to them. An instructor may say, "We will take that up at a later class. Will you please hold your question?" and the student may, in fact, find no subsequent class in which the matter is treated; as a result he may come to suspect the instructor of deliberate evasion. In general, student doubts probably ought to be resolved at the time they are expressed, even if the current discussion has to be temporarily diverted. It is always possible to say, "In brief, such and such is the situation" or "At a somewhat later point we have a case which bears on this in some detail; in the meantime, however, the typical practice is thus and so." Only rarely is a question asked which leads so far afield and is so foreign to the general interest of the class that the instructor feels disinclined to devote class time to answering the query and therefore suggests that the student drop in at his office to talk about it.

In the normal class there will be students who are reluctant to speak and students who talk too much. The instructor must be prepared to find both types. The student who wants to talk all the time gets on the nerves of the class, and good students may deliberately refrain from speaking because they don't want to be thought of in the same category. Unfortunately the student who monopolizes the discussion is likely to be somewhat obtuse and unaware that he is incurring disfavor with the class. After a time there will be boredom and inattention and complete loss of interest when this student is speaking, and eventually there will be outright manifestations of displeasure, such as shuffling of feet and rattling of papers. It is up to the instructor to rec-

ognize the signs and deliberately to take control of the situation, perhaps by means of particularly intensive questioning consciously aimed
at drawing the student out on a limb and disciplining him.

The student who is reluctant to speak likewise represents a problem
to the instructor. The reluctance may derive from a variety of causes.
Some students have speech impediments; others have impaired hearing and hesitate to speak either because they fear that they may be re-
peating what has already been said or because they are not sure just
what point the discussion has reached. Certain students normally are
of a quiet nature and seldom speak unless called on. Others speak
freely in small groups but are self-conscious and frightened at the
thought of speaking out in a large group.

In any class on a given day there are likely to be a few students who
are unprepared on the day's assignment and are in attendance primarily to absorb what they can from the class proceedings, not to
make any contribution of their own. Ordinarily the instructor finds it
helpful to be informed in advance that these men are unprepared. But
in any event their silence is temporary. More difficult to deal with are
the students who have a horror of being classed as "eager beavers" and
who refrain from speaking because of some notion that by so doing
they are improving their personal standing with their classmates. Here
the instructor needs to recognize that a powerful social pressure is at
work and that considerable tact and patience on his part may be
needed to bring these men into active participation.

Switching from an exposition of the instructor's philosophy by the instructor himself to a report from the other side of the desk, the next paper, by DeWitt Dearborn, presents one man's account of what he observed taking place in a series of meetings of a class with a particular instructor.

Observer's Report on the Role of the Instructor in
Case Discussions
DEWITT C. DEARBORN

This paper is based on observations made by the writer during fifteen class meetings at the Harvard Business School. The meetings, running for eighty minutes at a time, extended in broken sequence over a period of three months during the first part of the course in Finance, a required course in the first year of the two-year program. The observations were made in a section in which there were about ninety-five students.

The purpose of the observations was to record what the instructor did rather than what the students did in the classroom situations, with a view to determining whether any generalizations could be made about the function of the instructor in case discussion meetings. Attention was concentrated on the overt behavior of the instructor; thus the report presents very little subjective analysis of why the instructor did what he did or what specific or general effects on the class could be associated with his actions. It is pertinent to remark that the observer thought the teaching successful.

The paper is in three parts. The first presents a narrative description of three classroom sessions, with particular attention to the activities of the instructor; the second presents a topical treatment of the roles played by the instructor; and the third presents some general comments and tentative conclusions.

At the outset the observer kept notes which recorded content as well as interactions. On reviewing the notes after the first several days, the observer concluded that the instructor had been placed, or had placed himself, in situations in which he assumed "roles" that fell into an increasingly familiar pattern. From this point on, the observer turned his attention to isolating and defining these roles and to considering the performance of the instructor in each of them.

Over the period of the observations there was day-to-day fluctuation in the number of roles and their conformity to the tentative pattern;

121

but five distinct roles were finally identified and conceptualized, as follows: (1) discussion leader, (2) resource person, (3) helpful expert, (4) evaluator or summarizer, and (5) judge of performance. Without doubt, a different observer could have distinguished additional roles and might have combined some of those noted. The list is presented simply to facilitate the observer's task of reporting what he thought he saw the instructor doing in these fifteen class meetings.

NARRATIVE DESCRIPTIONS OF THREE CLASSROOM SESSIONS

Session on Santos Coffee Company Case[1]

ASSIGNMENT: 1. What action should the bank take regarding its loan to the Santos Coffee Company?
2. What criteria should be used in judging whether or not inventory represents satisfactory collateral for loans?
3. Would the company's receivables or inventory be satisfactory for collateral?

The instructor opened the meeting by commenting briefly on the next two assignments. He then asked, as a general question, "What action, in your opinion, should the bank officers take regarding the loan to Santos?" A member of the class replied that, in his opinion, if the inventory was given as security by Santos, the bank was making a mistake in ruling out a field warehousing arrangement and insisting on a public warehousing operation.

The instructor asked whether anyone in the class wished to comment on this idea. There was no response. He then encouraged the original speaker to "spell out" his reasons for this opinion. The student did so. At the conclusion of this contribution, the instructor recognized a student whose hand was raised.

This student asked which security arrangement was best for the Santos company. (This question shifted the point of view of the discussion from the bank to the company.) The instructor chose not to answer directly, and he did not encourage the student to explore the question. He did, however, present to the group the problem of deciding what to do with this question by asking the class, "Do you want to decide what the bank should do, or do you wish to look at this situation from the viewpoint of the officers of the Santos company?"

[1] This and a number of the other cases referred to in this paper are to be found in Pearson Hunt and Charles M. Williams, *Case Problems in Finance* (Homewood, Ill.: Richard D. Irwin, Inc., 1949). The remaining cases are in the mimeographed collections prepared by the Business School for the first-year course in Finance.

When the class chose the latter point of view, which was a departure from that indicated in the assignment questions, the instructor made no attempt to substitute a different goal. In the ensuing discussion there was considerable disagreement among the members of the class as to just how either a field warehouse or a public warehouse security arrangement would operate. The students made little progress here and could not reach a conclusion on the major question they had elected to discuss, i.e., "Which is best for the company?" They began to ask questions about the mechanics of such arrangements. The instructor addressed himself to each question, answered it directly, and did not refer it to the group. The group continued, for perhaps twenty minutes, to seek clarification and to defer tackling the judgment question.

Eventually a question on legal procedure came from the class. The instructor's reply was that he would not venture to guess; he would look up the answer and report to the class at the next meeting if the members were really interested and if they thought it significant to the decision they had to make. He commented that he himself had done considerable library research in preparing for the class meeting. He listed references and asked whether anyone else had done any reading outside of the case. Only a few students answered this question in the affirmative.

The instructor then stated that in his opinion the class was unprepared to deal realistically with the case and that rather than answer isolated questions he would give a short lecture on the significant factors. During the remainder of the period he discussed common security arrangements involving the use of inventory as collateral and outlined a procedure for organizing data in order to reach a conclusion as to the suitability of particular inventories for collateral.

The verbal participations by the class in this session may be summarized as follows:

Number of students who responded to a question 10
Number of students who asked a question 25
Number of students who contributed an idea 1
Number of different students who participated 25

SESSION ON HARBIN COMPANY CASE

ASSIGNMENT: 1. According to the final proposal, what are the obligations of Mr. Harbin and the Harbin Company to each other and to the bank?
2. Should the bank make the loan?
3. Describe how the loan against receivables will operate from day to day.

The instructor lectured for about fifteen minutes at the beginning of the meeting. His object was to clarify the changes in ownership and interests in the Harbin Company that would occur if Mr. Harbin's financial plans bore fruit. He made free use of "T" accounts and the blackboard during this period, and at the end he asked the class whether they had any questions about his explanations. This query gave rise to a series of exchanges, lasting about five minutes, between the instructor and individual students. The instructor concluded these exchanges when he asked the class, "Why didn't the bank officers attach any collateral value to Mr. Harbin's prospective stock holdings in the Harbin Company?" The students then discussed this question with little or no guidance or influence from the instructor. They established apparent agreement as to the reason for the bank's decision and also as to their concurrence in this decision. When, during this period, some questions were addressed to the instructor, he turned them back to the questioner or referred them to other class members.

A new contributor then offered an analysis of the case and proposed a plan of action for the bank. The plan was challenged by some group members, and an argument ensued. The instructor suggested that a systematic record of the facts and assumptions used by each participant would be helpful in isolating differences of opinion, which could then be more effectively compromised. He offered to serve as a recorder and to use the blackboard for the record. This proposal was accepted. In the course of the discussion it became clear that some of the students had imperfect knowledge of the facts of the case. The instructor began to insist on precision and accuracy. This procedure revealed inadequate preparation on the part of some students; and the instructor thereupon commented on the loss of time caused by the participation of individuals who were not familiar with the case.

A member of the group then directed the following question to the instructor: "Why should the bank insist that the Harbin Company pay the present note and then turn around and make the company a new loan?" The instructor himself did not answer this question; he referred it, as a general question, to the whole class. During the ensuing discussion, the students directed a series of judgment questions to the instructor, such as the following: "Did the bank officer pick the best security arrangement in terms of protecting the bank's interest?" "Was it the best arrangement from the viewpoint of the Harbin Company?" "Why did the loan officer think that the Harbin Company's receivables were the desirable security?" None of these questions was answered by the instructor. He turned them back to the questioner or called on specific students to answer or referred them to the whole class. Differences of opinion arose during the discussion. The instructor did not enter into the discussion in a dominant role; he did, however, offer his opinion now and then.

About ten minutes before the end of the class period, the instructor proposed that the class consider, from the standpoint of possible effect on the company, the covenant regarding net working capital restriction as it was drawn up in the loan agreement proposed by the bank. When no voluntary comments on this covenant were forthcoming, the instructor called on a student by name. This student responded by asking the instructor why the method of determining net working capital for purposes of the loan was not spelled out. Other members of the class asked whether this kind of covenant was usual, or unusual, in a loan agreement. The instructor replied directly to these questions, and a series of questions from students followed, all of which the instructor endeavored to answer, until one student asked, "Was it necessary for the loan agreement to contain this provision; couldn't the bank have avoided asking it?" The instructor called on a member of the class to comment on that query. A spirited discussion followed, and eventually the class concentrated on what it would mean to the operation of the company to have this restrictive covenant as part of the loan agreement. As the period ended, about a half-dozen students were ready to comment but could not get the floor.

The verbal participations by the class in this session may be summarized as follows:

Number of students who responded to a question......... 13
Number of students who asked a question................ 15
Number of students who contributed an idea............. 15
Number of different students who participated............ 30

Session on Adanac Packaging Machine Company Case

ASSIGNMENT: 1. Prepare the pro forma balance sheet requested by Mr. Cox.
2. Which is the better type of loan for the company to accept?
3. How should Mr. Cox present his decision to the board of directors?

A student opened this class session with the statement that he did not believe the bank should make the loan requested by the officers of the Adanac company. He then went on to outline his reasons for this opinion. He proposed that the class discuss whether the bank should make the loan rather than which alternative offered by the bank should be accepted by the officers of the Adanac company. (The student's proposal was, in effect, not relevant since, according to the statement of the case, the Adanac company already had in hand the bank's offer. The assignment questions, reflecting this fact, were oriented to the problem faced by the company officers.)

The instructor, to whom the student's proposal was addressed, referred the question to the class, as follows: "Do you want to discuss the situation from the viewpoint of the bank officers or from the viewpoint of the officers of the Adanac company?" The class began to discuss the question suggested by the student, some members supporting, some opposing, the view he had expressed. Their contributions seemed to imply their acceptance of the desirability of re-examining the decision of the bank's officers. The instructor did not discourage this move. He restated questions, added some comments, and acted as recorder, using the blackboard.

When a lull developed, the instructor asked the original speaker whether he had figured the "pay-back" period for the company in the event that it took either loan offered by the bank. (This question directed the discussion back to the company officers' problem.) The class accepted this shift in direction and embarked on a series of cash forecasts for the company. There seemed to be competition among the members to refine the arithmetic and achieve precision. At one point the students fastened attention on the interest expense to be incurred on the loan but were unable to agree on its treatment. Dollarwise the item was small; but the students apparently were determined to give exhaustive consideration to the whole pay-back problem, and the interest item seemed to them to be important.

Here the instructor entered the discussion with the proposal that he himself outline some ways of taking this expense into account and that the group then choose among them and get on with the whole calculation. He lectured for two or three minutes; then the students picked up the discussion and carried the cash forecasts to completion

A student remarked that in his opinion the group had not yet made the necessary decisions, that the question whether the bank should make the loan was not a realistic one, and that the task at hand was to decide which loan the company should take. He ended by saying that he thought the decision should be made in the light of the way in which the company proposed to use the funds. The instructor did not refer this proposal to the class, as he had the previous one. Instead, he encouraged this student to "put figures on his ideas" and offered to record these on the board. The student gave the data for a pro forma balance sheet, and the instructor wrote them on the blackboard. As the writing progressed, other students raised questions about the procedures and offered their own opinions as to certain of the estimates required for the statement.

After the pro forma statement was completed, the instructor asked the student who had first made the suggestion how he thought this calculation could be helpful to Mr. Cox in deciding which loan to recommend to the company's board of directors. The student spoke of the direct-judgment issue facing Mr. Cox. The class began to participate. And in the ensuing discussion ideas were expressed by students who manifestly had imperfect knowledge of the alternative loan arrangements offered by the bank. The instructor immediately called the deficiency to the students' attention and insisted that they support their comments with facts from the case. He pointed out that persons who did not know the details of the alternatives facing Mr. Cox could not realistically expect to make useful observations about these alternatives. Subsequently, persons who did not have their facts clearly in mind apparently did not participate in this discussion.

The instructor finally remarked, about fifteen minutes before the session was to end, that he thought the class was ready to make a decision on what Mr. Cox ought to do. The students, however, who seemed to wish to avoid the issue, suggested minor modifications in previous arithmetic calculations or proposed re-examination of some phase of the analysis of the case. The instructor continued, in various ways, to pose the question of what Cox should do, so that the class was always faced with this problem of decision. Finally some members of the class reached the point of making definite recommendations. Differences of opinion persisted, however, and the class continued to ask the instructor the following kinds of questions, in about this order, none of which the instructor would answer: "What did Cox actually do?" "Which loan did the company take?" "What do you think the company should have done?"

The verbal participations by the class in this session may be summarized as follows:

Number of students who responded to a question........... 9
Number of students who asked a question................. 9
Number of students who contributed an idea.............. 22
Number of different students who participated............ 34

THE FIVE PRIMARY ROLES PLAYED BY THE INSTRUCTOR AND SEVERAL INSTANCES OF EACH

The instances which follow were selected from the observer's notes on the fifteen class meetings. They are presented here in order to define and illustrate the several roles.

THE ROLE OF DISCUSSION LEADER

INSTANCE 1: At the first meeting of the class in the fall, mimeographed material entitled "Introduction to Financial Analysis" was discussed. The preparation of a statement of source and application of funds had been assigned when the material was distributed.

Questions raised by the instructor and replies from students took up the first part of the meeting. The questions seemed to be of two general types. The first type was used early in the period: "Do all accounting entries reflect transactions that affect company funds?" "Which ones do? Which do not?" "Why is an increase in the cash account labeled a 'use' of funds?" "Why is a transaction that reduces cash to pay a liability also labeled a 'use' of funds? Is this procedure consistent? What concepts make it consistent?" These questions provoked discussion at a higher level of abstraction than mere rehearsal of the mechanics of developing the statement would have stimulated.

After a period of about twenty minutes on this level, the instructor proposed questions that were on a still higher level: "Do you see how this technique [source and application] can be useful to financial officers?" "What purpose was served, if any, by having you do this exercise?" The class appeared unwilling or unable to move to this level. After several attempts to have specific individuals discuss these questions, the instructor asked, "Do you have any questions about the preparation of the S & A that was assigned for today?" This question seemed to stimulate a large number to participate. The rest of the period was characterized by active discussion by the class on a voluntary basis.

INSTANCE 2: At another meeting of the class the case of the Tremblant Company was discussed. Midway through the period the instructor paused to summarize the discussion. He noted the issues that had been developed and the conclusions that had been reached. When he finished, the class, which had been active up to that point, failed to pick up the discussion. The instructor then asked, "In your opinion, why is it necessary for the Tremblant Company, a profitable organization, to borrow funds at this time?" The class responded actively. The question had been included in the case assignment as one of several to explore. Increased participation by the group seemed to indicate that previous preparation had been made and was now appearing in the class discussion.

THE ROLE OF RESOURCE PERSON[1]

INSTANCE 1: In considering the issues in the Santos Coffee Company case, the class became entangled in the intricacies of warehouse arrangements. The instructor, in response to implied appeals from the students, halted the discussion and outlined the major factors in such arrangements, including public and field warehousing and trust receipts. He concluded by telling the class what material he had found useful in preparing for the day's class meeting and recommended several pieces for their reading.

INSTANCE 2: As the period devoted to discussion of the Santos Coffee Company case came to a close, the instructor took a few minutes to comment on the next day's case, that of the Harbin Company. He stated that in the past many students had found this case difficult—primarily, in his opinion, because they were unfamiliar with the operation of a pledge of accounts receivable. He then described briefly how such a pledge operated.

INSTANCE 3: During discussion of the case of the Southern Smelting Company, a student asked the instructor, "What is meant by 'subordination of the claim'?" The instructor called on a particular member of the class for comment on this query. It became apparent that this student had had legal training. The instructor engaged in a two-way discussion with him, and together they answered further questions from the class.

THE ROLE OF HELPFUL EXPERT

INSTANCE 1: During the first class meeting, as part of the analysis of the Berkshire Company case, the class had attempted to develop a statement of source and application of funds. Although able to carry out the calculations as required, many students expressed their con-

---

[1] A few words should be said about the distinction which the observer makes between the role of resource person and the role of helpful expert. The helpful expert solves, or helps directly in the solution of, problems in the immediate situation. The resource person, on the other hand, does not follow this procedure but confines his activity to supplementing the limited experience and knowledge of the class by himself supplying additional data or by suggesting ways in which the class can supplement its own resources. He then leaves the members of the class to work out their own solution to the particular problem, using, if they can and wish to do so, the additional resources he has helped to make available to them.

fusion as to why certain items on the balance sheets required adjustment by reversing entries whereas other items did not. When the class assembled for the second meeting on the Berkshire case, the instructor stated that, since he was aware that the students had problems, he had attempted to clarify for himself what these problems were and to develop some concepts that might help to clear up some of the confusion. He suggested that the class might wish to take notes on what he was about to say. He then lectured, using the blackboard as an aid, for about half an hour. At the end of this period, a question-and-answer session developed, which continued about twenty minutes longer.

INSTANCE 2: While analyzing the case of the Clarkson Lumber Company, the class became involved in estimating the company's probable future need for funds. After a time, several individuals in the class began to question whether anything worthwhile had been accomplished by all the suggestions contributed and implied that the estimates were worthless. At this point the instructor entered the situation, outlined what the class had done, made explicit the assumptions that underlay the figures, and suggested that the questions which were being raised might better be phrased so as to bring out the differences in assumptions rather than in such a way as to suggest that the class efforts had failed to improve the understanding of the case. His behavior appeared to reassure the members of the class that they had made progress, and they proceeded with the discussion.

(It was the observer's opinion that the problem had been attacked in a logical manner. During the discussion the group had developed a close approximation of a pro forma balance sheet. Up to that time the technique for the pro forma balance sheet had never been discussed explicitly, nor had it been illustrated in any of the material assigned.)

THE ROLE OF EVALUATOR OR SUMMARIZER

INSTANCE 1: Midway through the first meeting on the case of the Clarkson Lumber Company, the class began to lose direction in its discussion, with the result that some members suggested that they had been going nowhere in particular. They then began to retrace several parts of their previous analysis. At this point the instructor intervened and, using the blackboard, recapitulated the thinking of the group as evidenced by the class comments. He summarized the conclusions that they had reached and the logical processes that seemed to be implicit in their methods. He then described a method of estimating a balance sheet that they would use in the future and pointed out how similar their approach had been to this recognized technique for financial analysis.

He thereupon reviewed the issues which the class had raised but in his opinion had not resolved, and suggested that the students continue with one of these issues.

INSTANCE 2: Toward the end of the meeting devoted to discussion of the case of the Tremblant Company, the instructor used five or ten minutes to review what the class had done. He recounted the issues that had been raised, noted the analysis that had been made, and then stated that in his opinion this analysis had been sufficiently deep to serve as a realistic basis for indicating what action the officers of the Tremblant Company should take.

THE ROLE OF JUDGE OF PERFORMANCE

INSTANCE 1: For the second meeting on the case of the Clarkson Lumber Company, the class had been requested to prepare a pro forma balance sheet. In response to a request from the instructor for volunteers to present their estimates, a number of individuals, several of them by repeated participation, provided the necessary data as the instructor recorded the statement on the blackboard. The instructor next asked one of the most active participants to spell out the assumptions underlying the estimates. He insisted on precision and close analysis. After a few minutes the student became confused—whereupon the instructor called on other members of the class, with about the same result. These efforts continued for five or six minutes. The instructor then lectured for about ten minutes, spelling out the assumptions that appeared to have been made and pointing out explicitly, by example, how the resulting balance sheet would have differed if different assumptions had been made. He went on to comment that sophistication in the use of financial techniques, such as preparation of pro forma balance sheets, required that the user be able to make his mental processes explicit. Many times differing assumptions might be equally defensible, but full understanding would be hindered if the estimates alone were available for discussion.

INSTANCE 2: When the Wellington Shoe Company case was assigned, the students were asked to prepare a pro forma balance sheet. The instructor opened the class period by announcing that he would record the items of the statement on the board as each student contributed them. He said that each contributor should state the amount of the item, the assumptions made (if any), and the reasoning leading to the estimate for the item.

(This procedure had been unsuccessful when attempted some three weeks earlier, during the second day of discussion of the Clarkson case. Now, however, the class handled the problem with facility.)

INSTANCE 3: At the end of the class meeting devoted to analysis of the Santos Coffee Company case, the instructor remarked to the class, "The lack of familiarity with such terms as 'warehouse receipts,' 'trust receipts,' and the like, and the lack of understanding of the mechanics of the alternative arrangements proposed by the bank have operated to reduce the value of this meeting today. Next time, we have the Harbin Company case. If we are not to have the same problems with that case, I think many of you will have to do some reading in the library on receivables financing."

INSTANCE 4: Early in December an examination was given on the Sprague Tool Company case. In the middle of January a class meeting was devoted to reviewing this examination. The instructor arrived early and put on the blackboard certain "answers" to the calculations required in the examination. Mimeographed copies of three student examination papers had been distributed to the class a few days before.

The instructor opened the meeting by saying, "Let's compare each of these student papers with the others and compare the calculations with those on the board." These comparisons occupied the entire period. In the course of the discussion, the students tried to agree on grades for the three papers. They compared texts and calculations. When a student proposed a grade for a paper, he was usually challenged by the others to outline his criteria for assigning a specific grade. An interchange of ideas on acceptable and unacceptable performance was facilitated by this process. There were, in the end, large areas of agreement in the class.

SOME GENERAL OBSERVATIONS AND TENTATIVE CONCLUSIONS

In addition to the foregoing analysis, some other comments on the instructor's behavior may be noted:

(1) The instructor had complete command of the case facts. He rarely examined the case during the class session, and although he had notes on his desk he seldom referred to them.

(2) The instructor used questions frequently. These were either restatements of questions from the students or prepared questions. Some were assigned with each case; these usually were "key" questions, which served to shift the attention from one issue to another or to place the discussion on a different level of abstraction.

(3) The instructor frequently used prepared lecturettes on important concepts or difficult techniques.

(4) The instructor attempted to maintain a more direct control of the discussion when the discussion content was technique- or fact-oriented than he did when questions of judgment or decision were dominant.

Finally, a few generalizations may be offered with respect to the behavior of the instructor in handling case discussion classes:

(1) The instructor can rarely be a nonsignificant factor in the classroom situation.

(2) The instructor cannot, by his behavior, prevent the group from acting to place him in situations requiring him to make *choices* as to the role which he will assume and the way in which he will function in that role. The choice of "no role" is not a realistic alternative.

(3) The instructor has to make these choices frequently and quickly. He rarely has time to engage in a logical, consecutive thought process as a preliminary to behavior.

(4) The instructor must be able to perceive the needs, the resources, and the weaknesses of each class and of particular individuals in the class and to weave these into the over-all goals of the course in the process of discussing specific case issues. Case-method instructors are in situations which are fluid and constantly evolving into new situations. The experience of the class will be fruitful in direct proportion to the instructor's perception and ability.

(5) The choice of roles, as well as the manner in which the instructor functions in them, is significant in determining how much opportunity is permitted the class members for "developing judgment" and for "learning to exercise responsibility." The factors which affect the attitude of the class toward *taking advantage of these opportunities* appear to be less closely related to the instructor's own behavior.

Of special interest to the instructor, and particularly to the instructor embarking on the case method for the first time, is the question of the work which he needs to do on a case prior to the class period. This question relates not only to the analytical procedures which the instructor may need to employ in his preparation for teaching but also to the kinds of notes or other supplementary material with which he may wish to fortify himself as a basis for the conduct of the discussion. The following observations and suggestions are summarized from a memorandum, "Case Instruction for the Beginning Instructor," prepared by Robert W. Merry in his capacity as a member of the committee working on the general survey referred to in connection with the paper "Use of Case Material in the Classroom."

Preparation to Teach a Case ROBERT W. MERRY

To any case-method instructor the importance of his preparation for class is fully apparent. To the new instructor, however, it may come as something of a surprise that his task in preparing for a case class is more arduous than that of the students and more arduous also than that of a lecturer. If he were lecturing, the instructor would be the one to determine what material he would present and in what order he would present it. In embracing the case method, however, he has surrendered his sovereignty and yet undertaken to maintain control over the discussion. It would be a mistake for the new instructor to assume that he had only to read and reread the case and then go into class and ask one or two leading questions. Rather he must be so thoroughly conversant with the case that he is ready to deal with any angles which the class may introduce, to modify his approach at any time, or suddenly to change his outline in accordance with new ideas which may not previously have occurred to him.

Case teaching is a highly individualistic art, and the methods and approaches of one instructor seldom can successfully be appropriated by another. Every seasoned instructor develops an approach of his own. Each new instructor has to do likewise, and there are no general rules for him to follow. The instructor about to teach a case class for the first time, however, may be slightly at a loss as to what form his preparation should take.

The first step in the instructor's preparation of a case is to master the facts. The instructor needs to go over the printed case again and again, making outlines, marginal notes, and written summaries of essential details. If there are figures in the case, he will make many calculations, not only the ones which he himself believes to be correct but also others, which he anticipates that the students may put forward as appropriate and significant. He will scrutinize the apparent issues to make sure that they are the real ones. And if there are important subordinate issues, he will recognize that some questions probably will have to be settled before others. He may find it helpful to develop a conceptual framework which will show how the several pieces of the puzzle fit together.

Up to this point, the instructor's work on the case has roughly paralleled that of the students. The task has been to acquire a thorough familiarity with the facts, the figures, and the issues. Now the instructor may find it advisable to make a fresh start. In some instances he will at this stage need to consider the specific learning objectives toward which he wishes to point the case discussion. And here some appraisal of the relation of the major issues of the case to the instructor's course outline is appropriate. With an eye on the position of the particular case in the course outline, the instructor may wish to lead the students to emphasize some issues more than others. Also as a specific aspect of this consciousness of a course outline there is the frequent desirability of providing a transition from the case discussed at the preceding class meeting.

After these preliminaries the instructor needs to view the case itself as a whole, assessing it in terms of the principal areas for exploration and discussion, considering the relation of one to another, and devising key questions to lead into each of them. He may wish to give considerable care to the wording of these questions. By foreseeing the various avenues of connection the instructor can be better prepared to effect transitions from one issue to another, as well as to guide the class into the critical areas for discussion. Next he will note the answers that the class probably will offer to these key questions on the basis of the materials in the case, and the reasonable answers he will follow to their logical conclusion. Where weighing of considerations is involved, he will list the pros and cons and undertake to balance them. And in each area he will make the pertinent mathematical calculations. By these means he will develop what may be termed a teaching outline, which probably will differ markedly from his initial analysis of facts and figures and which may well cover several pages of foolscap.

In the classroom the instructor who is teaching by the case method for the first time may be inclined to adhere closely to this detailed teaching outline. He has put a great deal of thought into developing a program for the class meeting, he has followed through all the lines of argument which he thinks the students may reasonably offer, and he is pretty well convinced that the class discussion ought logically to develop according to his script. If the discussion should deviate from the course which he has laid out, he will be tempted to try, by narrow and specific questions, to set it back on the path in order to make sure that every point in his outline is accorded proper consideration.

In actuality, rigid adherence to a predetermined line of development may make for a discussion notably lacking in freshness and spontaneity. If, as they are put forward by the class, arguments and observations on the case are forced into the instructor's own outline, the students may soon be deterred from presenting an independent development of the case. To narrow questions they will give narrow answers, and the quality of the discussion will deteriorate rapidly.

After he has experienced the disappointing class discussion which results from an attempt at rigid control, the new instructor may resort to a procedure which involves almost no control. He will put to the class at the outset the major question to be discussed and will permit the students to bring up whatever points they choose, in whatever order they see fit. This procedure also entails difficulties. There is the danger that several important aspects of the major issue of a case may be overlooked if the students move on too rapidly to another issue. The discussion of one issue may be superficial or unsound because its development depends on another issue which has not yet been discussed. The treatment of points at random, following no logical system or pattern, is likely to have the result that at the end of the hour a student has no clear concept of an appropriate analysis of the case.

Something between these two extremes of tight control and no control at all is ordinarily called for. And the new instructor may find that he can most readily achieve this objective if he can free himself from close reliance on his notes. Having worked out his detailed teaching outline, he may do well to put it aside in favor of a mere list of the critical areas—such a list as may fit on an index card or two, which the instructor may glance at during the class hour simply to make certain that no important areas have been slighted. For the details of development he will rely on the thoroughness of his own preparation.

The instructor's preparation frequently will need to go beyond the bounds of the case itself. Many cases include a considerable body of technical detail, which may relate to an industry, a process, a machine, an institution, an instrument, or the like. Usually enough facts are given to convey the significant data. Sometimes, however, students request more information; and they may ask for an explanation of terms used in the case which are not clear to them. The instructor needs to anticipate student questions of this type and to make provision for them, certainly by taking steps to become well informed himself and also, wherever possible, by arranging for showings of industrial movies or for demonstrations, or by making available for inspection the items of merchandise or pieces of equipment which are under discussion.

In planning his strategy the new instructor ought not to overlook the potentialities of the chalkboard as a teaching aid. He will turn to it naturally to set down figures. But he will find it useful also for such things as listing the pros and cons brought out by the class, or jotting down notes as to major areas for discussion, or developing steps in a program of action to carry out a decision. When analysis of a case entails calculations, these very probably will need to be put on the board. Ideally the instructor will proceed by getting the students to tell him what figures to write, not by standing at the board and transcribing his own computations. But it will help him to make a quick mental verification if he has his own calculations before him. Hence he will do well to have with him the papers on which he has done his figuring. He may wish also to put on the board, as they are brought up in class, a series of headings which will indicate the major areas of discussion. These need not conform precisely to the instructor's own outline, but they are likely to approximate the headings noted at some point in his outline. Hence it may be useful for the instructor to devote some care to the phrasing in his own notes, and perhaps to underline in red the principal captions in the list to which he has reduced his teaching outline. Among the papers which he carries to class the instructor may also want to include some notes from which to make a summary at the close of the class hour. Generally, however, the instructor should not be dependent on his notes.

In a course which has previously been taught according to the case method or in a large course divided into sections and taught by several instructors, the notes of other teachers presumably will be available. After he has completed his independent preparation of the case, the new instructor may find it reassuring to refer to these. They may suggest fresh lines of approach or new ideas, and to this extent they will be useful. The new instructor may also achieve a feeling of greater self-confidence if he talks over the case with other instructors. The point can scarcely be overemphasized, however, that no instructor, under the case method, can effectively substitute another's notes for his own. Experience suggests also that notes prepared in an earlier year cannot be reused intact. Fresh preparation is essential each time. Old notes are useful for reference, and they may serve to recall to mind certain calculations which need reworking or certain difficulties which developed on an earlier occasion. But modifications will almost always suggest themselves, and fresh study and new analysis are essential each time the case comes up.

Nevertheless, for purposes of facilitating future use of the case, the instructor may find it advantageous to develop the habit of jotting down some notes as soon as possible after the end of the class hour, touching such matters as any corrections needed in the case, possible changes in the appended questions, new lines of thought or different methods of calculation brought out by students, a possible change in the position in the outline, and so on. Such notes should be included in the case folder, to be reviewed by the instructor when he next organizes his case outline for a term and when he comes again to the preparation of the specific case.

From what has gone before in this volume, and particularly from some of the cases that have been reproduced, it will be apparent that during the normal classroom periods of fifty or eighty minutes time does not permit complete analysis of all aspects of a case. Classroom discussion, under the guidance of the instructor, will highlight significant issues, direct the student's attention to angles of the case which he may not have perceived, and give the student an opportunity to exercise his judgment in making a rough balance of the factors involved. If the instructor in the classroom tries to pursue the objective of dovetailing all the pieces of the analysis into a neat and consistent pattern, he will inevitably destroy much of the spontaneity of case discussion and will tend to convert the case into a mere series of texts and illustrations for a lecture. Furthermore, no one student ordinarily has the opportunity in the classroom to pursue the complete analysis of a particular case from start to finish. If the instructor were to require one or two students to pursue such complete analysis, the result would be recitation rather than discussion. For these reasons, a necessary and important part of instruction under the case method consists in the periodic preparation by students of searching, comprehensive, and detailed case analyses in written form. The following paper by Thomas J. Raymond deals with this aspect of the case method.

Written Analyses of Cases   THOMAS J. RAYMOND

I. REPORT REQUIREMENTS

The requirement of written reports on cases has been a prominent feature of instruction in the Harvard Business School for many years. Indeed such written assignments have practically coexisted with the case method at the Business School since its early beginnings.[1] They are used in the curriculum of both the first and the second year.

At an earlier period, written reports in the first year formed an integral part of the instruction in particular courses—e.g., Finance, Marketing, Industrial Management, and so on. More recently, however, the written report work of the first year has been organized as a separate course, currently known as Written Analysis of Cases. This separate course organization for written work during the first year not only facilitates scheduling but has two other important advantages. First, this arrangement permits the use of cases which cut across the several first-year subjects, requiring the student to balance, for instance, production considerations, marketing considerations, and fi-

[1] See Dr. Copeland's description of the first offering of the course in Business Policy, supra, p. 26.

nancial considerations in order to arrive at a practical business decision. Second, it affords the opportunity to develop throughout the year a progression of written case assignments from short simple problems to longer, more complex, and more difficult ones.

These written report assignments in the first year are spaced at intervals of about two weeks, a total of sixteen or seventeen reports during the year. Assignments are made usually a week or ten days in advance. Therefore during his first year the student practically always has one written report assignment outstanding. The reports are graded and returned to students, usually with comments by the grading staff and sometimes with mimeographed analyses prepared by the instructor. First-year instructors take turns at preparing analyses and supervising grading.

In the second year, instructors use written report assignments at their option. A majority of them require one or more reports per term, and in some instances as many as five or six. These assignments are, of course, related closely to the management area which is the concern of the particular course. There is commonly more variation in the second year than in the first with respect to types of written reports. The second-year assignments may range from individual case reports, similar to those of the first year except for being more complicated and difficult, to more ambitious projects, ordinarily term papers, in which the students themselves, working either independently or in teams, undertake firsthand investigations of the business problems of particular companies.

This latter type of assignment deserves some special comment. Requirement of project reports has the merit of serving in part as a corrective to one of the deficiencies of the case method. This deficiency consists in the fact that the case method, as such, ordinarily does not give the student any practice in writing his own cases. He is handed a written statement of a business situation in which facts and figures have been assembled and attention has been focused on certain problems, or at least on certain aspects of the situation. The simulation of real business life, however, is not complete because, when schooling is over and the graduate has embarked on his business career, no one will hand him a "case." Instead someone will say, "Jones, you had better have a look at our shortage situation. I suspect there is some trouble there." Then Jones will have to go out and put together his case before he can begin analyzing it according to the approaches he has developed in school. To a limited extent the use of term project assignments serves to correct this deficiency. Confronted with such an assignment, the student must first find and recognize a case, then write the case, and finally write the analysis and recommend appropriate action.

The preparation of written reports on cases affords important training in analysis: What are the real problems at issue? What are the pertinent facts? What are the important unknowns? What are the critical questions bearing on each particular issue? How can logics and reasoning be employed to establish important inferences, connections, and relationships? How can opposing facts and arguments be weighed in making judgments? What is the appropriate timing of decisions? How can those decisions best be implemented? In order that the first-year student may cumulatively develop some facility in this kind of analysis, three things are needful:

(1) He should have some specific classroom guidance in the making of such analyses either as a part of the initial work in the regular first-year courses or as special classroom work connected with the course on Written Analysis of Cases.

(2) He should be required to write a fairly large number of these case reports during the first year.

(3) He should be encouraged, or even required, to work in collaboration with a group of his fellow students in the discussion and analysis of a report case up to the point where he actually begins writing his own outline or synopsis, from which point on, of course, all his work should be individual. This working in discussion groups not only prepares men realistically for what they will encounter in business but also affords valuable training in the give-and-take of day-to-day collaboration among people with different views, ideas, and personalities.

The preparation of written case reports affords training in communication also. A report commonly is addressed to somebody, either to the management generally or to a specific executive or possibly to the board of directors. Not infrequently the report assignment may designate the person to whom the report is to be addressed. As the year progresses and the student writes one report after another, he becomes more conscious of the fact that he is trying to communicate to people certain ideas, concepts, arguments, and recommendations. If, as not infrequently happens, the student receives a comment on his report to the effect that "A busy executive would not take the time to go beyond the second or third page of such a poorly presented report," he will begin to recognize that the job of written communication embraces substantially more than the mere accumulation of ideas plus an analysis. He will then begin to realize that the analysis which he has made of the problem is only preliminary to the work of writing the report and that the success of his efforts at communication may be influenced as much by the sequence of his arguments, the effective structure of his paragraphs, and the strategic positioning of summaries and recapitulations as by the strength of the supporting evidence and the actual cogency of the analysis.

It should go without saying that the student's use of the English language ought to be acceptable. Unfortunately, in actual fact, many students exhibit marked deficiencies in English, and special instruction has to be furnished in such fundamentals as grammar, punctuation, sentence structure, and paragraphing. The need of students for special work in English becomes apparent through the program of written case analyses, but of course this deficiency is by no means peculiar to the case method.

Akin to periodic written case analyses are examinations under the case method. In an examination the student is confronted with an unfamiliar case, preferably a fresh one, but in any event a case which he has not studied before; and he must apply to this case the analytical power and insight which he has been cultivating. Not only is the terrain unfamiliar, but the student is working under the pressure of time limitations—four hours at most, sometimes only three, in which to make his analysis, arrange his ideas, and present his argument and recommendations. A case examination thus is designed to test the student's analytical power, not his store of facts.

In grading an examination bluebook, the instructor naturally does not expect so finished a performance as if the student had had a week or ten days in which to formulate his analysis and recommendations. But in other respects the bluebook should closely resemble one of the periodically assigned written case analyses.

There follow, for purposes of illustration, the case of the Dexdahl Company, assigned for written analysis early in the fall of 1950, an analysis of the case prepared for the guidance of the grading staff, and a student report on the case.

II. DEXDAHL, INC.

On the evening of December 5, 1949, Russell Dexter and Norman Dahl, the owners of Dexdahl, Inc., met in the Boston home of Mr. Dexter to decide how many Ski Tree parts the company should order from its suppliers. Ski Tree, the company's only product, was a new type of external boot tree for ski boots. The first shipments of Ski Trees were delivered to stores on November 23, 1949. A substantial volume of orders received since that date had reduced the company's inventory to a low level. Thus, some action would have to be taken immediately if the company was to be ready to meet future demand.

Initial Organization

Mr. Dahl and Mr. Dexter met during the spring of 1949 through their wives, who had been classmates in a personnel management training course before the war. Mr. Dahl was a professor of mechanical engineering, and Mr. Dexter was employed by a large advertising agency in Boston. The two men, both of whom were in their early thirties, found that they had a common interest in skiing. One evening during the summer of 1949, Mr. Dahl told Mr. Dexter about an external ski boot tree he had invented. The idea sounded promising to Mr. Dexter, and he suggested that they look into the possibility of developing it commercially together.

Mr. Dahl had a model constructed, and the partners gave it the name "Ski Tree." The tree, a picture of which is shown in Exhibit 1, consisted of two plywood blocks sliding in steel channels with toe plates at one end and toggle levers at the other end, one on each side to clamp the boot heels to the wood blocks. The partners showed the model to a few ski store owners and ski instructors in Boston. The reaction of these people was mixed; some of them were very much interested and thought the product was salable. Mr. Dexter and Mr. Dahl then took a brief trip to New York City, where they showed the model to buyers of two leading sporting goods stores, two large department stores, and three leading small ski shops. Several of the buyers thought they could sell the item.

Competition at this time included a number of internal boot trees and two external trees. Most of the internal trees were priced from $2.50 to $3.00, though a few were sold by high-class stores for as much as $4.50. Some were manufactured by large ski boot manufacturers and sold by their salesmen. The only external tree distributed widely was made by a western firm. This tree was sold on consignment through a number of dealers for $3.95.

Mr. Dahl and Mr. Dexter were of the opinion that an external tree was superior to an internal tree. An internal tree had the disadvantages of stretching the boot, not allowing the inside to dry well, and not maintaining the original last of the soles because they were not held flat. Mr. Dahl and Mr. Dexter thought that the western firm's external tree was, by comparison with Ski Tree, complicated and clumsy in appearance. Mr. Dexter commented that one needed a third hand to operate it.

Estimating the potential demand for the Ski Tree proved to be a difficult problem since little specific market information was available. Estimates of the total number of skiers in the United States varied from 500,000 to 5,000,000. Various people in the trade said that each of the four large boot manufacturers sold 20,000 to 50,000 pairs of ski boots per year. Inconclusive though this information was, Mr. Dexter and Mr. Dahl believed that a large enough market existed to justify the venture.

By talking to dealers, instructors, and others, the partners acquired the following general information about the nature of the trade. In the middle

EXHIBIT 1

DEXDAHL, INC.

Advertisement in November 15, 1949, Issue of *Ski Magazine*

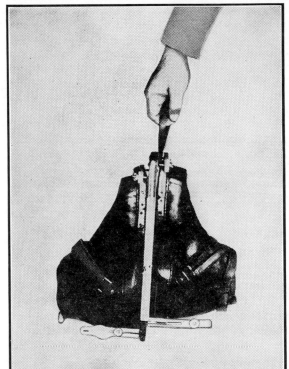

THE SKI-TREE

Manufactured by DEXDAHL, INC., COHASSET, MASS.

- fits all sizes and types of boots
- keeps the soles perfectly straight to ensure proper fit of the boots in the bindings.
- maintains the original last and contour of every ski boot.
- allows the ski boots to dry quickly and thoroughly, both inside and out.
- operates easily by sliding toe under plate and clamping boot with light push on heel lever.

See your Local Sporting Goods Dealer or write DEXDAHL, INC., Cohasset, Mass. $4.95

1920's, retail sales of ski equipment had been limited largely to sporting goods stores and department stores. In the early 1930's, as skiing grew in popularity, ski shops sprang up throughout resort areas. Their volume of sales steadily increased because of their excellent position to promote business directly. Regionally, sales were concentrated heavily in the northeast, northwest, and Rocky Mountain areas. Sales in the midwest were small, being limited chiefly to large city stores which supplied people who were about to travel to distant ski areas. Though there were no statistics, it appeared that sales of an item such as Ski Tree would be divided about equally between city stores and resort shops. The cities might obtain a slight edge because of the great volume of the New York department stores.

The seasonal pattern was vague, depending considerably on the weather. Most ski shops opened in October or November, but substantial sales did not commence until early December. The heaviest business in primary equipment (skis and boots) usually came in the first part of the winter, but sales of accessories were spread quite evenly over the whole season. It was thought that only a small percentage of people buying ski boots bought trees at the same time. In the cities sales tended to be stronger before Christmas because of gift buying, whereas at the resorts business picked up in January and February, when snow conditions were best. City stores started marking down ski equipment in late January; by Washington's Birthday sales had almost stopped; and during March the lines were replaced by spring sporting equipment. In resorts, sales might continue into April, depending on the length of the skiing season.

Mr. Dexter and Mr. Dahl discussed the organization of the business with a friend who was a successful Boston lawyer. The lawyer was interested in the project and agreed to render all assistance needed. He took care of forming the enterprise into the corporation known as Dexdahl, Inc. He also started work on a patent application, though he explained that the patent might not be obtained for years and that any patent infringement suit Dexdahl might wish to bring against competitors would probably be lengthy and expensive. Dexdahl paid the legal expenses. The lawyer's only compensation was two shares of stock in the new company. The remaining 98 shares were divided equally between Mr. Dahl and Mr. Dexter, who invested $2,450 each from their personal funds. Both men felt they could have put in an additional $1,000 each without jeopardizing their financial security. They were advised by several business associates, however, to limit their investment to a total of $5,000. These friends said that if a new enterprise such as Dexdahl could not get itself on a self-supporting basis with that amount of capital, it probably was not a good venture.

PRODUCTION PLANNING

During late September and early October, 1949, the owners proceeded with plans for production and marketing of their product. Mr. Dahl took care of most of the production work. He drew up blueprints and specifications. He purchased for $2,500 dies to be used in manufacturing the metal parts. One manufacturer had offered to make the dies for $800, but his offer was declined because he also wanted Dexdahl to agree to buy all the toggles from him at 66 cents each, a price considerably higher than the figures that other concerns had quoted. Mr. Dahl believed that, as production increased, a lower unit price for toggles would more than offset the higher initial cost of dies. The officers decided to purchase parts and assemble the trees themselves, since it would be impossible to find a single manufacturer to make all the components. They set the initial production at 500 units. This number, they felt, would be adequate to supply many dealers and test the market thoroughly without unduly risking the company's funds.

EXHIBIT 2

DEXDAHL, INC.

Contract Prices of Materials and Estimated Labor Costs for Ski Tree

	Number per Tree	Price Each	Cost per Tree
Toggles.............................	2	$0.407	$0.814
Channels............................	2	0.04	0.08
Toe Pieces..........................	2	0.08	0.16
Bolts...............................	5	0.015	0.075
Wingnuts...........................	5	0.02	0.10
Springs.............................	4	0.0025	0.01
Set of 2 Wooden Pieces..............	1	0.29	0.29
Leather Strap.......................	1	0.025	0.025
Materials Total.....................			$1.554
Assembly...........................			0.15
Packaging..........................			0.05
Total..............................			$1.754

The most complicated parts in Ski Trees were the toggle units, two of which were used in each tree. Mr. Dahl solicited bids for 1,000 toggle units from 20 metalworking concerns. From the blueprints the concerns made up samples to estimate their costs and submitted bids ranging from 30 cents to 66 cents per unit. Since he was uncertain of the reliability of the lowest bidder, Mr. Dahl accepted the 40.7-cent bid of a concern which he learned from other sources was thoroughly reliable. This concern also estimated that on an order for 5,000 units it could quote a price of 33 cents each. Fifteen bids for the plywood blocks were obtained, ranging from 15 cents to 60 cents per set of two. An agreement was eventually reached with a furniture manufacturer who, Mr. Dahl understood, had a reputation for high-quality work. This manufacturer had originally bid 40 cents, but Mr. Dahl was able by bargaining to have the price reduced to 29 cents. For each of the other parts, several bids were likewise solicited. Bids were finally accepted at the prices shown in Exhibit 2.

No quantity discounts were offered for items other than the toggles. Toggles had to be paid for immediately, whereas all other items could be paid for within 30 days after delivery. All suppliers promised that the first deliveries on each order would start 10 days or less after the order was placed, the longest time being required by the toggle manufacturer. The remaining deliveries on each order would follow within a few days at a rate faster than Dexdahl could assemble the trees.

Dexdahl was able to find a shop in Cohasset which the company could use, rent free for two months, for the assembly work. Because of their training, Mrs. Dahl and Mrs. Dexter were interested in production planning and consequently undertook to lay out an assembly and packing line in the shop. They made rough motion and time studies and estimated labor costs for assembling at 15 cents per unit. Labor and materials for packaging were figured at 5 cents per unit. These material, assembly, and packaging costs (listed in Exhibit 2) totaled $1.75 per unit. All labor costs were included, though the Dahls and Dexters intended to do the work themselves and not take any payment until the company showed a profit.

Considering their costs and the competitive situation, Mr. Dexter and Mr. Dahl decided that $4.95 was the best retail price for Ski Tree. Normal terms in the ski equipment trade were 40% off list price for retailers and 20% off wholesale price for distributors. A 2% discount would be given to customers paying for goods within 10 days. The initial expenses of the business ($2,500 for the dies, $1,200 budgeted for advertising, office supplies, personal cards, and other material during the 1949–50 season, and $200 for incorporation) were to be distributed over 25,000 units.

During the last week in October, the company placed orders with its suppliers for parts to make 500 Ski Trees. The intention was that these parts should arrive, be assembled, and be shipped to stores not later than November 15.

OBTAINING OUTLETS

In his initial investigations Mr. Dexter had found that there was no national distributor for ski equipment to whom a small producer could take one or two items and secure effective distribution over the whole United States market. As a result, most people who had novel products either did not develop them at all, as had been the experience of Mr. Dahl up to 1949, or distributed them in a small area which could be covered personally. Thus, though a national distributor would have been preferred, the company was forced to develop its own marketing system. At the same time the owners decided to give no exclusive dealerships. They were convinced that they had a superior product and believed that by relying on a strong promotion program, with the product in as many stores as possible, they would achieve the greatest sales.

Before commencing his field work, Mr. Dexter drew up the magazine advertisement shown in Exhibit 1. The same copy was used for 100 display cards. Mr. Dexter also incorporated parts of the advertisement copy in a red and gray design for a box. To economize, he planned to pack Ski Trees in a standard-size shoe box.

Investigating the advertising media available, Mr. Dexter discovered that *Ski Magazine*, published in Hanover, New Hampshire, was the only magazine providing national coverage of the ski market. It had a circulation of 30,000 copies among skiers, ski lodges, ski clubs, dealers, and the like. There were also five regional ski newspapers, published in New York, New England, California, Oregon, and Colorado. Since the partners had decided that the initial effort should be as broad as possible, the two-column advertisement shown in Exhibit 1 was placed, at a cost of $250, in the November 15, 1949, issue of *Ski Magazine*. Advertisements in some of the regional newspapers were considered for later in the season if Ski Tree showed promise of success.

Mr. Dexter established his first outlets in Boston late in October. One of the purchasers was a man engaged in custom-making expensive ski boots, who declared that Ski Tree was the best boot tree he had seen. In ordinary years he thought he could sell one with each of the 200 pairs of boots he made every year. Since he had already purchased a large stock of internal trees for the 1949–50 season, however, he ordered only six Ski Trees. Similar small orders were obtained from several Boston stores.

Mr. Dexter took the first week of November as part of his annual vacation and travelled through Maine, New Hampshire, Vermont, and Massachusetts. On this trip he visited approximately 30 sporting goods stores, ski shops, and ski lodges. All these outlets carried at least one type of internal ski boot tree. About five carried one of the other types of external tree. A few of the dealers were skeptical about Ski Tree and did not place any orders. Some, however, were very much interested, and Mr. Dexter was able to obtain orders of from one to six units from 25 outlets.

He then went to New York City, where he first revisited the two high-quality sporting goods stores to which he had gone on his earlier trip. Each of these stores, he thought, sold 200 to 300 boot trees per year. He believed that he had a quality item and that once it was placed in the best stores other outlets would follow in time. The buyer at the first store was interested but said he would not handle Ski Tree unless Mr. Dexter agreed not to sell it to the two large department stores noted for their policy of selling below list prices. Mr. Dexter said that he intended to sell it to everybody but that he would agree to "fair trade" the item at the price of $4.95. With this agreement, the store ordered 12 units. The buyer for the second store had shown some interest on Mr. Dexter's first trip, but this time he said that a boot tree at $4.95 was too high-priced for his store. Next, Mr. Dexter visited the two large department stores, whose ski boot sales were probably 300 to 500 per year. The assistant buyers in each case told him not to expect much, but they did order 12 each. Of the three smaller dealers visited earlier, one ordered one unit, one ordered 12, but the third did not want any. Mr. Dexter observed that all the New York stores carried, on consignment, the external boot tree made by the western firm, though it was not displayed and apparently was not selling.

In the meantime, Mr. Dahl had written to his brother, who was president of a large ski club on the West Coast. The brother agreed to help and subsequently enlisted an important local distributor to solicit dealers in that area. The distributor was given the regular 20% discount off the wholesale price.

In the next to the last week of November, Mr. Dexter flew to Chicago, where he talked to several ski equipment salespeople, finally persuading a distributor, who was a former ski instructor, to sell Ski Trees. This man handled only three products at that time, one line of skis, one of boots, and one of wax. Since all these were of the highest quality, Mr. Dexter was immensely pleased that this distributor was willing to handle Ski Tree. The distributor said he might sell 1,000 to 2,000 Ski Trees in a normal year, but he told Mr. Dexter not to expect many sales for the 1949–50 season because his salesmen were already off the road. Most stores purchased their annual requirements of ski equipment and accessories during August and September; hence it would be difficult to obtain any new orders. Because he did not expect to sell much, the distributor agreed to work as an agent, receiving a 15% commission for the 1949–50 season. In the following year he would serve as a distributor on the same basis as the West Coast man.

Though it might have been possible to negotiate an agency agreement with either of these men, allowing only a 10% commission, Mr. Dexter believed such an arrangement would not result in sufficient sales effort. He decided that, for all areas where a middleman was needed to reach dealers, distributors would be used who would be willing to purchase Ski Trees for their own account.

INITIAL PRODUCTION AND SALES

While Mr. Dexter was developing outlets, Ski Trees were beginning to move into the market. Operations had been delayed because of difficulties in the manufacture of the wooden parts. Mr. Dahl worked directly with the manufacturer, who had never done such work on plywood. (Plywood had been chosen because it would not warp.) Four transverse holes had to be bored perfectly straight for the pins that held the toggles. The operation proved to be very difficult because of the tendency of high-speed drills to edge off a fraction of an inch. A considerable number of pieces were spoiled before this problem was solved with special jigs designed by Mr. Dahl. As a result, assembly operations were delayed so that the stores did not receive their shipments until a week after the advertisement appeared in *Ski Magazine*.

In response to the advertisement, orders were beginning to come in from stores which had not been visited personally. Likewise, a few letters were coming in from individuals. For instance, a girl wrote that she had seen someone with a Ski Tree on a train and wondered where she could buy it. About 50 orders had been received by mail from persons in New England who were not located near a store carrying Ski Trees. These were filled by mail at $4.95, other mail orders (about 50) being referred to dealers or distributors. In the last days of November, the company also received a few reorders from stores visited personally. In order to handle the increasing volume of correspondence and bookkeeping, Mrs. Dahl left her job as personnel director of a large Boston hospital and devoted full time to work for Dexdahl. Both couples were spending practically all their spare time with the company. On occasion it had been necessary to work on assembling and packing until 1 A.M. or 2 A.M., but all orders were being filled quickly. The assembly process was working well. After production got under way, the time allowances were found to be a little too liberal since actual assembly costs were closer to 10 cents per unit than the 15 cents previously determined.

On November 29, a letter was received from a buyer for a large department store in Chicago. The buyer said the Chicago distributor had shown him Ski Tree and he would like to purchase one gross (144). He asked for a 9% discount in addition to the normal 40%. The order was the largest received by Dexdahl, and the personnel of the company were anxious to accept it immediately. Mr. Dexter pointed out, however, that, once a concession was made, every other concern in the trade would be trying to make some sort of "deal." He insisted that Dexdahl had a good product and that, if its marketing program was sound, sales would be made without concessions. The others agreed with his arguments; consequently Mr. Dexter wrote that Dexdahl could not fill any order except on the regular terms of 40% off list, and he accompanied the letter with a Ski Tree for the buyer's personal use. Within a few days an order was received for one-half gross on Dexdahl's terms.

Mr. Dexter was concerned because he had received reorders from two stores in New York, but had not received any from one of the big department stores. Believing that there must be some significant reason why the original stock had not been sold, he took a hurried trip to investigate during the last week in November. He went immediately to the ski department of the store, but he could not find any Ski Trees. The assistant buyer, whom he had seen on his first visit, said that the trees were in the accessories department. Mr. Dexter was somewhat disappointed that Ski Trees should be off among the laces, straps, and like articles. When he found that the trees had been assembled incorrectly so that they did not work, he became very much disturbed. He told the assistant buyer that this situation constituted the worst possible advertising for Dexdahl. He asked whether he could buy the whole lot back, saying that such selling was worse than nothing. The assistant buyer replied that he could not do anything and referred Mr. Dexter to the buyer.

Mr. Dexter explained the problem to the buyer and made the request that he tell his salesmen to spend 20 seconds per customer on selling Ski Trees, pointing out that it would be well worth while to earn $2 every 20 seconds. The buyer was skeptical but said he would give Mr. Dexter a chance to prove the possibility of selling Ski Tree so easily. They went out on the floor, and found two girls buying ski boots. When the boots had been sold, Mr. Dexter stepped up and demonstrated Ski Tree to the girls, one of whom bought a pair immediately, the sale requiring 35 seconds. The buyer was so impressed that he took Mr. Dexter to lunch and asked him what he could do for him.

Mr. Dexter replied that he would like to demonstrate Ski Tree to a meeting of all the salesmen, whereupon the buyer promised to arrange one for the second week in December.

Mr. Dexter observed that one of the biggest problems in the department stores seemed to be the new sales personnel hired for the Christmas season. In general, these people did not know much about their products, and mechanical devices such as Ski Tree, which had to be demonstrated, were either ignored or presented poorly.

The personnel of Dexdahl were encouraged by the results of the advertisement in *Ski Magazine*. Ski Tree was the only boot tree advertised in the November 15, 1949, issue, and the response indicated to Dexdahl that the advertisement was good. Therefore, the officers decided to place another advertisement, half the size of the first one, in the December 15, 1949, issue.

The Situation on December 5, 1949

The conference of Mr. Dahl and Mr. Dexter was called on December 5, 1949, because the inventory of Ski Trees was down to approximately 100, and it would be necessary to order more parts to meet the demand, which was at that time running at about 150 per week. The question was how much to order. Mr. Dahl suggested ordering parts for at least 2,500 Ski Trees immediately so as to be able to meet all orders and obtain savings on toggle prices. Mr. Dexter pointed out that it might be better to order fewer. He was afraid that Dexdahl might be left with a large inventory at the end of the season. There was already some evidence that changes should be made to perfect the product. Although these changes would not be radical, requiring only small alterations in the dies, he did not want to have to dispose of a large inventory of the original design. He felt that no great damage would result if Dexdahl fell behind on filling orders, because the company could send out letters saying that the tremendous reception of Ski Tree had made it impossible to fill orders immediately.

Under the pressure of operations and their other work, the Dexdahl personnel had not kept detailed records of sales performance. In order to size up the situation quickly, they made a few simple checks. They noted first that the number of dealers handling Ski Trees was growing steadily. In New England there were approximately 45, of whom one-third had ordered trees as a result of the company's advertisement. These dealers had placed initial orders totaling about 180 Ski Trees. Ten dealers had reordered. Orders for 92 units had been received from Chicago, and 108 units from the West Coast. The size and speed of reorders from a few dealers, as shown in Exhibit 3, gave some indication of the sales situation. It appeared that Ski Trees were selling in some places. They were not selling in others, especially in ski resorts. The latter situation might be explained by weather conditions. Despite one good snow in New England in late November, the winter had been generally mild up to that date, and skiing conditions were poor. Mr. Dexter was particularly pleased by the performance of Dealer A, who was located in

Exhibit 3
DEXDAHL, INC.
Selected Sales Statistics to December 5, 1949

Outlet	Original Contact	1st Order		2nd Order		3rd Order	
		No. of Trees Purchased	Date	No. of Trees Purchased	Date	No. of Trees Purchased	Date
A Sporting Goods Store (town)	Dexter	2	11/6	6	11/24	6	11/30
B " " " "	"	6	11/6	6	11/25	6	11/28
C " " " "	"	6	11/6	6	12/3		
D " " " "	"	12	11/5	3	11/25	3	11/30
E " " " "	"	6	11/3	12	12/3		
F Boston Dept. Store	"	3	11/3				
G Ski Store (city)	"	2	11/4				
H N.Y.C. Sporting Goods Store	"	12	11/9	12	11/26		
I Ski Store (resort)	"	2	11/7				
J Sporting Goods Store	Advert.	2	11/20	12	11/26		

a northern college town. When visited in November, the dealer had been very skeptical about selling any Ski Trees at $5 and had wanted an exclusive dealership, there being two other large ski suppliers in town. Mr. Dexter regarded Dealer A as a shrewd judge of ski products. The fact that he had reordered twice after an initial order of two units was encouraging. Ski Trees were also selling well in the other stores in that town.

The quality of the product was apparently good. Only one Ski Tree had been returned as defective. Payments on all sales were being received promptly. The company was in good financial condition, with $1,500 in the bank, $700 in accounts receivable, and no current liabilities.

Mr. Dexter had also been encouraged to learn on several visits to dealers that salesmen for competing tree manufacturers had been making derogatory remarks about Ski Tree. It appeared that the product was achieving recognition.

How many of each of the component parts of Ski Tree should Dexdahl order?

III. AN ANALYSIS OF THE CASE

A preliminary step in the analysis of this, as of any, case is thorough reading, in order to get a view of the over-all problem and of its component parts. Frequently also importance attaches to the time of the case. In the Dexdahl case, for instance, the student must bear in mind that the problem required a decision in December, 1949. Information regarding the weather during the remaining months of the winter of 1949 50 is not appropriate to introduce. Hindsight was not available to the executives of the company.

The Dexdahl case involves considerations of purchasing, finance, production, marketing, and accounting. All these aspects require treatment; and in assigning this case early in the year there was the added pedagogical objective of underscoring the importance of developing a questioning attitude about business data, their source, their validity, and their applicability. In the Dexdahl case the company records cover a very brief period of time, and the "market information" is very broad. Students are likely to place unwarranted significance on the company figures and to develop projections of marketing trends on the basis of too limited statistics.

A perceptive analysis of this case questions the usability of the data on skiers in the United States, ski boot purchases, the company's sales figures, and so on. It also recognizes the existence of differences among kinds of costs—some real in terms of cash outlay, others not out-of-pocket disbursements but bookkeeping charges.

One possible approach which is useful in case analysis comprises five steps:

(1) Defining the central issue

(2) Selecting the pertinent areas of consideration

(3) Analyzing the considerations and determining their relative importance

(4) Investigating other possibilities

(5) Drawing a final conclusion.

Applying this outline to the Dexdahl case, we see that the stated problem is to decide how many of each of the component parts of Ski Tree the company should order. In reaching a decision on this question it is appropriate to examine the profitability of this new enterprise and the demand for its product. Specifically the areas which have an important bearing on the decision are (1) profitability of the venture, (2) suitability of the product for the market, (3) long-run demand, (4) short-run demand, and (5) advisability of ordering 5,000 toggles. Since the immediate problem requires that sales for the rest of the season be estimated, the short-run demand has to be considered separately from the long-run demand. The advisability of ordering 5,000 toggles (enough for 2,500 Ski Trees) has to be considered because of the quantity discount available on an order of this size.

Analysis of the main considerations involves marshaling the evidence, evaluating its significance, drawing conclusions, and determining the relative importance of the several considerations. There follows a possible worksheet for such an analysis. This was prepared in the first instance for the guidance of the grading staff. When, in subsequent years, the case was used as a vehicle for classroom instruction in case analysis, mimeographed copies of the worksheet were furnished to the students for purposes of illustration.

WORKSHEET FOR ANALYSIS OF THE DEXDAHL CASE

1. Profitability of the Venture
   a. If the operation is to be self-supporting, the company will have to sell at least 4,000 units annually to break even. (See Exhibit A.)
   b. For the business to yield some compensation to Mr. Dexter and Mr. Dahl and show a profit, however, more than 4,000 units per year must be sold.
   c. Any estimate of the profitability of the venture is necessarily rough because the exact amounts of many of the expenses are not known.

CONCLUSION: Although these estimates are very rough, it appears that Dexdahl must sell somewhat over 4,000 units per year in order to be a profitable venture.

EXHIBIT A. BREAKEVEN POINT

Per Unit Contribution to Overhead

List price..	$4.95
Wholesale price...	2.97
Manufacturer's price..	2.376

Manufacturer's price less cash discount (2%)......................	$2.328
Cost to manufacture*..	1.55
Per Unit Contribution to Overhead†...........................	$0.778

Annual Overhead Charges

Rent for 5 months (11/1–3/31)‡..................................	$ 250
Advertising (4 issues *Ski Magazine*)................................	1,000
Other advertising expenses......................................	250
Office supplies..	100
Office manager's salary—5 months§..............................	500
Dexter's traveling expenses....................................	1,000
Total Overhead...	$3,100‖

Breakeven Point

$$\$3,100 \div \$0.778 = 3,985 \text{ or } 4,000 \text{ units}$$

* Assumes quantity discount on toggles and 10 cents per unit for labor costs.

† Assumes that all sales will be to wholesalers. If Dexter continues to sell direct to retailers, the wholesalers' commission should accrue to him personally and not to Dexdahl, Inc.

‡ Assumes that rent-free quarters will not continue to be available.

§ Dexdahl cannot continue to count on wives' services. Estimated salary for one person part time is $100 per month.

‖ Does not include depreciation of the dies or incorporation and patent expense. These are "sunk" costs.

2. Merchandising Considerations: Suitability of Product for the Market

Favorable

a. External tree is better than the cheaper internal tree. New England boot manufacturer said Ski Tree was the best tree he had seen.

b. Competing internal tree is clumsy.

c. Only one tree has been returned as defective.

d. Reaction of retail stores and ski equipment distributors is generally favorable.

e. Competitors have made derogatory remarks about Ski Tree, indicating that they have recognized it as a competitive product.

CONCLUSION: The product is good.

Unfavorable

a. Ski Tree may appeal only to buyers of expensive ski equipment. High-priced.

b. Competition may take some of Ski Tree's business.

c. Retail store owners had unfavorable experience with the competing products. Attitude may carry over to Ski Tree.

d. There exists the possibility of patent infringement by competitors. A law suit would be too expensive for Dexdahl, in all probability.

3. Long-Run Demand

Favorable	*Unfavorable*
a. There are 80,000 to 200,000 pairs of boots sold annually.	*a.* These figures are too vague to be very useful.
b. There are 500,000 to 5,000,000 skiers in the United States.	*b.* This is just an estimate and not reliable.
c. A Chicago distributor says he can sell 1,000 to 2,000 Ski Trees per year. It ought to be possible to sell more on the West Coast and in New England.	*c.* Experience thus far indicates that Ski Tree does not "sell itself"; a great deal of promotion is needed.
d. A New England manufacturer of expensive boots says he can sell one with each of 200 pairs of boots he sells per year.	*d.* Present volume of sales is due entirely to Dexter's missionary work.
e. First advertising brought immediate results.	*e.* Retail salespeople who sell Ski Tree require some training, particularly the temporary Christmas employees.
f. With proper sales technique it is possible to sell Ski Tree in a very short time. (Mr. Dexter sold one in 35 seconds in a store where the article had not been moving.)	

CONCLUSION: It is impossible to estimate accurately the long-run demand because the evidence is so inconclusive, but the potential demand is probably high enough to permit profitable operation. In any event, the long-run potential is dependent on the firm's willingness to continue its promotional efforts.

4. Short-Run Demand: Remainder of the 1949–50 Season

Favorable	*Unfavorable*
a. If weather conditions are favorable to skiing, sales at ski resorts and sporting goods shops may be high.	*a.* Dexdahl cannot count on large Christmas sales in retail stores.
b. Sales might pick up at the end of the season as skiers prepare to store their boots.	(1) Most stores purchase ski equipment in August and September.
c. Dexter's spasmodic vigorous promotional work may bear fruit.	(2) The bulk of the Christmas sales in retail stores will come within the next 15 to 18 days. Dexdahl has only 100 units in stock and could not ship more for about 12 days (delay of 10 days in procuring toggles).
d. Dexdahl might expect sales of 150 units a week, since orders have been coming in at that rate.	

Favorable   *Unfavorable*

(3) Stores have not been pushing the item, and Dexter doesn't have time to do much promotional work.

(4) The temporary Christmas sales employees are unfamiliar with the item.

b. After Christmas, sales in city stores gradually decline.

c. The Chicago distributor does not expect to sell many this year because his salesmen are off the road.

d. Sales at ski resorts are low and may continue to be low if

(1) Weather remains poor;

(2) Dexter doesn't have time for extensive promotional work.

e. Ski Tree is "fair-traded" and therefore can't be marked down for January sales.

f. Ski Tree has been out for only three weeks, and the figure of 150 units per week is an unreliable basis for projecting sales for the season.

g. Selected sales statistics indicate that reorders were larger than original orders in only two out of ten cases and smaller in five out of ten cases.

h. Chicago and West Coast distributors accounted for almost half of total orders to date, and Dexdahl has had no reaction from them.

i. Dexter is not optimistic about this season's sales since he is concerned about the possibility of having a large ending inventory.

CONCLUSION: The present rate of sales may not continue; whether sales increase or not depends largely on skiing conditions and the firm's willingness to continue promotional work. Prediction of orders for 150 Ski Trees per week for the next two weeks is probably safe.

5. Advisability of Ordering 5,000 Toggles at This Time

Favorable

a. By purchasing toggles for 2,500 units, Dexdahl gets a quantity discount of 19% ($385). (See Exhibit B.)

b. A purchase of this quantity may prevent delay in filling orders if sales increase substantially around the first of the year. Toggles cannot be delivered until 10 days after ordering.

c. Perhaps design changes will not affect toggles; design changes are probably not urgent.

d. There is a good possibility that business will be profitable in the long run.

Unfavorable

a. Until 4,054 toggles have been used (2,027 Ski Trees), there is no saving. (See Exhibit B.)

   (1) All parts except toggles can be ordered to meet current demand.

b. Dexdahl may have an obsolete inventory on hand after the current season.

   (1) Design changes are complicated, and Dexter does not want to risk carrying an obsolete inventory.

   (2) It is not certain that Dexdahl will want to stay in business another season.

c. Inventory on hand at the end of the season might involve storage problems.

d. Investment in inventory will impair working capital.

   (1) Cash on hand is only $1,500; receivables are $700; and an investment in 5,000 toggles would cost $1,650.

   (2) It is possible that other expenses would be incurred.

EXHIBIT B

COMPUTATION ON TOGGLES

5,000 units at 40.7 cents $2,035	5,000 units at 33 cents $1,650	$2,035 1,650 $ 385 saving

$1,650 ÷ $0.407 = 4,054
4,054 toggles (enough for 2,027 Ski Trees) must be used to break even.

TIMING: The minimum order for toggles would be 1,000. If Dexdahl is to be ready to fill 150 orders per week, toggles should be reordered when Dexdahl's inventory is down to about 500, since there is a 10-day lag in delivery of this item. Of an order of 1,000 toggles placed on December 6, about 500 would be used to fill the backlog of orders, and the remainder would cover production needs for the ensuing 10-day period. The reorder point can be recomputed in accordance with the sales trend.

CONCLUSION: If the contemplated design change either does not affect the toggles or is not urgent, then 5,000 toggles may be ordered along with enough other parts to meet only the immediate needs. It seems more reasonable, however, in the light of the potential demand for the rest of the season, to order the minimum number of parts.

The five areas of consideration seem to be of equal importance. They are closely interrelated and interdependent, progressively shaping the final conclusion.

A thorough treatment of a case includes not only an investigation of the specific choices presented as such in the case but also an exploration of other reasonable possibilities. The only other possibility that might be considered in the Dexdahl case is that of going out of business. This course does not seem warranted at the present stage of operations, since it is too early to predict the profitability of the venture and the potential demand seems significant enough to warrant continuation.

Although conclusive evidence is lacking, it appears that Dexdahl will be a profitable operation if sufficient promotion is employed to reach the fairly large potential market. Since funds for promotional work during the remainder of the season are limited, and since the contemplated design change (if it affects the toggles) may make an excess inventory undesirable, it seems wise to order the minimum number of toggles and parts.

IV. A STUDENT REPORT ON THE CASE

The student report which follows is somewhat better than average in clarity of presentation, in the use which it makes of the case evidence, in the broad recognition which it shows of the Dexdahl situation, and in the well-established perspective which it exhibits.

It immediately sets up a realistic approach by showing that considerations of future, as well as present, sales and finances have a bearing on the immediate problem. It then defends this approach by an analysis which seeks to prove the relevance of these factors to the final decision on how many Ski Tree parts to order.

DEXDAHL, INC.

The immediate problem of the Dexdahl company is how many of each of the component parts of Ski Tree should be ordered at this time. In making this decision the sales possibilities of the present season must be analyzed in relation to the financial limitations of the company. Further, it would be well for the owners to stop and re-evaluate the over-all future possibilities of their enterprise in the light of what they now know about their possible profits. I have come to the conclusion that they should proceed rather cautiously at this time, and should buy parts to assemble 600 Ski Trees.

It may well be that Ski Tree is a good product and has good long-range sales possibilities. We have evidence that a Chicago distributor of high-quality ski equipment thought he could sell 1,000 to 2,000 Ski Trees in a normal year. A New England manufacturer of an expensive ski boot thought he could sell one with each of 200 pairs of boots he made per year, and he thought that the Ski Tree was the best boot tree he had ever seen. Twenty-five out of thirty of the stores in New England were impressed enough to place orders on Dexter's first trip. Some ski instructors and store owners in Boston were interested and thought Ski Tree salable. The company's first advertisement brought immediate results. Total sales for the short period to December 5 were impressive. Dexter attributed derogatory remarks of competitors to the fact that Ski Tree was receiving recognition. That only one defective tree has been returned indicates the product is good mechanically.

I conclude that Ski Tree has definite long-range sales potential. There are indications though that its main appeal may be to buyers of more expensive ski equipment. There is also indication that sales will require considerable promotional effort. The personal salesmanship of Dexter has been responsible for a large amount of present sales. It was seen in one of the large department stores that a mechanical device like Ski Tree needs to be pushed, i.e., to be demonstrated to customers. Department managers and sales personnel must first be "sold" and indoctrinated, or the product may sit on the shelves unnoticed by customers, or even improperly assembled. Competitors' ski trees that were merely left on consignment were not selling, perhaps for this reason.

The sales prospects for the 1949–50 season are not so promising. There is much evidence that the company got started too late this year. The Chicago distributor said his salesmen were already off the road, and that most stores purchased their season's requirements in August and September. The New England boot manufacturer who was so optimistic about Ski Tree had already purchased a large stock of internal trees for the season. The partners are going to lose at least 10 precious days between now and Christmas because they became so engrossed in their work that they neglected to look at their stock picture until now, December 5. They know they have 100 Ski Trees on hand. Exhibit 1 shows they have sold at least 500. When present orders are filled they will, therefore, be out of stock entirely. Ten-day delivery on toggles will preclude their producing any further trees until at least December 16. The regular transportation tie-up at that date will probably make it impossible for Dexdahl to make deliveries by Christmas to other than local New England stores, at least. City sales are strongest before Christmas, and it appears they are going to miss the bulk of these sales.

Dexter has established his product as a fair-trade item. Therefore, the stores will not be able to take markdowns on it. Since ski equipment is in the markdown stage by the end of January, I don't believe the city stores will order any Ski Trees that they are not pretty certain they can sell by that time. Consequently, I feel that city sales are pretty much through at present. Since normally city sales account for about 50% of total ski equipment sales, they have missed a good portion of the total market this year.

Resort sales, estimated to be the other 50% of sales potential in ski equipment, present better possibilities. Thus far, Ski Trees have not been selling in the resort areas. This is possibly attributable to the poor skiing weather. If the season should turn to normal, there appear to be good sales possibilities

EXHIBIT 1

DEXDAHL, INC.

Sales Orders to December 5, 1949

Original Orders Accepted:

Mail orders...................	50
New England dealers...........	180
Chicago distributors...........	92
West Coast distributors..........	108
	430
Second orders...................	55
Third orders....................	15
Promotion gift..................	1
Total........................	501

through March or even April. Based on performance thus far, I think it conceivable that additional sales of 2,500 could be obtained before the end of the present season.

Then why not buy enough parts for 2,500 Ski Trees and have enough on hand, and save money as Mr. Dahl suggests? The 2,500 sales, if obtained, will be spread over the balance of the season; so 2,500 are not needed now. The $385 possible saving on the toggles is quite substantial, but I think we are

EXHIBIT 2

DEXDAHL, INC.

Computation of Average Selling Price

Weights:

10% of sales direct × 4.95...................	$0.4950
30% of sales to retailers × 2.97...............	0.8910
60% of sales to wholesalers × 2.376...........	1.4256
Average sales price........................	$2.8116

unable to take advantage of it at this time. Five thousand toggles would require an immediate outlay of $1,650. If at least 600 trees are now necessary, $444 would be required for other parts, making a total outlay of $2,094. We now have $1,500 cash, $700 accounts receivable, and 100 Ski Trees worth $281.16 at selling price (see my weighted sales figures as shown in Exhibit 2). Our total liquid assets are therefore $2,481. Our net cash position would then be $387.

In order to get resort sales, it is going to take promotion. I think it is going to take one person's full time. Is Dexter going to quit his advertising job and work full time traveling for Dexdahl? Where will the traveling expenses come from? More advertising will now be necessary. Rent, heat, light, and other expenses must later be paid. Shipping expenses in particular seem to have been ignored. I feel that if the 5,000 toggles are purchased now, Dexdahl will become insolvent. Of course, the partners could put their other $1,000

EXHIBIT 3
DEXDAHL, INC.
Computation of Average Profit

	Direct Sales	Retailers	Wholesalers
Selling price	4.95	2.97	2.376
Manufacturing costs	1.704	1.704	1.704
	3.246	1.266	0.672
2% discount	0.099	0.059	0.0475
Gross profit	3.147	1.207	0.6245
Shipping costs (estimated)	0.50	0.05	0.15
Total	2.647	1.157	0.4745

10% sales direct × 2.65	0.265
30% sales to retailers × 1.16	0.348
60% sales to wholesalers × 0.47	0.282
Average gross profit on each Ski Tree (less shipping costs)	0.895

Yearly Fixed Costs and Expenses (estimated)

Salaries (management, sales, promotion)	$5,000
Traveling expenses	1,000
Secretary	3,000
Rent for shop, heat, light, etc	600
Advertising	500
Depreciation—dies 10% per year	250
Incorporation and patent expense—20% per year	60
Office expense	100
Total	$10,510

$10,510 divided by $0.90 is 11,678 or the total sales necessary to break even.

each in the business. When they first supposed they had this extra money, Dexter may have been counting on retaining his advertising job, and possibly Dahl was figuring on his wife's income from the hospital. At any rate, they had better keep this money in reserve if they can. If the skiing season continues poor, they may find themselves with a large inventory and little cash at the end of the season no matter which course of action is chosen. In this event, if the 5,000 toggles were purchased, it would prove disastrous.

One reason why Dexdahl should end the season with no inventory is that there have been indications that slight changes in the dies may be advisable before next season. Also storage of inventory costs money. Mainly, however, the company needs to be in a good cash position to start the next season. Promotional expense is again going to be high. There seems a good possibility of strong competition, particularly if Ski Tree's initial success is noted widely. One girl said she saw a Ski Tree on a train, and I noted this was before any were on the market—maybe there is already a competitor they don't know about, or maybe the West Coast outside tree isn't as different to the customer as Mr. Dexter would like to believe. Ski Tree is high in price compared to the other trees on the market, and vulnerable to competition in this respect. One New York high-quality sporting goods store said the tree was too high-priced already.

Possibility of patent infringements was suggested by the Boston attorney. Dexdahl's financial position leaves them ill prepared for a lengthy law suit.

My recommendation for the immediate problem is to buy no more than enough parts to make 600 Ski Trees at this time. Each week the previous week's sales should be reviewed and orders placed to replenish that amount of stock. If, for example, sales are 150 next week, order enough parts at the end of the week to make 150 trees. I assume, of course, that suppliers will go along with this. If not, make the closest approach possible.

Whether Ski Tree will support two families, or whether Dexdahl in particular can make a permanent success of it, seems open to question. In Exhibit 3 I have estimated some of the costs that would be apparent in a normal season, and have made certain computations as to profit per Ski Tree. From a weighted average gross profit of approximately 90 cents per tree, I have figured that in order to absorb my $10,510 yearly estimated costs and expenses it would take yearly sales of 11,678 Ski Trees. If Dexdahl is unable next season to reach this figure and at least make salaries, I believe it would be wise to dispose of the business.

The discussions of the case method thus far in this volume have treated cases essentially as isolated phenomena, but the instructor who is going to offer a course on the case basis must deal with the problem of organizing his case material into some kind of outline. Depending on whether the instructor wishes principally to stress the analysis of cases as isolated bits of reality or whether he wishes to emphasize contrasts and interrelations among case situations, this course outline may be a loose one or a tight, closely articulated one. And depending further on the particular instructor's point of view, the logics of the outline may be those of the functional, institutional, or industrial field of the course, those imposed by the case material itself, or those deriving largely from pedagogical considerations. There is no general rule. In the following paper, Neil H. Borden, who has been in charge of the Advertising course in the Harvard Business School since the early 1920's, describes his experience in organizing case material for effective teaching in that field.

Development of an Outline for a Course Taught by the Case Method

NEIL H. BORDEN

This is a history of the development of an outline for a course taught by the case method. The beginnings of this course, Advertising Problems, date back more than a quarter century, to a period when I was a young instructor in the Harvard Business School. Although the time is long past, the memories of the problems faced are fresh and they are buttressed by notes still in my files.

The specific outline which I designed for my course in Advertising Problems is of importance only for illustration, as are the changes in the outline that have occurred since. The things which I wish to stress in this history are the problems faced in developing a case course and the procedures followed in resolving the issues. Such an approach may permit the drawing of observations which will be of help to others facing a similar task.

Up to the time when I took charge of the Advertising course, only a few cases had been used in the classes. My predecessor had taken his doctoral work in Psychology and had taught in that field, and currently he was pioneering in the application of pyschological methods to advertising work. Of particular interest to him was the development of field investigational methods to determine the charactcristics of markets for products. Accordingly his students devoted considerable time to constructing questionnaires and conducting actual field work

164

among consumers and the trade, at a time when market research was relatively new. Similarly his psychological leanings were reflected in a large section of the course devoted to consumer motivation and advertising appeals. Here again field investigations were emphasized as means of determining the appeals to use. The methods of the psychological laboratory also were studied as means of throwing light on such things as the strength of appeals, the relative effectiveness of advertisements and parts of advertisements, and the effects of size and color on consumer response. As in most college Advertising courses, considerable study was devoted to the techniques of advertising—headlines, illustrations, layout, and typography. Advertising media likewise came in for a fair share of attention, as was their due.

Thus the Advertising course, through its study and discussion of text material, its field and laboratory study, and its written assignments, had provided good training in procedures for men going into advertising and marketing work. When the responsibility became mine, however, it seemed to me that a change was desirable not only in pedagogy but in the substantive framework in order to make the course better conform to the objectives of the Harvard Business School curriculum.

The starting point in determining the framework of the course was to lay down clearly its objectives. Whom was the course to train? For what purposes were these men to be trained? What kinds of problems and what substantive areas needed to be considered to give them competency when dealing with advertising in their later careers?

The teaching objectives of the Harvard Business School in large degree determined the objectives of the course. This School at that time, as now, had as its goal the training of men to become effective business administrators. The aim was not to give skills in the techniques of their beginning jobs, but rather to train men to deal effectively with the problems which they would meet when they reached positions calling for administrative action.

On the basis of the School's training aims, it seemed clear to me that the Advertising course needed to be designed for two groups of students: first, men who as sales or general executives in a wide range of businesses would be interested in the use of advertising in their enterprises, but who would not direct the detailed advertising operations; second, those who would look to advertising for a career, as advertising managers, as advertising agency executives, or as advertising directors of newspapers, magazines, or other media.

The primary need of the first group was an understanding of the widely varying uses of advertising as a business tool. These men required training which would help them to decide the proper role of advertising in specific businesses. Or, to put this thought another way, as general executives they would profit from training which would help them determine the part to be assigned to advertising in the marketing mix of any business with which they were connected. Men in the first group also needed training which would help them either to design or to evaluate the strategy of selling campaigns of which advertising was an integral part. Moreover, they needed a background for appraising the soundness of advertising budgets; such appraisal might involve judgment either regarding the over-all role to be assigned to advertising or regarding the soundness of advertising schedules adopted. As general executives they would probably have occasion also to pass on media selection and copy approach. In short, they would profit from training which would help them as future sales or general executives to make sound decisions when formulating advertising policies for their businesses or when passing upon the advertising work of others.

For men in the second group, those choosing advertising as a career, it appeared to me in planning the course that the training needs were much the same as for the first group. I anticipated, however, that these men would probably desire a more extensive and intensive consideration of operating or procedural problems of the type which fall under the direction of advertising managers, i.e., problems of media selection, control procedures, the measurement of advertising effects, and the use of market research, either for planning or for appraising advertising and selling campaigns.

A main objective of the course, namely, the training of students to deal effectively with administrative problems, was to be attained in large part from the pedagogical method adopted. The students were to be required to analyze actual case situations. They would be called upon to recommend a plan of action in one business situation after another, basing their decisions on facts available in the cases. No matter what the order of cases, they would get the benefit of training in case analysis. But to be fully effective my course could not be a miscellaneous collection of advertising problems designed merely to give practice in case analysis. There needed to be a conceptual scheme from which the students could erect a systematic structure of useful generalizations to help them attack advertising problems in the future with dexterity and understanding. In short, the course needed to provide an orientation in the field which would help the future businessman to crystallize problems and to bring to bear on their solution the aid of his past thinking on similar problems. Accordingly the development of a logical framework was essential.

As I worked on the outline, it seemed to me that the first part of the course should be given over to cases designed to bring understanding of advertising as a business tool, and the second part should be devoted to advertising procedures.

In many ways it was easier to develop the second part of the outline than the first. The procedural problems met by advertisers were known. In the previous Advertising course there had been a logical division of the areas into which procedural problems might be assembled. It was clear to me that at some place in my outline I needed to gather operational problems dealing with the following:

(1) The selection of media, that is, choice among types of media, such as magazines, newspapers, outdoor, and so on, and also choice among competing media of a specific type

(2) The determination of copy approach

(3) The determination of advertising schedules, that is, problems relating to size, frequency, and position of advertisements

(4) The devising of methods to measure advertising effects, such as inquiry analysis, consumer opinion tests, and psychological tests relating to size and color

I decided to omit from my outline cases in one area of advertising procedure which was a part of the usual Advertising course, namely, the actual construction of advertisements. Such cases would focus attention on the techniques of layout and typography, headline writing, and copy writing. I had concluded that the objective of the course was not to train copy writers or layout men; hence I did not want to take any substantial portion of my limited class hours for the development of skills in these advertising techniques. Although I realized the importance of teaching students of advertising to think constantly in terms of consumer buying habits and motivation, I believed that the analysis of advertising campaigns which would be under study would provide opportunity to focus upon the consumer and his behavior; the selection of appeals and the determination of selling strategy would be constantly under scrutiny. I therefore omitted cases calling for actual preparation of advertisements and study of techniques.

A few years later I concluded that I had made an error in not providing for at least a limited amount of work in the construction of advertisements. Any man employing advertising must appraise advertisements, even if he does not prepare them. Such measurements as have been devised indicate tremendous variation in the effectiveness of advertisements. Part of this variation is a matter of selection of appeals. Much of it has to do with the techniques of presentation. Hence I introduced into the course experimentally a few cases requiring the writing of advertisements and a liberal assignment of background reading on the techniques, with the thought that the cases and the supplementary material would provide an understanding of advertising and an appreciation of the significance of techniques that could not be so well attained merely by analyzing advertisements included in cases. Six or seven cases spread over the term were set up, requiring the preparation of an advertisement to meet the needs of each situation and an analytical critique to explain the treatment adopted in the advertisement. Every written assignment, after submittal of papers, was discussed in an extra class hour, with attention focused each time on some specific phase of advertising technique. The assignments were admittedly too few to develop skills in the techniques, but they helped to develop an understanding which would serve the students well when they came to direct the use of advertising.

I recount this change in material included in the operational part of my outline because it illustrates a basic requirement in building a case course outline, namely, the need for a continuing analysis of course objectives and for experimentation as to the best method of attaining the objectives.

When I came to develop the outline for the first part of the course, experimentation was particularly necessary. I knew that what was needed was a series of cases which would bring understanding of advertising as a tool for the business administrator. But I faced real difficulty, for little or no study had been made of the widely varying role of advertising in different businesses or of the reasons for such variation. I felt the need for an arrangement of cases which might provide a good framework of reference for use in dealing with new situations. From my teaching of Marketing, I realized the value of comparison and contrast among cases as a basis for building generalizations that would be of value to the student. But I was plowing a new field. I could not be sure just what types of cases involving decisions about advertising would prove best for my class, or what would be the most advantageous order in which to arrange these cases.

In a situation of this kind the case method serves well. Cases provide material whereby the instructor can grow in his field. The teaching material is research material. From it the instructor learns just as he hopes his students will learn. Each case provides evidence for an inductive approach. Contrast and comparison among cases help the instructor to develop useful generalizations and concepts which provide the future framework of his course. Changes in the order of cases taken up in class are easily made. With each subsequent offering of the course, new cases may be added, others eliminated. Continual experimentation can be carried on to find the order of case analysis that serves best to develop the understanding desired. In the dynamic field of business administration, the significance of this continual collection of new cases to course development and to refinement of course outline cannot be overemphasized.)

When I took over the Advertising course, I fortunately had at my command a few cases on advertising and sales promotion that had been gathered for the Marketing and Sales Management courses of the School. I also had the help of knowing these courses well from having taken them as a student and from having assisted in both, either as case collector or as instructor. The underlying concepts in these courses afforded valuable hints regarding a teaching outline for Advertising.

Guided by such case material as was available and by the marketing and business knowledge which I had, I laid down my first outline to govern the collection of further cases for the Advertising course. This outline was frankly tentative, to be confirmed or modified by use. The plan divided cases on the use of advertising by business into three broad categories: (1) cases dealing with the advertising of consumer goods, (2) cases dealing with the advertising of industrial goods, and (3) cases dealing with the use of advertising by retailers. This division was based on the hypothesis that the advertising in these several areas was sufficiently different to warrant separate study.

From the Marketing course I had learned that advertising and selling were employed for two basic purposes: first, to stimulate primary demand, that is, demand for a certain type of product; and, second, to stimulate selective demand, that is, demand for a particular brand or a specific source. Accordingly, in laying down specifications for cases in the consumer goods areas, I sought some which placed emphasis on stimulation of primary demand and others which chiefly involved selective demand. I aimed also to secure at the start cases that varied widely as to type of product, size of company, brand policy, and other factors that might influence the use of advertising by the seller and the strategy he employed.

As I gathered cases in which analysis was to be centered primarily on an appraisal of the role of advertising in stimulating demand for specific businesses, I reached the conclusion that it was advisable to establish in my outline another group of cases which, while involving appraisal of the role of advertising, would center attention on questions of strategy, timing, and coordination among the various elements of selling and advertising programs. Business administrators must deal with such questions if they are to secure good results from their marketing programs.

Thus by the steps described I arrived at the following rough outline of cases for my first offering of the course:

I. Appraisal of Marketing and Advertising Possibilities—Consumer Goods
    A. Appraisal of Opportunity through Advertising to Stimulate Primary Demand
    B. Appraisal of Opportunity through Advertising to Stimulate Selective Demand
II. Determination of the Place of Advertising in the Sales Program—Problems of Coordination and Strategy
III. Appraisal of Advertising Possibilities and Determination of the Place of Advertising in Sales Programs—Industrial Goods
IV. Use of Research to Determine Markets and Advertising Policy—Research to Measure Effects
V. Determination of Copy Approach—Problems of Copy, Size, Frequency, Color, and so on
VI. Selection of Advertising Media
VII. Retail Advertising Problems

Within this outline the arrangement of cases was guided largely by expediency. The cases in hand at any time were analyzed and judgments made as to the arrangement that would be at once logical and teachable.

From this beginning came an evolving, changing outline. The continued gathering of new cases, and the subjection of these to contrast and comparison, aided me as a young instructor to advance my understanding of the advertising field. My teaching materials were research materials. New guiding generalizations regarding advertising and marketing came to light. Reasons for the wide variations in marketing mixes became evident. A conceptual scheme of the place of advertising in various kinds of business began to emerge. My effort at every stage was to arrange cases in such order as to permit students to find for themselves the significant relationships. In no two years was the course the same. New cases were introduced, old cases dropped. Sections were added to the outline, others were omitted.

To rehearse all these changes is not appropriate in this paper. But some of the steps taken and the considerations behind them have a general significance which makes them worthy of mention. Initially it may be noted that my course was introduced on a one-term basis, a practice now quite widely followed in the Harvard Business School whenever a new case course is offered. This practice assures a better course for students; the instructor is under less pressure in producing class hours that are full and satisfying; he does not have to stretch or pad; he has time for course development. As time went on, however, the situation changed. At the outset the number of cases and the number of subdivisions permitted under the main categories of my outline were necessarily limited. After several rounds, when the quantity of advertising case material had grown, the opportunities for developing a satisfying full-year course became evident. The course was then put on a full-year basis. At that time more elaboration in the subdivisions of the course outline became possible.

Another thing which had to be considered was the relationship of the Advertising course to other courses offered in the School. To illustrate, in the early rounds I included a section of cases on retail advertising. Soon I had to decide with my colleague McNair whether I should teach retail advertising or whether he should make this topic a part of his course in Retail Store Management. We agreed that the topic was his. Again, I thought it wise to drop out of my course detailed cases dealing with field research aimed at the determination of consumer buying habits and motives. Such cases involved duplication of material included in the course in Market Analysis and in some other Marketing courses. On the other hand, I kept and expanded my cases dealing with research designed to measure the effects of advertising. Measurement methods seemed to me to be of enough significance to deserve considerable study on the part of men planning to be operational advertising executives. Although students taking the Market Analysis course along with Advertising would find some duplication in subject matter, this duplication did not seem to me to be so serious as would be the omission from my course of specific consideration of measurement techniques.

This bit of experience prompts a further observation regarding the number of cases to be included in an outline at any time and the number of substantive areas to be comprehended in the ramifications of an over-all outline. After a period of time, what is to be included necessarily becomes a matter for compromise. The chief guide, I think, might be the importance of the cases and of the substantive material incorporated in them to the educational objectives of the course. Beyond these considerations, there is a danger to avoid, namely, the temptation to include too much. Under the case method, it is my experience that careful, full analysis of a limited number of cases gives far better training to students than hurried analysis of a large number of cases providing more coverage. The chief hope and aim is to train men to deal realistically with business problems when they meet them. Development of ability to analyze and to reach sound decisions in specific cases is preferable to the mere accumulation of a knowledge of advertising facts and methods such as might be had from consideration of a larger number of cases.

It is more important, also, that the student should develop the ability to draw pertinent conclusions from experience than that he should be exposed to voluminous exposition of generalizations made by others. Rather than asking students to read some text on advertising "principles," it is preferable to devote part or all of a class hour periodically to the development of currently useful generalizations drawn from a group of cases recently studied. (The term "currently useful generalizations" is used advisedly; it connotes useful precepts for action by executives in certain kinds of situations, not mere platitudes or generalizations; it is less grandiose and all-embracing than "principles"; and it takes cognizance of the fact that the generalizations of earlier periods are not always valid for new situations.) It is not the generalizations themselves that have value for the student, but rather the powers of discrimination that he develops by this practice in drawing generalizations.

Granted that the possession of substantive knowledge, by itself, is secondary to the ability to make a sound analysis and to draw useful generalizations, yet in the planning for a case course some attention needs to be given to the means by which general information in the field is best conveyed. Ordinarily the cases themselves provide a considerable volume of background material; but supplementary reading assignments at certain points are usually necessary also.

In the Advertising case book published in 1950 there are eighty-four cases, presented in nine groups interspersed with declaratory chapters designed to take the place of at least a part of the collateral reading formerly recommended from miscellaneous sources. The publication of declaratory text in the same volume with cases was experimental and was by no means intended to obviate reference to other appropriate materials. The purpose was to provide, within convenient compass, background and guidance to help the student in his analysis of the various groups of cases and in his understanding of the structural outline of the course.

My experience in the use of declaratory material is this: while students may find the background material of some help in case analysis, they do not find in the generalizations provided in the declaratory material any "answers," i.e., decisions as to the specific courses of action called for in the particular case. On the other hand, study of the background material in conjunction with analysis of the specific cases results in greater understanding of the generalizations carried in the text or in outside reading references.

The outline of the Advertising course, as it had developed by 1950, is shown by the table of contents of the case book, reproduced here, in slightly condensed form, as an Appendix. It is in sharp contrast to the initial outline set forth on page 170. And with each offering of the course, new arrangements and new cases still continue to be introduced. It is my belief that the instructor using the case method should seek an outline of cases that will provide for the student a helpful conceptual scheme of the subject, and that this outline should serve as an aid to orientation and thinking on specific cases but not as a formula providing answers.

APPENDIX

OUTLINE OF ADVERTISING COURSE, 1950[1]

I. Some Preliminary Considerations
II. Appraisal of Opportunities to Use Advertising Profitably to Stimulate Primary Demand
  A. Cooperative Advertising Campaigns by Associations of Manufacturers
    1. Associated Salmon Packers—Cooperative Advertising of Pink Salmon
    2. American Meat Institute—Industry Advertising of Meat
    3. Millers' National Federation—Long-Range Promotional Program as of January, 1941
    4. Irish and Scottish Linen Damask Guild, Incorporated—Cooperative Advertising of Linen Damask
    5. Hat Research Foundation—Industry-Wide Program to Promote the Sale of Men's Hats
  B. Campaigns by Individual Manufacturers to Stimulate Primary Demand
    1. The Expello Corporation—Advertising to Introduce a New Cleanser
    2. Holmes Manufacturing Company—Advertising of Stillson Wrenches to Householders
    3. Tonto Drug Company—Advertising for Skin Lotion
    4. Tennessee Eastman Corporation (A)—Advertising to Stimulate Primary Demand

[1] This is substantially the outline as it appears in Neil H. Borden, *Advertising: Text and Cases* (Homewood, Ill.: Richard D. Irwin, Inc., 1950).

III. Appraisal of Opportunities to Use Advertising Profitably to Stimulate Selective Demand
1. Sucrosa Sugar Refining Company—Advertising of Sugar
2. Morton Salt Company—Advertising of Salt
3. General Baking Company (A)—Advertising of Bread
4. Lydia E. Pinkham Medicine Company (A)—Advertising Policy for Proprietary-Medicine Manufacturer
5. Master Chocolate Makers—Advertising Fancy Candy
6. Waltham Watch Company (A)—Advertising Policy for Watches
7. Providence Clock Company—Advertising Policy for a Manufacturer of High-Grade Clocks
8. Personna Blade Company, Inc.—Advertising of Table Cutlery
9. Rand Company—Advertising of Vacuum Cleaners
10. Buckner Textile Machinery Company—Advertising Program for Textile Machinery
11. National Rock Drill Company—Advertising of Rock Drills to Mining and Contracting Markets
12. Waverly Manufacturing Company—Advertising of Bench Grinders
13. D'Arrigo Brothers Company—Advertising of Branded Fresh Vegetables
14. Rust Craft Publishers, Incorporated—Advertising of Greeting Cards
15. Hewes & Potter, Inc.—Advertising of Neckwear and Other Men's Accessories
16. Rasto Mills—Advertising and Promotional Program for Jersey Cloth
17. Textron, Inc.—Advertising for a Line of Textiles
18. Reber Silk Hosiery Company—Character of Promotional Effort for Women's Hosiery
19. George Host Company—Proposal to Increase Manufacture for Private Brands
20. Hartley Company—Advertising of Umbrella Frames
21. Pitt Rubber Company—Use of Advertising to Promote the Sale of Shoe Soles
22. Contook Manufacturing Company—Consumer Advertising of Gray Goods
IV. Problems Connected with Building Promotional Programs: Strategy, Scheduling, Coordination of Selling Efforts
1. General Mills, Inc.—Introduction of Crustquick
2. The Taylor-Reed Corporation (A)—Introduction of a New Product
3. Athena Corporation (A)—Type of Introductory Campaign for Small Company
4. Lavena Corporation—Introduction of New Product by Advertising over Dealer's Name

3. Davis Petroleum Company—Consumer Survey on Gasoline Purchases and Advertising Recall to Check Effectiveness of Advertising Program

F. Consumer Listening Research: Radio

   1. Bulova Watch Company—Use of Data on Radio Listening to Guide Spot Purchases

IX. Advertising Agency Relations

   1. Clapham Company—Proposed Formation of an Advertising Agency by Allied Manufacturers of Machinery and Mechanical Goods

   2. Etna Company, Inc. (B)—Selection of an Advertising Agency

In the preceding paper Professor Borden has described one approach to the organization of a case course by narrating the development, over more than twenty-five years, of his course in Advertising Problems in the Harvard Business School. The resulting course outline, as reproduced at the end of Professor Borden's paper, is one which might be termed broadly as functional in character. Such a functional course structure, however, is by no means the only possible one. Quite a different concept for the organization of a case course is set forth in the following paper by John G. McLean,* in which he explains the development, during the postwar period, of a course in Advanced Production Problems. The concept around which Professor McLean's course is built is that of the industry rather than the function.

The Industry Approach to the Teaching of Business Administration by the Case Method JOHN G. McLEAN

Many of the case problems dealing with the programs and policies of industrial companies require for their solution (1) a general understanding of the technological characteristics of the manufacturing process with which the company is working and (2) a thorough comprehension of the competitive situation, economic conditions, and trade practices prevailing in the industry in which the company operates. Typical of the problems which may require either or both of these two kinds of background understanding are problems having to do with such matters as the following: a company's over-all competitive strategy and the interrelationships among its manufacturing, marketing, financial, and research programs; the timing and extent of major plant expansion programs; the advisability of various types of vertical or horizontal integration moves and the balance to be maintained among manufacturing operations at successive levels in vertically integrated structures; the optimum composition of a company's product line from a manufacturing and marketing standpoint; the location of plant facilities and the desirability of centralized versus decentralized manufacturing operations; the wisdom of various types of industrial mergers; and the appropriate management responses to new technological developments or fundamental changes in the economic and competitive environment in which a company operates. In

* Parts of the material in this paper have been adapted from *The Development of Teaching Methods and Materials for a Course in Manufacturing Policy*, a thesis submitted by the author in partial fulfillment of the requirements for the degree of Doctor of Commercial Science at the Harvard Business School in May, 1948.

dealing with problems of this character, which may for convenience be referred to as "advanced management problems," the experienced industrial executive draws a large measure of his insight and judgment from long familiarity with the business economics of his manufacturing process and a keen awareness of what is going on in the industrial environment in which his company lives.

These advanced management problems cannot be handled readily in the conventional case course organized by topical areas. A typical case course in the industrial management field designed to deal with these problems might, for example, have sections of work on such topics as plant expansion, plant location, product policies, vertical integration, horizontal integration, production planning and control, shop organization, industrial research, and industrial mergers. Within each section there would ordinarily be a group of case problems drawn from different kinds of companies in different industries. Under such an arrangement, the student is required to jump from one industry and one type of manufacturing situation to another, day by day as the work progresses. As a result, he has difficulty in gaining sufficient understanding of any one industry or process to deal fully and realistically with the problems before him. The work of the course thus may engender habits of superficial analysis, a lack of assurance on the part of the student, and a sense of frustration on the part of both instructor and student because the class discussion is rarely able to probe the depths of the problems or to treat them in their full context.

The difficulties posed by the conventional topical outline may, of course, be somewhat mitigated by writing into each case, or presenting in appendices, certain essential information regarding manufacturing processes and industry conditions. This procedure, however, has two fundamental drawbacks. In the first place, if a full treatment of process and industry is undertaken, the case becomes long and unwieldy, and the student's labor of absorbing an understanding of the process and industry may dwarf, at least in his mind, the task of solving the business problem which the case is intended to pose. In the second place, if the facts about process and industry are selected to give the student what he needs in dealing with the case problem, a certain amount of "spoon feeding" is inevitable. In other words, the student's job becomes one of merely correlating a preselected and predigested set of facts about process and industry with the facts of the business situation outlined in the case. In actual business practice the real problem of the executive is that of using his imagination and judgment to decide just what developments in the industry and what facts about the technology of his manufacturing process are pertinent to the particular situation.

The pedagogical problems involved in handling the advanced management cases in the conventional topical outline immediately suggest the possibility of using an industry approach, that is, of arranging the material by industry groups and of giving the student an opportunity to study the technological characteristics of the process and the competitive and economic conditions in an industry before tackling a series of case problems drawn from companies in that industry. Such an arrangement is diametrically opposed to the more usual topical outline, because in the latter the cases are grouped by topic or function and the industries are mixed, whereas under the industry approach the cases are grouped by industries and the topics are mixed.

As an illustration of what the industry approach is and how it may be used in the teaching of business administration, there follows a description of how one course is organized and taught in the second-year curriculum of the Harvard Business School. The course was introduced in 1947 under the title Advanced Production Problems, which name will be used throughout the discussion although it is somewhat of a misnomer for the work of the course.

I. OBJECTIVES AND ORGANIZATION OF THE ADVANCED PRODUCTION PROBLEMS COURSE

The Advanced Production Problems course takes as its primary objective the task of training students to deal with the programs, policies, and management problems of industrial companies in the full light of the basic characteristics of the production processes with which the companies are working and in the full light of the current trends and conditions in the industries in which the companies are situated. The course has two secondary objectives which follow almost as corollaries from the prime objective. The first of these is to develop the students' ability to analyze a manufacturing process and to determine quickly the things about it which are important for top management to understand; the second is to develop the students' ability to analyze industries and to evaluate the competitive, economic, and technological forces at work in them.

The course is designed to build upon the groundwork established by the first-year program, which provides basic training in Production, Marketing, Finance, Control,[1] and Administrative Practices and gives the student an initial acquaintance with the economic, political, social,

---

[1] A course dealing with the use of figures for management purposes; it embraces many aspects of both accounting and statistics.

and legal environment within which business decisions are made. In particular, the Advanced Production Problems course builds upon the first-year course in Production, which includes fundamental training in nearly all the basic subjects and techniques of industrial management, such as the use of machines and equipment, methods work, worker training, time study, wage incentives, job analysis, merit rating, plant layout, scheduling, production control, and shop organization. The Advanced Production Problems course is intended to give the student an opportunity to make extensive application of the knowledge of subjects and techniques gained from the first-year Production work and other first-year courses in dealing with the top management problems of industrial enterprises.

The Advanced Production Problems course is designed also to supplement the work of the other second-year courses. A second-year student's program normally comprises a full-year course in Business Policy and eight one-term elective courses. The elective courses are chosen from a total offering of about fifty different courses, approximately twenty-five of which are scheduled in each term. Nearly all these elective courses have a topical organization and provide training in certain functional, institutional, or subject areas. These courses rarely can afford the time to consider in full detail the effect exerted on management programs and policies by both the technology and the current trends in the particular industry. The Advanced Production Problems course thus is designed to supplement in two ways whatever combination of elective courses a student may have in his program: first, it deliberately cuts across functional boundaries and subject areas and requires the student to draw together his training and knowledge in several different fields in reaching management decisions; and, second, it is one of the few courses in the School's curriculum which require the student to do intensive work correlating the facts of business problems with the facts of manufacturing technologies and industry conditions.

The cases for the Advanced Production Problems course are drawn from five, or sometimes six, different industries and are arranged in the outline by industry. The course runs for one term, extending over a period of about fourteen weeks; hence two or three weeks are allotted to each industry section. The work for each section is divided into three major parts. First, one or two class meetings and a field trip are devoted to an examination of the characteristics of the manufacturing process. Second, one or two class meetings are devoted to a study of economic and competitive conditions in the industry. And, third, four or five class meetings are devoted to a series of cases dealing with the management problems of particular companies in the industry. Each of these three phases of the work is discussed in greater detail below.

The number of industries studied in the course is necessarily a matter of compromise. On the one hand, it is desirable to include several industries in order to give the student the experience of making management decisions in a variety of different technological and industrial situations. On the other hand, the inclusion of a large number of industries would obviously result in superficial treatment and would defeat the main purposes of the course. Experience thus far has indicated that four or five industry sections are enough to accomplish the objectives of the course and that six is definitely the maximum number which can be handled effectively in any one term of work. It is presumed that the skills and abilities which the student develops from the program of the course will be readily transferable to, and useful in, whatever industrial situations he may ultimately encounter.

The particular industries currently represented in the course are the furniture, cotton textile, plastics, radio-television, steel, and petroleum industries. The selection was guided largely by the desire to confront the students with a variety of different managerial situations, but certain other considerations were also important. Thus a deliberate effort was made to select industries which would have a good deal of natural interest and appeal to the students, and industries in which graduates of the Business School are commonly employed. The metalworking industries were avoided, however, because the metalworking processes serve to provide the main teaching vehicle for the first-year course in Production.

The diversity of the managerial situations presented by the six industries is readily apparent. The furniture and textile industries are for the most part made up of relatively small, nonintegrated units, whereas the steel and petroleum industries are made up primarily of large, vertically integrated corporations. The furniture and textile industries are literally thousands of years old and have long since attained much of their growth and maturity, whereas the plastics and radio-television industries are among the newest in our industrial economy and have in recent years been characterized by extremely rapid growth and expansion. The bulk of the output of the furniture, cotton textile, radio-television, and petroleum industries is for consumer markets, whereas the bulk of the output of the steel and plastics materials industries is for industrial markets.

The furniture and textile industries draw their basic raw materials from replenishable supplies, the one on a long and the other on a short cycle, whereas the steel and petroleum industries draw their basic raw materials from depletable natural resources. Entry into the up-holstered furniture, cutting and sewing, plastics molding, and oil producing industries can be accomplished with relatively small capital accumulations; in the steel, petroleum refining, and plastics raw materials industries very large capital accumulations are necessary. In the radio-television and petroleum refining industries patent or license arrangements may be extremely important determinants of a company's competitive situation, whereas in the other industries such arrangements are usually of minor significance. Finally, the managerial problems of the petroleum industry are frequently international in scope, whereas the problems of the other industries are more likely to be confined to the United States.

The foregoing are but a few of the many differences which exist in the technological and economic environments of the six industries; they are mentioned merely to suggest the differences in the managerial situations which the student faces as the work of the course progresses from one industry section to another. Needless to say, there are innumerable other industry groupings which might serve the purposes of the course equally well.

The program of the Advanced Production Problems course requires an average of about fourteen hours of student time per week. The classroom work consists of three eighty-minute discussion periods weekly. The work done outside the classroom consists of the reading and preparation of the case material and the writing of about half a dozen two-page memoranda during the term on cases assigned for class discussion or on problems assigned for study on a field trip. Most of the cases are long and complex, and a minimum of two or three hours is required for each class preparation. The field trips, which are scheduled every second or third week, require about four or five hours of student time on each occasion.

II. THE WORK ON MANUFACTURING PROCESSES

The fundamental purpose of the work on manufacturing processes is to provide the student with such understanding of the processes as is necessary to deal effectively with the case problems taken up in each industry section. From this work it is intended also that the student should develop some skill in analyzing the economic characteristics of manufacturing processes, gain an appreciation of the kind of knowledge about a process which is necessary to top management personnel in formulating management programs and policies, as distinct from the kind of knowledge which is necessary and appropriate to the

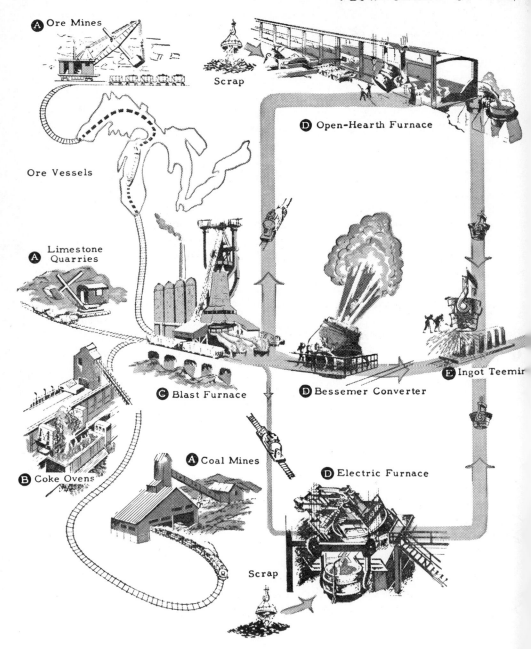

Ⓐ Ore Mines

Scrap

Ore Vessels

Ⓐ Limestone
Quarries

Ⓓ Open-Hearth Furnace

Ⓒ Blast Furnace

Ⓓ Bessemer Converter

Ⓔ Ingot Teemir

Ⓑ Coke Ovens

Ⓐ Coal Mines

Ⓓ Electric Furnace

Scrap

STEEL MANUFACTURING
STEEL MAKING PROCESS

(A) The three principal raw materials, iron ore, coal, and limestone, are mined and shipped over water and rail routes to the steel mills.

(B) Coal is converted into coke in by-product coke ovens.

(C) Pig iron is extracted from iron ore in the blast furnace. The coke and limestone are the reducing and purifying agents.

(D) Steel is made by refining pig iron and scrap in the open-hearth furnace, Bessemer converter and electric furnace. Pig iron and scrap are used in about equal proportions in the open-hearth furnace; pig iron accounts for almost the entire charge in the Bessemer converter; scrap iron and steel account for almost the entire charge in the electric furnace.

(E) The steel-making furnaces are tapped and the molten steel is poured or "teemed" into an ingot mold.

(F) After cooling the mold is stripped away from the ingot.

(G) Ingots are heated in soaking pits to a uniform rolling temperature.

(H) Ingots are rolled into three semi-finished forms: (1) blooms in the blooming mill, (2) slabs in the slabbing mill, and (3) billets in the billet mill. To roll billets the ingot is first reduced to a bloom, which is then further reduced to a billet in the billet mill.

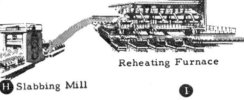

Reheating Furnace

(H) Slabbing Mill

(G) Soaking Pit

(F) Ingot Stripping

(I)

Scale Breaker

Spreading Mill

Slab Squeezer

Roughing Stand

Roughing Stand

(I)

Roughing Stand

Semi-finished forms are rolled into a variety of products in hot finishing mills: (1) blooms are rolled into structural shapes and rails in structural and rail mills, (2) slabs are rolled into flat-rolled products such as coil, sheet and strip in continuous hot strip mills, and

(3) billets are rolled into rod in continuous rod mills. The hot finishing process illustrated below is the continuous rolling of slabs into coil, sheet and strip. Further finishing of flat-rolled products is frequently performed in cold finishing mills. The coil is given a further reduction in thickness and a variety of coated finishes depending on the end use of the product.

(I) Finishing Train

operating engineer, and obtain some practice in the use of firsthand observation as a means of learning about the management problems arising from particular technologies and production processes.

The teaching program for this phase involves the use of three major components: illustrated process descriptions, field trips, and industrial movies. In the following paragraphs each of these components is discussed, and attention is then directed to the way in which the three components are used in a typical section of the work.

ILLUSTRATED PROCESS DESCRIPTIONS

The first component of the teaching program on manufacturing processes is a series of specially prepared, illustrated notes on each of the processes. These notes are written from the point of view of the business administrator and represent a compromise between the highly technical material found in the literature of science and engineering and the popularized descriptions of processes which have occasionally been prepared for the general public. The notes are arranged in several different ways, depending on the nature of the process; but typical of them are the notes on the steel process, which consist of three parts. The first two pages present a pictorial flow chart (see pages 184–185) which is introduced to give the student an immediate impression of the major steps in the process and their general relationship to one another. The next two pages show an aerial photograph of a typical steel mill, which is intended to give the student a general impression of what an entire mill might look like and also some idea of the relative space requirements for the various units of processing equipment. The remaining thirty pages of the notes are a step-by-step, illustrated description of the process. A large photograph is shown of each major unit of equipment, and the text material accompanying the picture presents a brief statement of the facts about the operating characteristics of the unit.

In both the preparation and the use of the notes on the manufacturing processes, an effort is made to distinguish between the knowledge about a process which is useful for general management purposes and the knowledge which is useful for engineering purposes. From his study of the notes, it is intended that the student should develop an understanding of what might be termed the "production economics" of the process. It is anticipated, for example, that he should seek the answer to such questions as the following: What raw materials does the process require, and in general what has to be done to them to produce a finished product? What do the various units of equipment cost, and what is their approximate economic life? How easily can the volume of output be expanded or contracted, and how will such changes affect unit costs? How flexible is the process in its adaptability to changes and variations in the product line? What procedures are required for the satisfactory control of output, quality, and costs? What limitations does the process impose on the arrangement of shop departments and the subdivision of the supervisory job? How large must the plants be to operate economically? What are the economic factors which influence plant location?

It is not intended that the student should develop from the notes an understanding of such things as the design and construction of individual machines, the techniques by which equipment is set up for particular jobs, the methods used to correct specific quality defects, or the various other technical matters which are normally the concern of the plant engineer. To cite some specific examples: From the notes on the textile process, it is intended that the student should learn the range of yarn counts and weave constructions over which a mill can operate economically, but not the procedures by which spinning frames and looms are adjusted for particular changes in yarn size and fabric construction. From the notes on the furniture process, it is anticipated that the student should learn how long lumber must remain in dry kilns and approximately what quantity of lumber a kiln will hold, but not what temperatures and humidities are used for drying particular species of wood. From the notes on the steel process, it is intended that the student should learn that for economical production a blast furnace must be operated continuously for two or three years at a time, but it is not required that he master the chemistry of what goes on within the blast furnace.

The notes on the processes in all instances stop short with a presentation of the facts about the process; the job of correlating and interpreting the facts is deliberately left to the student. In other words, the notes are designed to serve merely as a starting point from which the student may develop, through study and class discussion, his own ideas as to the basic characteristics of the processes and the way in which those characteristics influence management policy decisions, the organization of industries, and the operating methods of particular companies. To a considerable extent, therefore, the notes on the manufacturing processes are treated in a manner similar to any other "case problem," in which the student is called upon to analyze the business facts of a situation and to form judgments and opinions regarding them.

PLANT INSPECTION TRIPS

In connection with each process studied, the students are taken on an afternoon trip through a typical plant. The purpose of the trips is to provide the student with impressions of speed, size, working conditions, and various other things which cannot be conveyed easily to him in the classroom. The trips also serve to impart a sense of realism and practicality to the work and are helpful in stimulating the imagination, curiosity, and interest of the students. In addition, the trips give the students some training in how to make a plant inspection, a skill which is useful in a great many business situations.

The plant inspection trips require about four or five hours of student time, and it has been found that, in order to make the visits worthwhile, a great deal of attention must be directed to the arrangement and conduct of the trips, the briefing of the students, and the specific assignments. A preliminary visit is usually made by the instructor to make certain that the plant is suitable in terms of size and type of operations performed. During the preliminary visit, the company officials are acquainted with the purposes of the work and shown the illustrated process descriptions and other materials which the students will study before and after the plant visits. By this means the instructor seeks to put the officials in a position to supplement and not duplicate the classroom work in their talks with the students. At the same time, plans are worked out with respect to the guiding of the groups, the particular departments to be visited, and the approximate length of time to be spent in each area of the plant. An effort is always made to secure one qualified guide for each six or seven students. If the groups are larger, the students have difficulty in hearing what the guides are saying and in asking questions on points which are of interest to them, a difficulty which arises from the noise in the plants and the problem of finding sufficient space where the students can assemble around the guides.

Experience shows that the field trips have little value unless the students are given in advance of the visit some understanding of the plant operations and some knowledge of the things to be observed. Most industrial establishments are confusing to an individual going into them for the first time unless he has some background for appraising the things he sees and some basis for correlating and organizing his impressions. In no case, therefore, are the students taken on a trip before the illustrated process descriptions have been studied and discussed in the classroom. During the class discussion a careful effort is made to indicate the exact parts of the process which will be seen in the plant and the points at which the particular company's practice may differ from that described in the illustrated process description. Attention is also directed to operations and processes which are especially important to observe, and suggestions are made regarding problems which the students should consider in the plant.

On all the trips, the students are given some specific job to do. The purpose is to take the student out of the role of a passive spectator and to require him to make a general correlation of, and mental commentary on, his observations and perceptions. Sometimes the students are asked to work out a simple sketch indicating the general relationship of the several manufacturing departments to one another and to the products which the company makes. On other occasions each student is told to assume that he is the plant superintendent making his daily trip through the plant and is asked to prepare a memorandum for himself covering actions to be taken, things to be investigated, points to be talked over with others in the organization, and ideas for future contemplation. On still other trips the students are given special problems to study, such as that discussed on page 190 in connection with the field trip to a textile mill. In no case are the students permitted to take notes while they are in the plants. The intent of this restraint is to place emphasis upon observing and thinking rather than upon observing and recording.

INDUSTRIAL MOVIES

Industrial movies are used at certain points to supplement the illustrated process descriptions and the plant inspection trips. In some instances the movies serve as one means of preparing the students for a plant visit. In other instances they are used to impart specialized information which cannot be presented readily in the illustrated process descriptions or obtained from a field trip. In the study of the textile process, for example, it is judged important that the students should gain some understanding of what is meant by variations in fabric construction. Adequate coverage of this topic in the illustrated process descriptions would require a great many words and several diagrams, and the knowledge could not be gained easily on a trip through a single textile mill. A movie has been found, however, which treats the subject satisfactorily in a fifteen-minute period through the use of animated diagrams. Movies employing animated diagrams are very useful also in giving students an understanding of processes which are ordinarily not visible, such as the oil producing and oil refining processes.

TYPICAL TEACHING PROGRAM ON A MANUFACTURING PROCESS

The program of work which is followed in connection with the study of the cotton textile process will serve to illustrate how the process descriptions, plant visits, and industrial movies are used in conjunction with one another in developing the students' understanding of manufacturing processes.

As their first assignment, the students are asked to read the illustrated notes on the process and to familiarize themselves with the operation and purpose of each piece of mill equipment. In addition, they are given a sketch of a mill site and asked to prepare a very rough floor plan for a mill which might be built on it, assuming the mill to require approximately the same equipment as that outlined in the process notes. The purpose of this assignment is merely to get the students to think about the flow of work through the mill and to work out the general orientation of the various mill departments with respect to one another and to such external facilities as railroad sidings and highways.

In the first class meeting, the students are shown a color movie which follows the process through the same mill that is subsequently used for the field trip. The film is stopped at frequent intervals to permit the students to ask questions and to permit the instructor to elaborate on the more difficult parts of the process with blackboard sketches and comments. If time permits, the first class meeting is also used to discuss and compare the mill layouts which the students have prepared as a part of their assignment for the day.

The class is next taken to visit the textile mill shown in the movie. As the assignment for the trip, the students are told that the mill is producing a 90-inch combed percale sheeting with the following construction: plain weave, warp count 100, filling count 100, warp yarn 30's, and filling yarn 33's. They are also told that the speed of the looms is 180 picks a minute. They are then asked to determine how the operations and balance of equipment at the mill would be affected if a shift in market demand made it necessary to change over to (1) a combed percale sheeting with a cloth count of 120×120, (2) a combed percale sheeting with a cloth count of 100×120, (3) a carded muslin sheeting with a cloth count of 70×70, warp yarn 20's, and filling yarn 22's, (4) a combed shirting with a cloth count of 128×68, (5) a twill, satin, or figured weave, or (6) a rayon staple fabric, a rayon filament fabric, or a cotton-rayon blend. The objective of this assignment is to require a fairly careful study of the flexibility of the cotton textile manufacturing process in making adaptations to product changes, a matter which is important in many management situations and which has a significant bearing on the way the industry is organized.

At the beginning of the class meeting following the field trip, the short movie concerning fabric constructions referred to on page 189 is shown in order to illustrate the nature and extent of the variations which are possible in textile products. The remainder of the class period is then devoted to a discussion of the problems assigned for study on the field trip. In the course of the discussion, the students develop not only an understanding of the management problems involved in altering a mill's product line but also, of necessity, an understanding of the operating characteristics of much of the mill equipment.

III. THE WORK ON THE ANALYSIS OF INDUSTRIES

Like the work on manufacturing processes, the work on the analysis of industries is designed to provide the student with such information and understanding as he will need in dealing with the case problems in each industry section. The work on industries is designed also to give the student some experience in correlating and interpreting statistical information about an industry, in evaluating competitive conditions, and in appraising the significance of long-term trends and new developments. Finally, the work on industries is intended to give the student an appreciation of the kind of information about an industry which is useful in dealing with management programs and policies.

NOTES ON THE INDUSTRIES

The teaching program on the analysis of industries is built almost entirely around a series of specially prepared notes on the industries. In preparing these notes, a great deal of time and effort is expended in culling from the large mass of material usually available on an industry the particular data which are of pertinence to the business administrator and his job. The composition of the notes varies somewhat from industry to industry, but ordinarily three basic types of material are included: a brief outline of the business structure and practice of the industry, a review of some of the more important competitive and economic forces at work in the industry, and selected historical and statistical data about the industry.[1]

The material on the business structure and practice of an industry is essentially a synopsis of the policies and experience of the companies which make up the industry. It usually includes information on such things as the distribution of the manufacturing and marketing activities of the industry among different kinds and groups of companies; the number, size, and location of the manufacturing plants in the industry; the major markets in which the products of the industry are

---

[1] The notes on the industries usually comprise about fifteen printed pages of text (equivalent to about thirty mimeographed pages) and about twenty charts and tables.

sold; the experience which companies have had with various types of equipment and different arrangements of the production process; the brand, product, and price policies which are commonly followed by companies in the industry; the distribution channels which are normally employed by manufacturers; the types of wholesale and retail intermediaries which exist in the industry; the experience which companies in the industry have had with various types of vertical and horizontal integration arrangements; and the strength and character of the labor organizations that are active in the industry.

The material on competitive and economic forces is intended to give the students some feeling for, and understanding of, the many and diverse pressures to which company managements are subject as they undertake the task of formulating programs and policies. Data are usually included in the notes on such things as the changes which are taking place in the established practices and traditions of the industry and the nature of the forces which are prompting the changes; the intensity of competition in different phases of the industry and the various forms in which competition characteristically manifests itself; recent technological developments in products and processes both inside and outside the industry which may be of significance from a managerial standpoint; the short- and long-run demand-supply situation and the general availability of manufacturing capacity in relation to demand; government regulations and tax laws which are of critical importance in management's planning, such as the prorating laws and the tax allowances for depletion in the oil industry; and the social and political pressures which may be of significance in shaping management judgments, such as the agitation against crude oil imports which developed in 1949 and the pressure for accelerated expansion of steel producing capacity in 1949 and 1950.

The historical and statistical information in the notes on the industries is included for the purpose, among others, of giving the student perspective and a sense of proportion in evaluating current developments in an industry. Charts and tables are usually inserted to present records of such things as the principal factors ordinarily involved in the analysis of demand-supply relationships in the several product markets; the prices of raw materials, intermediate products, and finished products; the growth in the manufacturing capacity for the various products which the industry produces; common operating ratios for the different groups of companies engaged in manufacturing and distribution; wage rates in the several geographical areas of the country; and the return on borrowed and invested capital earned by companies in the industry.

As in the case of the illustrated descriptions of manufacturing proc-esses, the notes on the industries stop short with a presentation of the facts about the industry. The evaluation of the facts and the inter-pretation of their significance are left to the student. In other words, every possible effort is made to avoid a passive, textbook kind of ap-proach and to leave as much room as possible for imagination and constructive thinking on the part of the student. The notes may, for in-stance, tell the student a good deal about the new technological devel-opments taking place in any industry, but the student is required to form his own opinions as to the probable impact of the new develop-ments on management situations.

TYPICAL TEACHING PROGRAM ON AN INDUSTRY

The manner in which the notes on industries are used in the teach-ing program and handled in the class discussions may be illustrated by a description of the work on the analysis of the cotton textile industry.

Two full class meetings are devoted to study and discussion of the industry notes. As their first assignment, the students are asked to jot down the two or three most significant facts for management purposes which may be drawn from each of the charts and tables. During the first class meeting, the charts and tables are then taken up one by one, and the students are asked in each case to explain what they regard as significant in the data and why they think it important. In the dis-cussion of Exhibit 2 of the "Notes on the Cotton Textile Industry" (pages 194–195), for instance, the students are expected to point out that there has been a long-term decline in the total plant installed and total plant active in the cotton textile industry, which persisted throughout the entire period of World War II; that the great increase in demand generated by the war effort was met by an increase in mill running hours and by an increase in spindle output per hour; and that the increase in spindle output per hour probably resulted from long runs, during the war years, on fairly coarse fabric constructions. The students are also expected to note from the exhibit such things as the very slow rate of equipment replacement in the industry, the mod-erately fluctuating proportion of the industry's output normally sold in foreign markets, and the changes in export demand which occurred in the period following World War II. Facts and information about the industry and conditions prevailing in it are drawn from the other charts and tables in a similar fashion. As the discussion progresses, the students raise many questions of their own, challenge one another's interpretations, and begin to explore the relationships of the data in one table to those in another. The class activity is always far more

Sample Page from Notes on the Cotton Textile Industry
Exhibit 2
Summary Statistics[1]

	1933	1934	1935	1936	1937	1938	1939	1940	1941	1942
EQUIPMENT										
Spindles in place at beginning of year	31,442,174	30,938,340	30,889,484	29,253,444	27,700,194	26,704,476	25,986,620	24,943,302	24,532,146	24,146,130
Increase or (decrease) from preceding year	(884,352)	(503,834)	(48,856)	(1,636,040)	(1,553,250)	(995,718)	(717,856)	(1,043,318)	(411,156)	(386,016)
New installation, additions and replacements	348,568	529,840	214,874	469,316	772,724	178,280	349,416	414,974	449,848	210,456
OPERATION										
Spindles active at any time during year ending July 31st	26,894,860	27,742,462	26,700,946	24,664,428	25,419,110	24,774,004	23,731,050	23,585,938	23,389,454	23,607,508
Spindles idle during same period	4,547,314	3,195,878	4,188,538	4,589,016	2,281,084	1,930,472	2,255,570	1,357,364	1,142,692	538,622
Average number of active spindles based on twelve monthly reports	24,873,270	25,119,435	23,421,150	23,373,147	24,079,936	22,042,442	22,306,734	22,410,483	22,945,121	23,037,332
Intermittent spindles (being the difference between average active spindles and those active at some time during year)	2,021,590	2,623,027	3,279,796	1,291,281	1,339,174	2,731,562	1,424,316	1,175,455	444,333	570,176
Percentage relation of average active spindles to spindles in place	79.11%	81.19%	75.82%	79.90%	86.93%	82.54%	85.84%	89.85%	93.53%	95.41%
Spindle hours run	86,580,232,828	75,711,412,882	76,017,361,534	91,773,252,676	95,591,131,816	75,925,187,178	92,559,108,308	98,183,985,391	121,772,205,730	133,492,717,810
Hours run per average active spindle	3,481	3,014	3,246	3,926	3,970	3,444	4,149	4,381	5,307	5,795
Raw cotton processed (millions of pounds)[2]	3,053	2,655	2,755	3,470	3,657	2,904	3,627	3,954	5,167	5,637
Cotton processed per spindle per hour (pounds)[3]	.0353	.0351	.0362	.0378	.0383	.0382	.0392	.0403	.0424	.0422
MARKET										
Production in square yards	7,866,040,000	6,878,579,000	7,135,276,000	8,613,837,000	9,445,914,000	7,502,168,000	9,044,979,000	9,593,557,000	11,327,903,000	12,418,160,000
Exports in square yards	302,042,000	226,306,000	186,565,000	200,501,000	236,251,000	319,634,000	367,466,000	357,925,000	500,000,000*	450,000,000*
Imports in square yards	41,348,000	41,533,000	63,674,000	114,195,000	147,320,000	58,282,000	111,817,000	84,344,000	75,000,000*	25,000,000*
Available for domestic consumption	7,605,346,000	6,693,806,000	7,012,385,000	8,527,531,000	9,356,983,000	7,240,816,000	8,789,330,000	9,319,976,000	10,902,903,000	11,993,160,000
Population at July 1st	125,770,000	126,626,000	127,521,000	128,429,000	129,257,000	130,215,000	131,200,000	131,970,000	133,217,000	134,713,000*
Available for per capita consumption in square yards	60.47	52.86	54.99	66.40	72.39	55.61	66.99	70.62	81.84	89.03

	1943	1944	1945	1946	1947	1948	1949	1950	1951	1952
EQUIPMENT										
COTTON-SYSTEM SPINDLES										
Spindles in place at beginning of year	23,757,844	23,342,922	23,105,942	23,789,000*	23,928,000*	23,727,000*	23,751,000*	23,341,000*	23,149,000*	23,152,000*
Increase or (decrease) from preceding year	(388,286)	(414,922)	(236,980)	584,058	141,000	(201,000)	24,000	(410,000)	(192,000)	3,000
New installation, additions and replacements	7,752	82,736	323,668	323,056	416,555	607,358	858,623	649,780	771,065	295,642
OPERATION										
CONSUMING COTTON ONLY										
Spindles active at any time during year ending July 31st	23,429,252	23,018,828	22,674,882	N.A.	N.A.	N.A.	N.A.	N.A.	N.A.	N.A.
Average number of active spindles based on twelve monthly reports	22,744,106	22,332,080	22,018,529	N.A.	N.A.	N.A.	N.A.	N.A.	N.A.	N.A.
Average number of spindles active on last working day of month	N.A.	N.A.	N.A.	21,475,000	21,588,000	21,391,000	20,063,000	20,449,000	20,632,000	19,924,000
CONSUMING FIBERS OTHER THAN COTTON, OR BLENDS										
Average number of spindles active on last working day of month	N.A.	N.A.	N.A.	1,174,000	1,198,000	1,337,000	1,174,000	1,295,000	1,261,000	1,337,000
ALL COTTON-SYSTEM OPERATION										
Spindles idle during year ending July 31st	328,592	324,094	431,090	N.A.	N.A.	N.A.	N.A.	N.A.	N.A.	N.A.
Average number of spindles idle on last working day of month	N.A.	N.A.	N.A.	1,212,000	1,066,000	1,050,000	2,334,000	1,372,000	1,264,000	1,887,000
Spindle hours run:										
On 100% cotton	125,413,065,000	114,984,489,000	107,354,187,000	109,474,292,000	116,040,000,000	115,346,000,000	97,874,000,000	117,753,000,000	118,285,000,000	109,328,000,000
On other fibers, blends	N.A.	N.A.	N.A.	5,875,300,000	6,346,000,000	7,432,000,000	5,816,000,000	7,502,000,000	7,563,000,000	7,583,000,000
Hours run per average active spindle	5,514	5,149	4,876	5,094	5,371	5,424	4,882	5,760	5,748	5,499
Raw cotton processed (millions of pounds)2	5,269	4,792	4,511	4,803	4,568	4,461	3,838	4,680	4,908	4,479
Cotton processed per spindle hour run on cotton (pounds)3	.0420	.0417	.0420	.0439	.0402	.0385	.0392	.0397	.0415	.0410
MARKET										
COTTON TEXTILES										
Production in square yards	11,569,224,000	10,572,421,000	9,779,238,000	10,171,225,000	11,083,383,000	10,863,125,000	9,391,578,000	11,206,659,000	11,415,218,000	10,589,410,000
Exports in square yards	538,502,000	628,675,000	673,601,000	774,345,000	1,480,025,000	938,796,000	880,255,000	558,678,000	802,427,000	761,595,000
Imports in square yards	19,695,000	11,216,000	80,029,000	43,758,000	15,962,000	31,749,000	19,743,000	47,799,000	45,779,000	34,881,000
Available for domestic consumption	11,050,417,000	9,354,962,000	9,185,666,000	9,440,038,000	9,619,320,000	9,556,082,000	8,531,066,000	10,695,780,000	10,658,570,000	9,862,696,000
Population at July 1st	136,739,000	138,397,000	139,928,000	141,339,000	144,126,000	146,631,000	149,188,000	151,677,000	154,360,000	156,981,000
Available for per capita consumption in square yards	80.81	71.93	65.65	64.77	66.74	67.90	57.18	70.52	69.05	62.83

* Partly estimated.

1 Unless otherwise noted, data were assembled by The Association of Cotton Textile Merchants of New York from Bureau of the Census reports, WPB estimates, and information obtained through the courtesy of machinery manufacturers. Reproduced from *Ten Years of Cotton Textiles* through the courtesy of The Association of Cotton Textile Merchants of New York.

2 From Textile Economics Bureau, Inc., *Rayon Organon* and *Textile Organon*, annual review numbers published in February of each year.

3 Calculated from preceding data. Figures for the years from 1943 on are somewhat overstated because a certain portion of the raw cotton was consumed in fiber blends.

vigorous than would be anticipated from a cursory examination of the charts and tables. The discussion of Exhibit 2 alone frequently requires thirty to forty minutes, and it is rarely possible to get through more than five or six of the charts and tables in the eighty-minute class period.

As their assignment for the second class meeting, the students are asked to study two questions: (1) What are the dominant characteristics of the organization of the cotton textile industry, and why have they developed? (2) What is the significance of the new developments which are outlined in the last section of the notes on the industry? In the class discussion of the first question, the students are expected to call attention to the fact that the industry is composed largely of small companies and small manufacturing plants, that relatively little vertical integration has taken place in the industry except in the case of certain products and under certain special conditions prevailing during World War II, and that there is a great deal of product specialization both by the companies engaged in the manufacturing and by those concerned with the distribution of textile products. The students are then asked to express their ideas as to why these conditions exist and why more large, vertically integrated units with wide product lines have not grown up in the industry. The discussion of this matter calls for a comprehensive examination of almost every aspect of the industry, including particularly the competitive conditions and selling problems in the various textile markets, the limitations imposed by style changes and the need for variety, the relative inflexibility of many of the textile processes in the face of product changes, and the multipurpose character of many of the wholesale and retail outlets employed by the industry.

The new developments which the students are asked to appraise in their assignment for the second meeting include the recent surge of progress in the development of new textile machinery, the development of a large number of new textile finishes, and the increasing use of synthetics and fiber blends. In considering the implications of the new textile machinery, the students are expected to call attention to such things as the fact that the availability of new, improved equipment may lead to an even greater degree of excess manufacturing capacity in the industry than has existed heretofore, will inevitably pose problems with respect to the timing and financing of equipment purchases for many mills, and may (together with lower wage rates) give the Southwest somewhat the same manufacturing advantages over the Southeast that the Southeast had over the North after World War I. In discussing the new textile finishes and new fiber blends, the students are expected to note that the new products made possible by the new finishes and fibers will tend to increase the complexity of the styling and merchandising job and may tend to reduce the average length of manufacturing runs that can be secured on any one textile item. In addition, the students are expected to point out that the practice of blending fibers tends to press the styling and merchandising job back into the spinning and weaving mills and may, in the case of many mills, call for the development of some entirely new skills and interests within the executive group.

As the work of the course progresses, it becomes possible to ask the students to analyze and explain the economic circumstances underlying the differences and similarities in the structures and practices of the industries which they have studied. Questions such as the following may be raised: Why have the petroleum and steel industries developed large, integrated units as the prevailing form of business organization, whereas the furniture, textile, and plastics molding industries have not? Why do we find the phenomenon of price leadership in many of the petroleum and steel markets but not in most of the textile and furniture markets? Why are prices in the steel and petroleum markets generally less sensitive to reductions in demand than are prices in most of the furniture and textile markets? What accounts for the disparity between plant and company concentration in the petroleum and steel industries? In view of the increasing tendency of government agencies to regulate, or at least question, both the structure and the business practice of industries, it is important that the business administrator should be able to answer questions of this type.

IV. THE WORK ON CASE PROBLEMS

The group of case problems in each industry section is designed to provide the student with a series of experiences in formulating programs and policies for industrial companies in the light of what he has been able to learn about the technological characteristics of the process and the industrial environment. The cases are broad in scope and also provide an opportunity for the student to give considerable attention to the highly important task of correlating management policies in several major areas, such as manufacturing, marketing, research, and finance. The study of the case problems is the most important phase of the entire teaching program; to a considerable extent the work done on the analyses of manufacturing processes and industries is merely a means of putting the student in a position where he can do a comprehensive, penetrating, and realistic job of case analysis.

TYPES OF CASES USED

The chief criterion used in the selection of case material for the course is that the problems should, in fact, require a broad comprehension of the process or the industry, or both, for their successful solution. It goes without saying that there are a great many business management problems which can be handled with relatively little understanding of the technical processes which a company is using or the general economic background of the industry in which it operates; such problems constitute the bulk of the material in the Business School's teaching program and in most case courses in business administration. The general nature of the particular types of cases which seem to require the industry approach and which are used in the Advanced Production Problems work may be illustrated by four examples: Mengel Company, Textron, Incorporated, Bates Manufacturing Company, and Armco Steel Corporation.[1]

Mengel Company. The Mengel Company case deals with the program which the company initiated immediately after World War II as a means of gaining entry to the furniture industry and of securing the volume of business necessary to keep its two large woodworking plants in Louisville, Kentucky, in operation. The situation is outlined in the opening paragraphs of the case, which are quoted from *Business Week*, June 1, 1946:

This month the Mengel Company of Louisville, largest manufacturer of hardwood products in the United States, will make one of the very few attempts on record to market furniture under a brand name on a national scale.

The nation's 3,500 household furniture makers usually sell their product locally or regionally to 20,000 retailers. This restricted pattern of production and distribution results from (1) the manufacturer's original desire to stay close to a lumber supply, (2) the dealer's inclination to buy as near home as possible to cut down freight costs, and (3) the great variety of products in the furniture field.

A result is that brand names in furniture usually are a secondary consideration with the consumer. Price and dealer reputation come first. . . . Mengel will try to buck this situation by spending $500,000 in national advertising in 1946 to plug its brand name "Permanized" and to make the average consumer style-conscious. . . .

[1] The typical case used in the course consists of about fifteen printed pages of text (equivalent to about thirty mimeographed pages) and about fifteen pages of statistical tables, charts, maps, and pictures of the company's plant or products.

Mengel's profits are expected to come from volume production and complete integration. In addition to cutting its own oak, maple, and other American woods, and importing its own mahogany from Africa, the firm also makes plywoods and veneers and follows through every step in the manufacturing operation, even to doing its packaging in containers made in Mengel factories. . . . The final assembly line is a two-mile system patterned after assembly lines in the automotive industry.

To facilitate the use of mass production methods, the company's program also involved restriction of the product line to five or six suites, as contrasted with the thirty to fifty normally offered by furniture manufacturers. The distribution program involved the use of carefully selected, franchised dealers operating under annual quotas and under restrictions as to minimum resale prices. No participation in the industry's periodic furniture shows was contemplated by the company for the immediate future. In contrast, a great majority of furniture manufacturers offered their products at the furniture shows, on equal terms and with no restrictions, to all retailers who were willing to buy.

Analysis of the case clearly requires an opinion, which can be formed only after careful study of the manufacturing process, on such questions as the following: Are the characteristics of the process such that economies can, in fact, be obtained from mass production methods and vertical integration? Will those economies be sufficient to offset the additional expense which the company is planning to incur for advertising purposes? Will the mass production process be susceptible to sufficient control so that the quality of product necessary to support the brand program can be obtained? How far do the proposed manufacturing techniques commit the company to a program of manufacturing only five or six suites?

The analysis likewise requires judgment, which can be formed only after a study of the furniture industry, on such questions as the following: Is the demand for furniture and is the character of the product such that consumer preference for a manufacturer's brand can be developed? In view of the size of the total market, the buying habits of consumers, and the competitive situation in the industry, will it be possible to secure the desired sales volume ($12,000,000) with only five or six suites? In view of the traditions and existing practices of the industry, can adequate support for the program be secured at the retail level?

The remainder of the analysis requires, among other things, the isolation of the critical points in the undertaking and the formulation of a manufacturing and marketing program which will reduce the risk at those points to a minimum and give the best possible support to the company's program as a whole.[1]

Textron, Incorporated. Textron, Incorporated, was one of several large concerns in the textile industry which embarked on programs of vertical integration during World War II. Within a period of about six years beginning in 1940, the company changed from a processor of rayon yarns to a manufacturer of cotton and rayon consumer products, performing all operations from the spinning of yarn to the sewing and marketing of finished garments and household items. At the same time, the company expanded its assets from about $3,000,000 to $55,000,000 and its net sales from $7,500,000 to over $100,000,000 a year.

The case presents a fairly complete picture of the company's entire program and raises at least three fundamental issues. First, the case poses the classical problem of the advantages and disadvantages of vertical integration in the textile industry, a matter which can be studied and discussed only in the light of a full knowledge of the nature of the textile manufacturing processes at all levels in the industry and in the light of a keen appreciation of the behavior of the various textile markets and the nature of the prevailing competitive conditions. In appraising the wisdom of the company's program it is, of course, necessary to analyze the particular set of economic, tax, and market conditions which combined during the war years to prompt the formation of integrated structures, and to consider the effect of the possible removal of those conditions in the postwar period on the competitive position of a vertically integrated structure.

The second major problem posed by the case has to do with the balance to be maintained, under integration, among the manufacturing capacities at all levels in the integrated structure. In other words, should the company undertake to hold its spinning and weaving, finishing, and cutting and sewing capacities approximately in balance; should it plan to set up a tapered structure which will call for purchasing a certain volume of fabricated products, finished cloth, and greige goods from outside suppliers; or should it plan to set up a tapered structure which will call for the sale of a certain volume to outsiders at the greige goods and finished fabric levels of the market? The problem of balance is close to the heart of the company's entire competitive

---

[1] For the sake of the record, it is appropriate to note that in the period 1946–1952 a number of other furniture manufacturers began to sell on a branded basis. To meet the competition of these firms, the Mengel Company made several changes in its program. Among other things, the company increased the number of suites in its line, added to the number of its dealers, and began participating in the furniture shows.

strategy, and a satisfactory judgment on it can be rendered only after careful consideration has been given to the manufacturing and marketing problems of the industry and to the competitive conditions that are likely to prevail in the future as the industry passes through the various phases of the economic cycle.

A third major problem implicit in the Textron case has to do with the character of the management problems which the company faces in attempting to operate the integrated structure. One possible analysis yields the conclusion that the fundamental management problem is that of resolving three somewhat conflicting sets of requirements. From a production standpoint, the situation seems to call for long production runs with relatively few changes, because for the most part the process is rather inflexible in its adaptability to product variations. Moreover, an integrated structure results in a long production cycle and means that production plans must be formulated well in advance of the selling seasons. From a marketing standpoint the requirements are just the reverse; the situation calls for an ample variety of fabrics and for freedom to make changes on short notice. A third set of requirements has to do with the executive personnel. In view of the conflicting production and marketing requirements, it is obvious that extremely skillful merchandising ability will be necessary. The more skillful the ability, however, the more likely it is to resent the kind of controls and restraints necessary for the operation of the integrated structure. It thus may be argued that the venture will stand or fall on the ability of the company to develop a form of organization and a set of operating procedures which will permit the quick and wise compromising of production, marketing, and human requirements at all times in accordance with current conditions in the industry.[1]

Bates Manufacturing Company. In 1951 the Bates Manufacturing Company, one of the few large textile concerns remaining in New England, operated five spinning and weaving mills in Maine and also did some of its own finishing and sewing work. The company was the largest manufacturer of Jacquard-woven bedspreads in the United States and a major producer of fine cotton goods, rayon fabrics, and coarse cotton fabrics. Approximately 46% of the company's products, mainly matching bedspreads and draperies and finished fine cotton fabrics, were advertised nationally and sold under the brand "Bates Fabrics"; the remainder were sold as unbranded greige goods. The branded goods were sold in the medium- and high-price brackets and

---

[1] It is interesting to observe that by early 1953 Textron, Incorporated, had divested itself of all consumer goods manufacturing and was devoting its activities to the production of greige goods.

were noted for their quality. The management had for some time given a good deal of attention to the development of nonstandard and specialty products which would not face direct price competition from southern manufacturers.

On March 5, 1951, the management of the Consolidated Textile Company, Inc., a firm with two spinning and weaving mills in North Carolina and Virginia and a large finishing plant in Massachusetts, wrote to the Bates stockholders offering to exchange eleven shares of Consolidated capital stock for ten shares of Bates common stock. The Bates directors and management were not a party to the offer and were emphatically opposed to it. The case situation, therefore, promptly poses three broad questions: What arguments can the Consolidated management offer to induce the Bates stockholders to make the exchange? What arguments can the Bates management advance to persuade the stockholders to reject the offer? What decision should the Bates stockholders make?

A judgment of the situation requires, first of all, a fairly complicated financial analysis of the relative values of the two stocks. In the course of the financial analysis it sooner or later becomes necessary for the student to evaluate the future earning prospects of the Bates Manufacturing Company. One of the key considerations in the evaluation is the fact that Bates is standing almost alone in the face of one of the most sweeping industrial migrations our economy has ever witnessed. Analysis of the migration reveals that it has been prompted largely by manufacturing disadvantages inherent in the northern locations; and the student has to appraise the nature, extent, and probable duration of those disadvantages. Finally, the situation requires an appraisal of the probable effectiveness of the efforts of the Bates management to offset the company's manufacturing disadvantages with marketing advantages, that is, by emphasis on brand names, styling, merchandising, and the development of specialty products. In following the trail of the analysis, therefore, the student is called upon time and again to look at the Bates situation in the light of the total industrial environment in which the company is operating.

Armco Steel Corporation. The Armco Steel Corporation is a fully integrated steel producer with facilities for performing all steps in the steel process from the mining of coal and iron ore to the manufacture of finished steel products. The company, which was approximately the seventh-largest producer in the industry in 1950, specializes in the production of flat rolled sheet and strip in standard and special-purpose grades and, through its subsidiaries, also manufactures many other items, such as structural shapes, pipe, wire fencing, and nails.

The steel producing plants of the parent company are located at Middletown, Ohio; Ashland, Kentucky; Butler, Pennsylvania; and Baltimore, Maryland. One subsidiary, the Sheffield Steel Corporation, operates steel producing and fabricating plants at Kansas City, Missouri; Sand Springs, Oklahoma; and Houston, Texas. A second subsidiary, Armco Drainage and Metal Products, Inc., operates more than forty small fabricating plants located in all parts of the United States and Canada.

The case history gives a fairly complete outline of the company's entire operating situation and presents the substance of a report which the management committee submitted to the board of directors in 1949 concerning a proposed capital expenditure of $12,000,000 for the construction of three new open hearth furnaces at the company's main plant in Middletown, Ohio. In appraising the wisdom of the project, the student finds it necessary to make a comprehensive analysis of the effect of the new furnaces on the company's operating costs and profits, an analysis which cannot be undertaken without a good understanding of the general economics of the steelmaking process. Among other things, it was anticipated that the new equipment would increase the company's ingot capacity, reduce processing costs per ton, alter the scrap-to-pig ratio in the entire bank of open hearth furnaces at Middletown, alter the balance among the blast furnace, open hearth, and rolling capacities, and require changes in the normal furnace maintenance and downtime schedules. All these factors must be correlated in quantitative terms before an estimate can be made of the number of years required to return the capital outlay and of the average return which can be expected on the capital investment.

At this point the analysis is by no means complete, because it is apparent that the financial results are largely dependent on the future course of scrap, pig iron, and finished steel prices and on the level of open hearth operations which the company is able to maintain. The student thus finds it necessary to evaluate the issues in the light of all the information he has gained from his earlier study of the steel industry. The ability of the company to maintain a high level of operation for the new furnaces rests to a considerable extent on the soundness of Middletown as a location for steel manufacturing operations. The analysis of the Middletown location, in turn, requires a judgment with respect to the country's future sources of iron ore and an appraisal of the probable course of government action with respect to basing point pricing practices in the steel industry.

Finally, the situation poses questions with respect to the timing of the expansion project. In 1949 plant construction costs in the steel industry were at an all-time high; and there was, moreover, a great deal of talk in the industry about new steel processing techniques that might soon be ready for commercial development. Both these considerations suggested the desirability of deferring any major capital commitments. On the other hand, there was much political and public sentiment in 1949 to the effect that the steel industry had a national responsibility to expand steel capacity as rapidly as possible in order to relieve inflationary pressures and meet the expanding needs of the economy. With respect to this latter point, there were sharp differences of opinion among economists both in industry and in government; some maintained that the growth in steel capacity was lagging behind the growth in the requirements of the economy, while others insisted that the growth in steel capacity was outstripping the need and that the existing shortages were only temporary.

SELECTION AND ARRANGEMENT OF CASE MATERIAL

Since the case material in each industry section is designed primarily to give the student a series of experiences in formulating programs and policies for industrial companies in the light of what he has learned about the process and the industry, the instructor has a great deal of freedom in the selection and arrangement of the cases in the outline. There are, however, certain special techniques which have been found to be particularly effective in implementing the objectives of the course.

Use of Competing Companies. It has been found highly desirable to draw at least two of the cases in an industry section from companies which are in direct competition with each other. Companion cases of this type serve several different purposes. In the first place, they provide an opportunity for the student to contrast and compare the policies which different managements are developing to meet the same industrial situation. Moreover, the cases frequently require the student to form his own judgments with respect to issues on which the opinions of two different groups of competent and equally successful executives in an industry are diametrically opposed, an experience which corrects decisively and abruptly the tendency of some students to concur uncritically in the policies developed by a well-known, successful concern. Finally, it has been found that the policies and programs of one company may seem entirely sound and provoke no comment or discussion when considered by themselves. When considered in the light of what a competitor is doing, however, those same policies and programs immediately become highly controversial.

The technique of using companion cases may be illustrated by the cases on Durez Plastics and Chemicals, Inc., and the Catalin Corporation of America, which deal with the programs of the two companies in the immediate postwar period. Both these firms were highly profitable, medium-size concerns operating primarily in the materials manufacturing branch of the plastics industry. The Durez company had a clearly defined policy of integrating backward to manufacture raw materials in every possible instance. The company was also revealing a strong tendency to specialize in the phenolic field. The Catalin Corporation, on the other hand, had a firmly established policy of manufacturing no raw materials whatsoever. Furthermore, it was making every effort to broaden its product line to include a well-balanced selection of several different plastics. There were, in addition, several secondary differences between the policies of the two companies. The students are required to use their knowledge of the processes and the industry to pick out the major points of strength and weakness in the two programs and to form an opinion as to which of the companies is likely to develop the stronger position in the industry over the long run.

Use of Leading Companies. It has been found desirable to include in each of the industry sections a case on one company which by virtue of its management policies stands out from the common run of companies in the industry in the sense that it is departing from the generally accepted practices and traditions of the industry. In the furniture industry section, for instance, the Mengel Company is used because of that company's attempt to manufacture medium- to high-quality furniture on a mass production basis, to reduce to five or six the number of suites offered, to develop a manufacturer's brand, and to distribute through franchised dealers. All these policies were at variance with those customarily followed by the industry in the immediate postwar period. In the textile industry section, Textron, Incorporated, serves as an example of a firm departing from the general pattern because of its aggressive attempt to develop an integrated position in an industry which is characteristically nonintegrated. Such cases provide an excellent focal point for discussion of the relationships among management policies, process characteristics, and industry conditions; they also provide an opportunity to present some of the thinking of the more aggressive managements in the several industries.

Use of Case Series. In the more complicated industries, it has sometimes been found desirable to take up a series of cases each of which throws light on a certain segment of the industry, before treating the larger problems which require consideration of the industry as a whole. In one arrangement for the textile industry section, for instance, the first case deals with the problems of a greige goods mill in controlling quality; the second case deals with the activities of a finishing plant, the characteristics of the finished fabric markets, and the relationship between lot sizes and processing costs in the finishing processes; and the third case deals with a cutting and sewing company and the relationship between the characteristics of certain garment markets and the problem of plant layout. The final case in the series is on the integrated company, Textron, Incorporated, and requires a simultaneous consideration of all levels and several different branches of the industry and their relationship to one another. The use of the three preliminary cases increases the capacity of the student to pass judgment on the issues in the Textron case and makes it possible to proceed immediately to the central problems in the case without spending a great deal of time on subordinate questions.

Approaching Policy Issues through Operating Problems. In dealing with major policy problems, it has sometimes been found desirable to approach the issues through consideration of one or more operating problems at subordinate levels in the organization. A case on the White Furniture Company, for instance, poses three problems. The first, which is a problem for the production engineer, involves the laying out of a new conveyor system to handle the company's finishing operations. The second problem requires a determination of the effect which the new conveyor system will have on the company's manufacturing activities as a whole, a matter appropriate for consideration by the chief executive of the manufacturing division. The final problem requires consideration of the advisability of using certain funds for the new conveyor system rather than for research, product design, or advertising purposes and is a policy question which the manufacturing executive would be called upon to discuss with the other top executives of the company. In this instance, the understanding gained from the solution of the first problem contributes to the solution of the second; and the understanding gained from the solution of the second helps the student to go to the heart of the argument on the third problem.

Use of Undisguised Cases. It has been found generally desirable to draw the cases for the industry sections from well-known companies and to avoid disguises. Such cases arouse the interest and attention of the students and increase their willingness to undertake whatever program of work on the cases may be suggested. For instance, it has been found much more feasible to give the students long, difficult assignments on cases dealing with companies such as the Mengel Company, Textron, Incorporated, and Sylvania Electric Products, Inc., about which they have probably read in newspapers and magazines, than it is to give such assignments on disguised cases. The use of the well-known companies also serves to establish an important liaison between the work of the course and the students' outside reading and general grasp of business and national affairs.

CLASSROOM DISCUSSION OF THE CASE PROBLEMS

The classroom techniques for handling cases under the industry approach are not greatly different from those used in other types of case courses and need not, therefore, be discussed at any great length. Suffice it to say that the classroom discussion ordinarily has four general purposes. First, it is intended that the classroom discussions of a case should give each student an opportunity to corroborate the thinking which he has been able to do by himself in the preparation of the case. Second, it is intended that the discussions should provide a stimulus under which each student, in the development of judgments and conclusions, will carry his thinking a few steps beyond the stage that he was able to achieve by himself. The third general purpose of the classroom discussions is to provide the students with an opportunity to make a joint effort in the solution of the case problems. The instructor ordinarily attempts to guide the cooperative effort in such a way that it will result in (1) a marshaling of all the facts, ideas, and opinions pertinent to the problem, (2) a laying bare of the skeletal relationships among process characteristics, industry situation, company policy, and the facts of the problem, and (3) a comparing of opinions with regard to final judgments. Finally, the classroom discussions give each student an opportunity to tell his ideas to someone else, a process which usually helps the student to clarify his own thinking and stimulates him to still further mental activity.

In the Advanced Production Problems course, the students are expected to participate in the classroom discussions in at least four different ways. Each student is expected, in the first place, to throw into the common hopper all facts and ideas which he believes are pertinent to the problem. The second responsibility of the student is to raise penetrating questions which will aid in the analysis of the case. The contribution of a skillful question to the discussion is just as valuable as the contribution of a helpful idea, and sometimes a large part of the hour is devoted solely to the task of formulating such questions. A third responsibility of the student is to react creatively to the things that are said by the other students and the instructor. It is usually the hope of the instructor that a "chain reaction" of ideas may be set in motion in which a comment or question of Student A will create an idea in the mind of Student B, which, when expressed, will stimulate a thought in the mind of Student C, and so on through the classroom. The eventual responsibility of the student is to formulate and offer for appraisal his considered judgments on the cases.

The most difficult problem which has developed for the instructor in connection with the classroom work on the case material is that of deciding how much guidance to give the discussions through the use of questions and responses. When company policies and programs are considered against the broad background of general industry economics and process characteristics, the reasoning may become very complicated and the student may have to achieve a high order of mental activity before his mind can encompass and see clearly the full problem in all its ramifications. It is sometimes very difficult, therefore, for the students to work their way through to the heart of the interrelationships involved in the cases and to make progress in the formulation of final judgments in the short time which is available for classroom discussions.

If strong guidance is given to the discussions, it is possible within the allotted classroom time to lay bare the essential relationships involved in the cases and to give the students an appreciation of the way in which company policies and programs can be worked out within the network of those relationships. Classroom experiences of this type make a valuable contribution to the learning process but deprive the student of the opportunity to develop the mental strength and sense of mastery which he can gain only from thinking his way through the problems under his own power. On the other hand, if the instructor reduces the degree of guidance, there is a real danger that the average student will come out of the classroom with nothing but a series of unorganized mental impressions and a feeling of frustration.

The problem thus is one of determining for each class period precisely how much guidance can be given in the interests of avoiding confusion without jeopardizing the objective of teaching the students to think independently. It is to be borne in mind that the extent of guidance desired by the students is not necessarily the extent which yields optimum pedagogical values. Furthermore, the solution apparently depends somewhat on the composition of the class. In the first postwar classes, for instance, the average age of the students was 28 to 29 years, and many of the men had had previous business experience as well as several years of training in the armed forces. In these classes there were usually ten or a dozen outstandingly competent men who were able to carry the rest of the students through the more difficult parts of the cases. In the later classes, however, the students were two or three years younger and had had considerably less experience. In these classes, there were perhaps three or four topnotch men, but not enough to exercise a strong formative influence on the thinking of the class as a whole. As a result, the later classes could not accomplish so much in a given period of time as could the first classes, unless they were given a good deal more guidance.

As a matter of general policy, the instructors in the Advanced Production Problems course have found it desirable in the early part of the term to give enough guidance to make sure that the students do not depart from class in a state of confusion. The degree of guidance is then gradually reduced as the mastery of the students increases.

V. THE RESULTS SECURED FROM THE INDUSTRY APPROACH

On the basis of experience with the Advanced Production Problems course during the six-year period 1947 to 1953, it is possible to make a number of observations with regard to the general effectiveness of the industry approach as a means of training students to handle case problems:

(1) The industry approach provides a powerful vehicle for training students in the handling of advanced management cases in the industrial field. In the judgment of the instructors, there is an unmistakable difference in the level, range, and depth of case analysis work which the student can be trained to do with the industry approach and that which he can be trained to do in the conventional industrial management course developed along topical or functional lines. As the work progresses through the various industry sections, there is a slow, but clearly perceptible, growth in the student's capacity to relate the problems of a particular company to the pertinent aspects of the industrial environment and to the technological characteristics of the process with which the company is working. By the end of the term most of the students automatically treat company programs and policies, industrial situations, and process characteristics as an integral whole. Most of the students likewise develop from the work of the course a considerable capacity to correlate their thinking on the manufacturing, marketing, research, financial, and other programs of a company and to correlate their solutions to operating problems with a company's over-all competitive strategy. Many students, in fact, report that the results obtained in these latter two areas represent the most important single contribution of the course to the work of the School.

(2) The industry approach provides a framework in which the stu-

dent may be given some training in the viewpoints and capacities of industrial leadership. Presumably an industrial leader is a man whose point of view is broader than that of the individual company. He is a man who can see and understand the problems of his own concern and likewise those of other companies in the same and related industries. He is a man who can distinguish among the interests of the individual company, the interests of the industry, and the interests of the national economy as a whole. He is a man to whom other business executives turn for counsel and advice, a man who is selected to head industry committees, and a man whose opinions are respected and valued by government officials. The industry approach, and particularly the work it involves on the analysis of industry conditions, offers an opportunity to develop in the students some of the viewpoints and habits of thinking which must be added to those of the company leader if he is also to become an industry leader.

(3) The greatest single hazard involved in using the industry approach is that the student will become so absorbed in gaining an understanding of processes and industries that he will regard such work as the primary mission of the course and view the case problems merely as a source of further information about the industries or as a device for analyzing further the forces at work in the industries. This viewpoint is an inversion of the one desired for the work of the course, but it is not necessarily an incorrect or undesirable one. On the contrary, it is entirely in keeping with the philosophy of the industry approach that an industry should be analyzed, in part, through a study of the practices and policies of the companies which constitute it. If, however, the inverted viewpoint is the only one which a student develops, for him the course fails to accomplish its primary objective, namely, that of developing his capacity to use a knowledge of process and industry in formulating judgments on management programs and policies. It must, of course, be recognized that any gains made in a student's capacity to handle cases can at best represent only a small increment to a large amount of skill which he acquires from the sum total of his other case courses. The work on process and industries, on the other hand, is done in more or less virgin territories and will inevitably tend to assume a disproportionate emphasis in the thinking of some students.

(4) The primary sacrifice made in using the industry approach is that of forgoing the opportunity to develop particular topical subjects on a systematic basis. The Advanced Production Problems course, for instance, has a number of problems involving the financial analysis of capital investment proposals. These problems, however, are scattered

throughout the several industry sections and do not have the cumulative impact that might perhaps be secured if they were grouped together in a single, well-rounded section. The teaching of topical subject matter or skills in functional areas is not, however, the primary responsibility of a course using the industry approach, and is not necessary when most of the students' other work is in courses organized on a topical or functional basis.

(5) The simple logic of the industry approach appeals to the students. To them it seems eminently reasonable that they should first study the manufacturing process used by an industry and the competitive and economic conditions prevailing in that industry before attempting to tackle the major problems in the formulation of management programs and policies. There is, in fact, considerable reason to believe that the industry approach supplies a "missing link" in the training which a student receives from case courses taught on a topical basis. It appears that the handling of isolated cases in other courses leaves the student with a slight feeling of insecurity because he is frequently called upon to make decisions without any real understanding of the production processes involved or of the industrial situations in which the companies operate. This sense of insecurity develops whether or not the understanding of processes and industries is actually necessary for a solution of the problems at hand. Never having gained an understanding of any industry or process, the student has no means of knowing when the understanding is necessary and when it is not. From his sense of insecurity, the student gradually develops a desire to orient the administrative skills he has acquired to the total situation in which a company operates. In providing a brief experience of this type, the industry approach gives the student a sense of fulfillment and lends new meaning to many things he has learned in other courses.

That the case method, properly understood, involves something more than just cases and instructors is the contention of the authors of the next paper. C. Roland Christensen and A. Zaleznik point out that this method imposes certain burdens on instructors which in turn require an appropriate administrative environment if the case system is to flourish.

The Case Method and Its Administrative Environment

C. ROLAND CHRISTENSEN AND A. ZALEZNIK

The major purpose of this book is to describe the case method as it has been experienced and applied by many individuals in various courses of instruction. In this paper we should like to explore an aspect of the case method which is not commonly considered, particularly where the method is being experimented with for the first time. We refer to the kind of administrative environment which the case method demands for its effective application. The environment in a school is developed through the activities and relationships of students, teachers, and academic administrators. In this piece we are focusing attention on the contribution which the academic administrators make toward the creation of a favorable environment for the case method.

The case method is much more than a simple teaching technique. It is an educational process which provides a means for examining and learning from our experience, whether as students, teachers, or administrators. The constant examination and re-examination of our own experience through the medium of the "case" lead to an atmosphere in the school which is marked by change and new relationships rather than by stability. The main idea which we want to state in this paper, therefore, is that the case method demands a unique contribution from the academic administrator which makes it possible for all participants to learn in an environment of change and uncertainty and to gain satisfaction in doing so. An academic administrator examining the case method for possible use in his school must consider his own function in addition to the availability of cases, teachers, and qualified students. While we feel fairly confident about what the academic administrator's contribution must accomplish, we are far less sure as to what it is and how it is developed. Nevertheless, this variable—the academic administrator's contribution to the case method environment—is so important that we should like to explore it.

In the following remarks we first aim to present the characteristics of the case method which lead inevitably to an environment of change and uncertainty, and, in so doing, to indicate what pressures these characteristics exert on instructors as well as students; second, we hope to present in broad outline the goals of the academic administrator at the case method school; and, finally, we will discuss possible approaches to the implementation of these goals.

THE CHARACTERISTICS OF THE CASE METHOD

The case method makes some unusual and exacting demands on the participants. From our own experience as instructors, we have found that it places us under certain stresses because, as applied in teaching business administration, the case method creates an environment of change and uncertainty which we attribute to three facts: first, we are dealing with *business* as a world of risk and uncertainty; second, we are dealing with *administration* as an evolving concept; and, finally, we are dealing throughout with a *situational approach*.

1. BUSINESS AS A WORLD OF RISK AND UNCERTAINTY

Despite some views and, perhaps, hopes that business as a "science" will be a world of predictable probabilities, it is now and most probably will remain a world of risk and uncertainty. The businessman's stock in trade is his *willingness* and ability to take risks, to decide upon and implement action based on limited knowledge. No amount of reason and logic can postpone indefinitely the point where the businessman says, "This is it," and then looks for results into the future.

Business education, to be realistic, must face up to this risk and uncertainty. We doubt whether one can "teach" the willingness to take risks; student and teacher alike have to "live" the process. One of the features of the case method, as an inductive process, is that it provides an opportunity to participate in risk-taking and decision-making in the face of uncertainty through the medium of dealing with concrete situations. Those feelings associated with "making the plunge" are with us all the time.

The job of developing a willingness to live with the business world as it is lies on the instructor fully as much as it does on the student. In fact, the job for the instructor is the more difficult because of the pressures to which he is constantly subjected. He has to live with his own feelings of uncertainty as well as those of the students. He is under pressure from the class to provide a bag of tricks which will show everyone that decision-making is "really" selecting the sure choice out of several possibilities. If he moves in the direction of yielding to this pressure, classroom performance may seemingly be better; but is it realistic, and how much of a compromise with realism should an instructor make in the interest of effective pedagogy? There is always the temptation to make the problem look easy; but oversimplification not only is unrealistic, it also may be harmful in preventing the development of the spirit of risk-taking which is so essential.

The first fact, therefore, that contributes to an environment of change and uncertainty is the essential nature of the business world. The case method reflects the business world, and the participants involved in this learning process must find for themselves the willingness to deal with risk-taking.

2. ADMINISTRATION AS AN EVOLVING CONCEPT

In addition to their problem of learning to deal with the risk inherent in the business world, the fact that instructors are working with *administration*, a new and evolving concept, also contributes to a volatile environment. The implications of working with the concept of administration are quite complex.

It is fairly common experience that new fields of learning have great difficulty in becoming established. The pioneers in the field operate on a tenuous basis. They find it difficult to make progress in their work and easy to become discouraged. Even more important for their personal security, the pioneers frequently must work without much support and recognition from their academic brethren and the community at large. Only deep-rooted convictions and the vigorous support of the academic administrator will enable the pioneering work to progress.

Of course, administration as an art is far from being in the pioneering stage. From all appearances, too, the teaching of business has advanced far beyond the exploratory stage; it is easy to impute maturity when looking at the number of business schools, students, and graduates at work in business. Despite these appearances of maturity, we suggest that there is fundamental newness in the concept that administration is eminently worthy of research and teaching and that skills of administration can be made explicit and are communicable. If it should be thought that this concept is really not anything new, but simply part of "business," we urge a pause for reflection: we are thinking about more than teaching people technical skills and knowledge; we are concerned with *the processes through which work is accomplished in organizations*.

The teaching of administration viewed in this way is truly a pioneering endeavor. All the difficulties resulting from working with the new and unexplored have to be surmounted. To function with some assurance where the purposes and the relationships with the business and academic communities are evolving requires a measure of maturity on the part of the instructor, and consequently support from the academic administrator, not demanded by better-established fields of learning.

3. THE SITUATIONAL APPROACH

The case method is, in considerable part, a process of developing clinical skills, that is, skills for dealing effectively with concrete situations. The clinical approach of the case method forces us, students and instructors alike, to face up to the fact that dealing with concrete situations is a far more complex and demanding task than working with any set of generalizations or theories. We see very readily the uniqueness of situations, and we easily recognize the limitations and inadequacies of existing ideas and generalizations. We are therefore constantly being challenged by new situations. While we see in the challenge of the new and unique a great adventure, we can also see and feel the uncertainty which this constant process of evaluation and re-evaluation tends to develop.

If the academic administrator recognizes these three basic characteristics of business education by the case method, he will then be in a position of helping to create, through his administrative actions, an environment favorable to the development of this method.

THE GOALS OF THE ACADEMIC ADMINISTRATOR IN A SCHOOL USING THE CASE METHOD

Without intending any all-inclusive listing, we suggest what we consider to be five important aims of the educational administrator in the case method environment.

The first and perhaps the broadest goal is the acceptance of the case method environment as one of change and uncertainty. The academic administrator must help the individual student and teacher alike to accept this environment, achieve growth in it, and attain satisfaction in the process.

The second goal should be to give a sense of direction and purpose to the endeavor. With so many individual activities going on in a school, the administrators need constantly to lift up the common pattern, interpret it to the organization, and reaffirm its worthwhileness. Achieving this goal helps provide a measure of stability and individual security where inherently the forces at work tend toward change and uncertainties.

Third, the academic administrative group needs to aim at achieving the difficult balance between individuals' objectives and organizational requirements. An educational institution places a premium on individual creativeness, but it must function as an organization. Rather than have a conflict between what is good for the individual and what the organization needs, the practical emphasis should be on merging both, that is, ordering activities so that both individual creativeness and organizational requirements are achieved.

Fourth, the academic administrators need to encourage the development of bridges between the work of the faculty and the outside world. The establishment of these bridges helps in the communication of purpose and in the translation of the results of a school's work into practical applications. Equally important, if not more so, is the function of such bridges in keeping faculty members steadily in contact with emerging new facts and trends in the business world, thus preventing the erection of ivory towers.

Finally, the academic administrators need to make possible the conduct of affairs with a sense of humor. When working with a long and difficult educational process, it is easy to become discouraged and frustrated, particularly if some results do not begin to appear promptly. Then the danger grows that instructors will no longer find themselves getting a feeling of satisfaction out of the work they are doing. Hence the administration needs to be particularly careful not to conduct affairs in such a manner that the participants feel they are getting no fun out of it.

KINDS OF APPROACHES USEFUL
IN ATTAINING THESE ADMINISTRATIVE GOALS

What are the approaches which may help an educational administrator to achieve these goals for the effective operation of the case method? It is not possible to outline any all-inclusive list, but we are attempting to note some of the administrative approaches which have been observed to be useful. Alone, each is of little value, but their multiple and complementary functioning can help to create an atmosphere conducive to successful case method teaching and learning.

1. ATTAINING A SENSE OF DIRECTION THROUGH "SELF-DIRECTION"

One of the basic goals of the educational administrator working in the case method environment is to help provide leadership for a highly individualistic faculty group. As we observe the situation, an effective way of securing this sort of direction is by encouraging the participation of the faculty in the process.

The self-direction process may be encouraged through the operation of faculty committees. Often the typical procedure is for a problem to be raised by a faculty member, sent to the major committee, on educational policy, worked on by a subcommittee, deliberated again by the full policy committee, and then considered by the faculty in a regular meeting as a committee of the whole. Before the problem has been resolved, there has been ample opportunity for everyone to become self-educated on the issue. The pros and cons have been voiced from every angle and with every degree of emotion. When the faculty finally arrives at a decision, most of its members are willing to go along, if not on the grounds of logic, then on the basis that they have heard enough about the particular subject and wish to get on to something else. Such self-direction leadership may be time-consuming and awkward in its movement. After one has been to his second or third committee meeting in a short period of time, he may well feel that he could do with a little less of this self-direction. Yet letting the group work out many of its own problems tends to make for decisions which a highly individualistic and independent faculty will accept.

Effective committee operations depend upon keen administrative discretion in the selection of problems and areas to be considered. A distinction needs to be made, by the educational administrator, between matters which should be considered by the faculty and matters which should be handled by the administrative officers. A further distinction is useful between problems of a policy nature, such as those having to do with changes in the curriculum, and problems of a current administrative character, such as admissions, scholarship, and so on. The first type may be handled by policy committees; the second may be handled partly by administrative officers and partly by administrative boards on which faculty members sit.

The philosophy of faculty self-direction implies substantial interest on the part of faculty members in what other faculty members are doing, and it is part of the job of the administrator to promote general acceptance of the idea that there is no monopoly of ideas or methods under the case system, and that policy committees will from time to time carry on functions of review, criticism, and suggestion with respect to all parts of the curriculum.

2. Emphasis on Individualistic Patterns

A second major approach is to help the individual to function in the changing environment of the case method by encouraging each instructor to find his own way of learning and teaching within the framework of the general philosophy of the case method. Such a policy looks to the development of a series of individual approaches to the problem of teaching administration. The instructor is given the freedom to help the student learn in any way which he finds best suited to his own way of living and teaching. Within a course, working from the same case situation on the same day, various instructors may be stressing different points, using the case situation in many different ways. Also on the same day other instructors in the course may be using different case situations which they believe better suited for the development of their own particular students. Typically, there are no lists of standard questions to be answered. This emphasis on the personal nature of teaching creates some real problems for the academic administrator, such as scheduling, preparation of teaching material, and manning of courses. Certainly it is the opposite of neatly packaged coordination.

With regard to the individual's own growth, he is given an opportunity to voice his interest in teaching assignments, to choose fields of research, and to select areas of consulting work which will best broaden his capabilities as an instructor. From the point of view of the administrative group, this concern for the proper development of individuals requires hours of time, careful attention, and adequate financial resources. It means that the organization will be run not from the point of view of what is easiest to administer but rather from the point of view of what will make for the maximum development of the faculty and student groups.

3. RESEARCH AS A WAY OF ACADEMIC LIFE

Closely related to the encouragement of individualistic approaches to teaching and learning is the emphasis given to research as an integral part of educational activities. At the Harvard Business School, research is part and parcel of the everyday academic living. Research involves both project assignments ending in a published report and case collection and research for material for course development. Faculty members participate in both types of undertaking.[1]

How does the administration maintain this close working relationship between research and teaching? There is a definite policy that, unless unusual circumstances obtain, an instructor is given an opportunity to participate in a major research project of his own selection once every three years. He can select his subject, with the assistance of the director of research, so long as it is a problem of management interest to more than a single company. During the other years he is

[1] See Andrew R. Towl, "The Use of Cases for Research," infra, pp. 223–229.

quite frequently supervising a research assistant in the securing of current business cases for his courses. Also in any one year approximately one-third of the Faculty themselves typically collect one or more cases. It is the object of the administration to make it possible for the Faculty to be constantly participating in research as well as teaching.

By maintaining a vigorous research program closely tied in with its teaching activities, the educational administration achieves certain gains. The frequent research assignments in the field mean that the teacher constantly has an opportunity to check his own assumptions and conclusions against what he finds in the business world. He is able to keep up to date on the current problems of business and to bring his own case material up to date. Furthermore, case situations which he has personally observed and written up come "alive" to him in the classroom and enable him to build enthusiasm for the material with which he is teaching.

Research in this sense is a way of accelerating the learning of the instructor; it is a way of awakening interest in new fields; it is a way of bridging a gap between the reality of administrative problems and the classroom. Particularly incumbent on administrators is the obligation to see that the new instructor sets his feet on this path at an early stage of his career. In our experience certainly, important values were received from a substantial apprenticeship in the collection of cases and the subsequent opportunities to carry out research projects in our fields of teaching interest.

4. CONTROL OF CONSULTING ACTIVITIES

Research, whether project research or case research, notwithstanding its importance, cannot successfully furnish the sole connection between the case teaching faculty and the realities of the business world. Business consulting relationships for individual faculty members afford opportunities for intimate insight into business decision-making and for intimate contact with executives which constitute a valuable supplement to research.

An important part of the administrative task is to stimulate and at the same time guide and control such business counseling activities. As professors become eminent in their particular fields they are bound to receive many invitations to enter into business consulting relationships, and the danger is that such work will be too heavily concentrated on senior members. Thus may arise the twin difficulties that older men will take on so many outside activities as to impair their usefulness in the educational program and that younger men may not have adequate opportunities to obtain this particularly useful kind of experience. Keeping an eye on the consulting engagements of the faculty and striving at all times to maintain a proper balance are among the most important duties of the educational administrator who seeks to maintain a healthy environment for the case method.

5. A Premium on New Educational Enterprise

A major part of the educational administrator's task in a case method school is to encourage and foster bold new ideas in the teaching of administration. In any faculty there is a certain degree of inertia. Once an individual or a group has developed a program which has demonstrated reasonable success, complacency may slow down the desire to embark on new and unexplored educational ventures. A typical reaction to a suggestion to break with past precedent and experiment in a new area is likely to be that there is still much perfecting to be done on the existing courses and programs. Some repair work, of course, frequently must be completed before wholly new schemes can be undertaken; but such an attitude, if carried very far, stifles change. When the proposed experiments require the dropping or drastic modification of older courses or disciplines, it is only natural that those affected will query the worthwhileness of the new venture. An instructor may have put in many years of work on a particular problem and may properly consider himself an authority in that area; it is understandable, then, if he does not jump eagerly at abandoning that project for the uncertainties of a new field in which he may truthfully say, "I'll have to learn along with the student."

In this kind of situation, where the new and untried is uncomfortable, some action by the academic administration not infrequently may be needed to encourage new ideas. In the first place, at the Harvard Business School every attempt is made to encourage the development of a "general Faculty" spirit rather than the building up of strong departmental and special loyalties; there are no formal departments, and most teachers carry the title "Professor of Business Administration." Secondly, the administration encourages mobility of Faculty personnel. Particularly at the lower levels of professorial rank men are shifted from one teaching assignment to another in a new area on a fairly regular basis. For instance, an assistant professor within his normal six-year period may work in two or three fields, such as Finance, Marketing, and Production. When full professorial rank is achieved, interests in other fields are still maintained but development of an area in depth is encouraged. Furthermore, when new ideas and opportunities are brought out, the administration provides time and Faculty strength to work with that idea—for instance, the development of the Advanced Management Program. This experiment with education for the mature businessman represented a new enterprise fostered by the Faculty of the School and made possible by an administrative group which was willing to go along with an experiment involving years of study, much trial and error, and concentrated attention.

Only thus can an administrator make sure that the curriculum of his school is truly living and organic, that some courses are continually being abandoned and new courses are being developed. Helping changes to happen is a primary job for the administrator of the case method school.

A CAVEAT FOR THE READER

It may be well to repeat the warning stated in the introduction to this section. The simple listing of these several approaches must not be interpreted as an "answer" to the problem of effective administration in a case method educational venture. These approaches must be applied with balance and with adaptations to particular situations before they can be made useful. In encouraging new educational enterprise, for example, as we have noted, an educational administrator working with the case method may find helpful the policy of encouraging mobility of faculty personnel, in order to widen the range of the individual instructor's knowledge and experience. But such a policy may also raise problems. If it is carried to a degree where faculty members are not permitted time to build professional competence in areas of special interest, it may weaken faculty development. Also the policy of encouraging research is not without its dilemmas. What should be the "mix" of the research effort? A heavy emphasis may be put on project research, where a published book may furnish visible evidence to a larger audience of a writer's ability and knowledge in an area. On the other hand, unless the administrator specifically encourages it, not enough attention may be directed to course development and the collection of cases for the day-to-day teaching program.

All in all, there is much still to be learned about how the administrator functions in an educational institution using the case method.

AN ADMINISTRATIVE POINT OF VIEW

In this paper we have attempted to explore the environment of the case method and the contribution which the educational administrator makes toward helping people to live effectively in this environment. We conclude that the effective administrator in the case method environment is one who is willing to make his own job a more difficult job. He must be ready to work with a situation that is constantly changing. He must be willing to take the time to listen to, and to understand, the problems of a faculty no member of which can be sure of what he is teaching a particular student on any one day or when learning actually does take place, but every member of which is nevertheless sure that somewhere in the process intellectual development is definitely occurring. The administrator must be willing not only to accept change but to encourage it. He must live with an educational organization which defies attempts to be neatly categorized and packaged for ease of administration.

The educational administrator would find his job far simpler if course content and objectives were limited to the traditional format. He would have fewer headaches if he employed a system in which instructors were made entirely sure of what they were teaching, knew what points they were expected to get across, and could test for definite results from their educational endeavors. But effective case method leadership does not yield to this temptation to have its job more standardized and less difficult. On the contrary, it is willing to accept a more difficult administrative role in order that the volatile and disturbing atmosphere which surrounds case method teaching and learning may become a positive influence.

Cases have a usefulness that extends beyond the walls of the classroom; they can be addressed to business executives as well as to students. Thus, from a fairly early point in the development of case collecting at the Harvard Business School, cases were conceived to be a method of business research as well as a medium of instruction. In the paper that follows, Andrew R. Towl recounts some of the experiences with the use of cases in project research and shows how the concept has evolved.

The Use of Cases for Research   ANDREW R. TOWL

Cases are useful not only for instruction but also for research purposes. As a research tool, the case method is opening new ways to better understanding of administration. To illustrate what this research method is, its evolution at the Harvard Business School is briefly reviewed, with comments on some of the characteristics which make it widely applicable to the study of administrative situations.

The idea that cases might be useful for research as well as for instruction appeared early in the thinking of the Business School Faculty. Dean Donham in the first article in the first issue of the *Harvard Business Review*[1] gave attention to the use of cases for both purposes:

Unless we admit that rules of thumb, the limited experience of the executives in each individual business, and the general sentiment of the street are the sole possible guides for executive decisions of major importance, it is pertinent to inquire how the representative practices of businessmen generally may be made available as a broader foundation for such decisions, and how a proper theory of business is to be obtained.

.   .   .   .   .   .

. . . [The] reasons which have led us to the present technique of presenting cases to the classroom, under which conclusions are generally omitted, limit the use of case books for businessmen. The executive finds that other people have faced problems like his own, but he gets no light from their experience.

.   .   .   .   .

While the cases in our present case books have a value as teaching material in advance of anything which we have been able to supply through lectures or texts of the ordinary sort, there is need of further developments in the technique of presenting business situations. . . . Isolated business cases have been published with their solutions in various places, but the number of such cases which have been worked out with the detail necessary, if they are to be useful for solving executive problems arising in the future, is lamentably small

---

[1] "Essential Groundwork for a Broad Executive Theory," *Harvard Business Review*, Vol. 1, No. 1, October, 1922.

compared with the field to be covered. Both the case system for its proper development and business itself need something like the court reporter who systematically reports numerous cases for current publication.

Thus at an early point there was seen to exist a genuine need for the reporting of business management experience in a way which would convey the flavor of individual situations in a vital fashion, as no mere statistical procedure, whether on a comprehensive or a sampling basis, could convey it. The idea at that time was that by the systematic reporting of cases a "body of precedents" could be developed for the guidance of management.

During the 1920's some 8,000 cases were gathered at the Harvard Business School. These were obtained in large measure for purposes of course development, and many of them were collected into case books to furnish the basic material of instruction. In line with Dean Donham's suggestion there was set in motion also a project for reporting business executive decisions on a basis intended to be analogous to the reporting of law cases. In 1925 the first volume of *Harvard Business Reports* was published, presenting 148 cases, drawn from a wide variety of industries, with a statement of the decisions and likewise of the results, where these were known. The comments of executives who used this volume indicated, however, that the material did not go far enough. Businessmen obviously were seeking guidance and authority; they wanted to have pointed out to them the factors which were significant in each of the cases. Although "answers" manifestly could not be furnished, the desire for guidance was recognized; and succeeding volumes of the *Harvard Business Reports* were compiled accordingly. Thus the second volume included commentaries by members of the Faculty on each of the new cases reported, as well as an appended section of commentaries on most of the cases which had been published in Volume I. Over a period of years six such volumes of miscellaneous cases appeared.[1]

While the work on the *Harvard Business Reports* was going on, experiments were being undertaken with the publication of specialized case collections concentrated in limited areas. The Bureau of Business Research, which then supervised the collection of cases as well as the compilation of statistics on operating costs, issued two small volumes on merchandise control,[2] one volume presenting twenty-one cases in

---

[1] The entire series was under the editorship of Professor Charles I. Gragg, with the advice of a Faculty Publication Committee.

[2] Harvard Bureau of Business Research, Bulletin No. 55, *Cases on Merchandise Control in the Wholesale Grocery Business* (1925), and Bulletin No. 59, *Cases on Merchandise Control in Women's Shoe Departments of Department Stores* (1926).

the wholesale grocery field and the other volume ten cases on shoe departments in department stores, with commentaries highlighting significant aspects of the experience reported. It is interesting to note in passing that both these undertakings were suggested by the recurrence, in the Bureau's studies of operating statistics, of a discernible pattern of relationships among margins, expenses, profits, and stock-turn, and that both were financed by special grants from trade associations.

Subsequently five specialized volumes in the series of *Harvard Business Reports* were published, presenting cases in particular fields: industrial marketing (two volumes), cooperative advertising, the marketing of airplanes, and problems of the motion picture industry. Each of the specialized volumes (except the first of the two on industrial marketing) included, in addition to the cases and individual commentaries, an over-all discussion of the topics emerging from the individual groups of cases. The work on these volumes too was financed by special grants from the industries most concerned.

The *Harvard Business Reports* never achieved the widespread use which had been envisioned for them, and for a number of reasons the undertaking was abandoned in 1932. Experience up to that time seemed to indicate that efforts to derive a broad body of precedents from a large number of recorded cases were of limited usefulness and that a more productive approach was to concentrate on collecting and analyzing cases concerned with a particular kind of issue or problem, with the specific objective of developing a better understanding of that problem. From such a case study it was thought that useful conclusions might be drawn by researcher and executive alike.

Since 1932 the topical approach has been more and more used in research undertakings at the Harvard Business School. The publications have included, in addition to the volumes of cases with commentaries, histories of individual companies, cooperative undertakings such as the seven-volume study of the effects of taxation on business decisions, and a program of research in aviation, to cite only a few examples of the range of studies using the case approach.

The decision to base a research project on cases carries with it an obligation to adhere to the inductive method and not to gather material primarily with a view to demonstrating the validity of preconceived ideas. In the planning of a case research project, lists of the executives to be seen and the cases to be released by them are a better assurance of direct sources of data than an outline of topics. The pattern of the investigation and the report, however, is by no means rigid. To suggest the latitude which is possible, four reports from among many are described below.

James W. Culliton's *Make or Buy*[1] is a report developed from a study of cases. The author set out to consider what problems were paramount in a decision whether to manufacture or to buy materials, equipment, parts, and supplies. He himself gathered a series of cases from companies which had faced such a decision; and these cases he supplemented with others from the files of the Harvard Business School, with instances narrated by executives in the course of interviews, and with other material from a variety of sources. His survey covered a wide enough range of experience to reveal the major considerations affecting the issue of make-or-buy and to permit a useful interpretation of the experience of a number of companies in dealing with a common administrative issue. On the basis of his observations, he offered some generalizations about the interrelationships of cost, quality, quantity, and other influences on the decision to make or to buy. His study was not a quantitative one; that is to say, it did not furnish such statistics as, for instance, what proportion of the companies in the United States manufactured their shipping containers rather than purchasing them. Case research by no means serves the same purposes as a census or a systematic sampling.

A somewhat different type of research project developed through a case approach is reported in *Administering Changes*,[2] by Harriet O. Ronken and Paul R. Lawrence. This is a study of the introduction of a new product in terms of the human beings who worked on it. The report is presented within the framework of narrative of the development of an electrical device, intricate to conceive and exacting to manufacture, from its design to its routine mass production. It recounts the tangible changes occasioned by the addition to the company's line—development of new production methods, addition of a new production department, building of new equipment, and so on—but particularly it traces the impact of the technological change on the people concerned—the realignment of relationships among individuals, rearrangement of communication channels, and reassessment of the activities of functional groups.

The research was carried on in a single plant but against a background of wide case research experience. The report describes in detail

---

[1] Harvard Bureau of Business Research, Business Research Studies, No. 27 (December, 1942). This report is essentially the author's Doctoral thesis and illustrates an approach, through the study of cases, which has become fairly common among Doctoral candidates at the Harvard Business School.

[2] Harriet O. Ronken and Paul R. Lawrence, *Administering Changes: A Case Study of Human Relations in a Factory* (Boston: Harvard Graduate School of Business Administration, Division of Research, 1952).

what took place in the period of more than a year during which observations were made. Essentially it is a long series of cases, presented with a running commentary and with conclusions as to the broad significance of the findings.

The comment has been made that case studies and statistical sampling do not serve the same purposes. That the two approaches can be effectively combined, however, is demonstrated by Harry R. Tosdal's *Salesmen's Compensation.*[1] This report presents thirty cases, with detailed individual commentaries; it gives statistical data from a questionnaire survey indicating the frequency of occurrence and the importance of various problems and methods of compensating salesmen; and it offers twelve chapters of facts, analysis, and conclusions with respect to problems of salesmen's compensation. Professor Tosdal developed the text specifically from the case and statistical surveys; but he brought to it more than thirty years' experience in observing and studying problems of sales management. It is interesting here to note that the case studies suggested what considerations might appropriately be surveyed by statistical sampling, and that the sampling, in turn, through the frequency distributions which it revealed, indicated that certain modifications in the choice of cases presented would enhance the usefulness of the published report.

Other combinations of case studies with statistical sampling and other research methods appear in the exhaustive entitled *Effects of Taxation.* In one volume of this series, *Corporate Mergers,* for instance, the approach is described as follows:

First, we have conducted very extensive field interviews, covering one or more participants in over 100 merger transactions and also a considerable number of other individuals—mainly investment bankers, lawyers, and accountants—who were in a position to observe such transactions. We have used these interviews in forming our judgments on the relative importance of different motivations for mergers, as a source of illustrative material throughout the study, and in our analysis of the tax motivations for the sale of closely held companies. . . .

Several of the mergers covered by our field interviews are reported in detail in the text . . . because they furnish particularly apt illustrations of points under discussion. We obtained approximately the same amount of information on numerous other transactions, but there seemed to be little point to multiplying illustrations simply to fill up space. Needless to say, however, our conclusions are not based to any significant degree on the

---

[1] Harry R. Tosdal, with the assistance of Waller Carson, Jr., *Salesmen's Compensation* (Boston: Harvard Graduate School of Business Administration, Division of Research, 1953, 2 vols.).

individual cases reported in detail in the text; they rest on the combined weight of all our empirical and analytical evidence. Individual cases reported in detail serve an invaluable purpose in *illustrating* complicated problems with full emphasis on the complexities involved, but by themselves they do not constitute *proof* for the type of conclusions reached in this study.[1]

The four examples just cited suggest the flexibility which is possible in the planning and execution of a case research project. What is accomplished by such a project is indicated, to a limited extent, by the following observations.

The recording of experience in itself is one of the most important objectives for case research. When managers have such a record of experience before them, they find a focus for contributions from their individual experience. The issues in the situation come to light. Alternative courses of action appear more clearly. Much of what was perplexing to the executive at the center of the situation may dissolve when the situation is pulled together in a written record. This phenomenon, observed so often in the history of case research, is for management one of the most important results of the case approach.

Interpretation of experience is a further objective of case research; but how best to present such interpretation is a problem. When the case researcher goes into print, no means equivalent to the exercise of group discussion have been fully developed. Nevertheless the reader wants to know the meaning of the case to the researcher, the meaning in terms of the researcher's knowledge of other situations, in terms of the significant considerations and how they are related. To the researcher this sort of interpretation comes more readily than formulation of broad principles and generalizations. To the executive it is more useful.

Communication of the researcher's insight to the executive in his own situation is perhaps the prime objective of the research report. If the research report stimulates an administrator and his staff to "search" their own organization more fruitfully, the research undertaking has justified itself. Through contact with a broadened base of experience, a reader may see his own situation more clearly and take more effective action.

The objectives of recording experience, interpreting findings, and communicating understanding need to guide both the field work and the writing of the report of research by the case method. Elsewhere the

[1] J. Keith Butters, John Lintner, and William L. Cary, assisted by Powell Niland, *Effects of Taxation: Corporate Mergers* (Boston: Harvard Graduate School of Business Administration, Division of Research, 1951), pp. 5–6.

process of collecting and writing individual cases has been discussed.[1] A case by itself, however, generally has not been effective as a medium for presenting the results of research. Analysis of a case takes far more time than an ordinary reader of a book brings to the task and requires a quite different frame of mind.[2] It is now clear that the notion behind the early series of *Harvard Business Reports*, namely, that useful precepts for management could readily be distilled from groups of cases, was a substantial oversimplification. The immediate product of case research is insight and interpretation, not a set of management principles.

The final task of writing the research report is in itself an integral step in the process of gaining full insight from the data. Attempts to write for the executive audience are a part of working with the data which is essential to the emergence from individual cases of meaningful topics around which the report eventually takes shape. There remains then the art of putting down one word at a time so as to recreate in the reader an appreciation of the administrative process as a whole. Because administration balances many elements at the same time while only one word can be written at a time, this writing stage takes fully as long as the field work. This observation from the experience of many researchers may profitably be taken into account in planning a research project by the case method.

One who is interested in studying administration can get out into the field, locate executives, and learn of their experience. That experience can be recorded in cases, and interpretations can be made. Thus insight and communication can be improved. These are all values worth the effort. Cases and their interpretation become steps which the researcher and the executive may take together toward more effective action by private firms and governmental agencies in the world of concrete things, people, and events—the world in which the creative arts of administration must be exercised.

---

[1] See James W. Culliton, "Writing Business Cases," infra, pp. 256–269, and John Fayerweather, "The Work of the Case Writer," infra, pp. 270–276.

[2] In recent years there has been a trend in industry toward the use of cases for analysis and discussion in training programs. See A. Zaleznik, "The Possibilities of the Case Method in Supervisory and Executive Development in Industry," infra, pp. 230–243.

A logical extension of the idea that cases may be of interest to business executives as well as to students envisions the possible use of cases in leadership training programs in industry. In the next paper, * A. Zaleznik looks at some of the problems involved in this kind of educational activity as conducted by conventional methods and speculates on the feasibility of a case approach.*

The Possibilities of the Case Method in Supervisory and Executive Development in Industry   A. ZALEZNIK

If the generation of businessmen of the late 19th century could observe today's industrial society, they would undoubtedly marvel at our technical achievement. They would, however, be even more astounded at all the talk, plans, and programs associated with the idea of "improving human relations" in industry. Not the least source of their amazement would be the "back to school" movement. Business management today is much concerned with supervisory and executive development. Executives are leaving their jobs to return to school, and schools are being established within companies for continuing in-plant training of supervisors and executives.

Many varieties of training programs are to be found: in economics, in technical subjects, in company policies, and, of course, in human relations. Although problems exist in these first three types of training programs, the last one mentioned—training in human relations—appears to present the widest range of challenging possibilities and controversial problems.

Human relations training programs seem to encompass many topics. They may include courses in psychology which deal with the definition of terms and the identification of so-called characteristics of individual behavior. Other courses teach "principles of supervision" and attempt to tell supervisors how to behave in certain situations. For instance, in connection with disciplinary problems, the supervisor is told never to reprimand a subordinate in public: "Always call the subordinate into your office and issue the reprimand privately." Still other courses are based on the "pep talk." The intention here is to stimulate the trainees to go back and do a "real" job for the company. Executives and supervisors are lectured to, they are conferred with, and they engage in case discussions and role playing.

* The material is adapted from A. Zaleznik, *Foreman Training in a Growing Enterprise* (Boston: Harvard Graduate School of Business Administration, Division of Research, 1951).

Although an observer may become confused in the face of so many "training" activities, he soon recognizes the importance of their purpose. Whether this purpose is made explicit or not, human relations training efforts have grown out of recognition of the fact that the administrator functions as part of a system in which his own behavior, feelings, perceptions, and assumptions come together with the behavior, feelings, perceptions, and assumptions of other people. The administrator has to develop a way of thinking about his job, and skills in behaving on the job, so that both group objectives and individual satisfactions are achieved. To develop these ways of thinking and these skills is the purpose of training in human relations.

A question naturally arises as to what is being accomplished in the formal training programs in human relations. We have no statistical answer to this question. But research experience and discussions with executives and training personnel suggest that the traditional training approaches have little, if any, relationship to the kinds of problems which administrators meet on the job. In particular there is a conviction on the part of some observers that the case method approach in industry training situations may offer greater possibilities for the advancement of executive skills and understanding than do some of the more traditional approaches.

To clarify the picture of what the human relations training problem consists of, it may be useful to introduce a fragment of experience from a postwar, modern factory. This experience is presented to demonstrate the complexity of the human problems in administrative situations. It will also serve as our anchor when we examine an actual experience in supervisory training and likewise when we subsequently explore the applicability of the case approach. Training approaches need to be viewed in relation to real life experience because supervisory and executive training must make sense to the participants in terms of their concrete problems on the job. This test of training approaches is at once severe and realistic. Administrators who participate in training meetings and who do not see that the discussions have relevance to work problems are all too likely to feel that they have not received much help and may experience the uncomfortable feelings associated with being unable to practice what "experts" preach.

A FRAGMENT OF EXPERIENCE IN AN ADMINISTRATIVE SETTING—THE INTRODUCTION OF A TECHNICAL CHANGE IN A FACTORY

The experience to be described took place in a modern factory which manufactured a relatively new consumer product. This consumer product, as might be expected with an advanced design, developed certain "bugs" which were difficult to catch by plant inspection but became known through field tests and consumer reports. Certain field tests revealed one fairly serious bug, and reports were sent back to the plant with instructions to eliminate it as quickly as possible. Engineers assigned to the job came up with the answer, which involved the assembly of one very small component. Instructions for the changed assembly were sent to the manufacturing department, and the change had to be introduced in the assembly of the product. It developed that, to introduce the change, all the operators on an assembly line had to be instructed in the change so that they could modify completed units which were on the conveyor belt.

There were several characters involved in this episode. One was Harry, a middle-management executive who was in over-all charge of the major production job in the manufacture of this consumer product. His work unit consisted of 500 operators, twenty group leaders, five or six foremen, and a supervisor who was Harry's next-in-command. This supervisor's name was Dan, and he was the second character in this story. The third was a foreman, Tony, who supervised the assembly line on which the technical change was to be introduced. Tony had working for him three group leaders and from thirty-five to forty operators. Finally, two engineers, Roy and George, and a methods man, Bob, rounded out the list of characters; these three were the technical experts. There is presented below a diagram indicating the people involved in the change and their formal relationship to one another:

Early one morning rumors began circulating along the assembly line that a change was going to be made, but no one had any details. Tony, the foreman, had heard these rumors too, but he knew little more about the matter than most of the operators. He tried to continue operation of the line in normal fashion, but the operators were excited and there was considerable hubbub. Tony went down to the end of the line to check output. Meanwhile the two engineers and the methods man arrived on the line. They went over to chat with the operators but said nothing to Tony to explain their presence. At about 9 A.M., Harry and Dan arrived on the assembly line and made some "quick-fire" decisions.

HARRY: This change is very delicate and we have to be careful about it. Now I want this done right the first time. If it isn't done right we'll have to do it all over again and we'll be in a hell of a mess. I want it done right this time and avoid trouble later. Now let's get Bob, Roy, George, and everybody else connected with this to come in on it.

Dan called for these three men. Tony was still at the end of the line, and no one called for him.

DAN: Look, the best way to get this done is to shut the line down completely for a half hour and to throw all the girls to making the modification of all the completed units on the line. That'll be much better than having repairmen come in for overtime tomorrow. And that'll only confuse us. It's simpler to get the thing done once and for all.

HARRY: That's right. We'll shut the line down and get this over with. [Bob, Roy, and George agreed.]

DAN: O.K. Now let's get all the group leaders over here. Dottie, Helen, Jean! Over here. [The group leaders assembled.] We're putting in a modification on one of the leads. We have to change all the completed units on the line. Now, we'll shut the line down for a half hour, and all the girls will go right down to the units and change the lead. Do you get me? All right now. Bob, Roy, George, will you instruct the group leaders on this change, and then the girls? [They nodded.] O.K. Now shut the line down. Oh, wait a minute. The girls over there, be sure they've completed the unit in front of them. That'll save some confusion. Now this is a very tricky change, so we have to be careful and see that the girls do it right.

HARRY: All set? Well, I'll leave it now. Remember, I don't want to have to see this job done over again.

Harry left, and Tony came sauntering down to the group assembled around Dan. No one addressed him or otherwise acknowledged his presence. He in turn offered no comments.

DAN: O.K. Shut the line down.

Roy explained the modification and change to the group leaders, demonstrating on one of the units on the line. The line was stopped, and the girls rapidly completed the work on the units in front of them. The group leaders then called the girls down to the end of the line where the instruction and modification were to take place. Tony, meanwhile, walked back and forth from one group to the next, but he still said nothing. The group leaders and Roy, Bob, and George began the instruction. There was some confusion because the girls had not brought their hand tools with them; so they were told to go back to their work stations for these tools. Then some of the girls called out that there were no soldering irons available at the last half section of the line, and this caused further confusion.

Tony was then spoken to for the first time. "What about the soldering irons, Tony?" He did not answer. Someone suggested that only a few soldering irons be brought down and spaced evenly along the section of the line where the work was being performed. Tony called for one of the repairmen and told him to bring up some soldering irons and to plug them in along the last half of the line. The repairman looked confused, shook his head, and went for the irons. Dottie commented, "What a mess. This goes on all the time. What can you do?" The girls who were awaiting instructions sat at their work places, and there was considerable joking and laughing. One of the girls commented, "Gee, this is fun. I hope the line stays shut down for a while." Another girl spoke up, "This makes time go by faster." The instruction proceeded, and soon all the girls were busy modifying units.

The repairman came up to Tony with four soldering irons that were still hot. "Tony, what should I do with these?" Tony took them, and when Helen came over he handed two of them to her, holding the others. They held the irons for a moment, and then Helen started to giggle. "Look at me holding these soldering irons. Am I supposed to hold them all day?" Tony walked over to the other side of the aisle and laid the irons he was holding on a roller conveyor. Helen followed him and did the same.

The girls completed the modification work in a little more than an hour. As each girl completed her work, she returned to her position and sat down. Soon all the girls were seated and resumed their laughing and joking. No one gave the order to start the conveyor until a little later. About one hour and twenty minutes had elapsed since the belt was stopped.

This ends the story of the introduction of a technical change on an assembly line.

From the standpoint of the sheer physical problems involved in com-

pleting the change, the job purpose was achieved: units were successfully modified to meet the new specifications. From the standpoint of
the human processes involved, the experience was a failure and contributed to a subsequent breakdown in relationships in the work
group.

Tony was completely frustrated as a result of the behavior of his
bosses. Here is what he said: "This isn't my idea. Aw, this is terrible.
I wouldn't do it this way. They come up here and tell me to shut the
line down. They say only half an hour. It'll be at least an hour. Then
I'm going to lose all those units. Hell, they won't want to know from
nothing in the front office. All they'll ask is where's the production.
That's where I'll get it in the neck."

Harry and Dan, throughout the change, showed a complete lack of
awareness of the effects of their behavior on Tony and others. Even
after the change had been accomplished, Harry could not see that
he had done anything but the "right," logical thing to do. Here is
what he said about the experience: "Well, it's the darnedest thing,
these changes. They just knock hell out of our production. You saw
that we had to shut the line down. Well, what could we do? I guess
it's just the nature of the beast, and we just have to live with it. Well,
anyway, when they came to me about the change, I figured there
were two ways of handling it. One, we could have authorized overtime for about twelve repairmen tomorrow all day. That would have
meant overtime pay, and even then I'm not sure the work would
have been completed. The other way, and that's what we did, we
could shut the line down for half an hour and throw all the girls over
on the modification and have it cleaned up once and for all. Well,
I explained it to Nixon [Harry's boss], and he bought it. Well, what
else could he say? I mean there it was. Unless he could think of a
better idea, that's all he could do, buy my way. So that's how it was."

This oversimplified thinking on Harry's part, his total lack of awareness of himself as a person interacting with other people in an administrative situation, represents the kinds of defective thinking which
create and intensify human conflicts. Harry was not alone in his inadequate ways of thinking about administrative problems. Anyone in
a position of responsibility in the situation, from Tony up, and including the staff specialists, was in a position to have altered the course of
events described. But no one evidenced the understanding which this
situation demanded.

All the characters in this story, with the exception of the operators, were members of training groups which met periodically for
discussions intended to improve relationships on the job. What con-

nection was there between the training meetings and these work problems?

At this point it may be useful to examine the record of one training meeting typical of many, to see what, if any, relevance it had to job problems such as the introduction of a technical change. Presented below is a fairly detailed account of such a meeting, quite representative of the series of meetings that were conducted for supervisory and staff personnel at all levels in the manufacturing organization.

A TRAINING MEETING

CL:[1] Last week we were talking about habit. You will remember that we said that habit is applied to assembly operations and to cycle time. Today, we will start on instincts. What is your concept of instinct, Mr. . . . ?

T: Instincts are a method of acting upon unlearned ideas. It's something you're born with.

CL: Are there any questions?

T: Instinct can come out of habit. Take the German children that were raised in camps. What you do in childhood will affect the way you do things. Instinct is based on habit and environment.

CL: If you said that action is based on habit, I could agree with you. Right now, we are defining terms. Instinct is arbitrarily defined. Everything that you said is true, but under our terminology, instincts are inborn.

T: Well, that's drawing a fine line.

CL: Yes. Instincts are inborn. Everything else that you said is perfectly correct. We can bring out the point by going through the list of instincts. [*The conference leader then lectured on the "instincts," including the food-seeking instinct, the combat instinct, and others. He spoke on how modern society curbs instincts, and he presented illustrations on the instincts in primitive as contrasted with modern societies. He spoke on the instinct of self-preservation and was interrupted by a trainee.*]

T: Can I present a problem on that? Suppose you have two people who are deeply in love and would lay down their lives for each other. Suppose you put them in a room that's separated only by a glass panel and give them only water. If you open the glass door in ten days and put some bread in the room, what would happen?

CL: The case of some prisoners in the Japanese prison camps is an example of that. Some of them didn't share.

---

[1] "CL" designates the conference leader, and "T" designates a trainee.

T: Don't you think that years of love would override this?

CL: I can't answer that question. But if the people are not sufficiently hungry, then the male will give way to the female, who will then share the bread. But it's different if they are crazed with hunger.

T: Isn't love an instinct?

CL: If a mother and child were involved, the mother would give way to the child. There's a strong bond there. What would you do, say, in the Coconut Grove fire? Probably we would answer, "Help the women first."

T: We're not there.

T: We'd try to save face.

T: Society demands that we give way.

CL: If we said we would not give way, we would be called a coward.

T: But people would think you were a liar.

CL: In an emergency we would trample over women. The Chicago theater fire is an example. Well, the point you bring out is that all these urges are present, but that society has rules to tell us how to act. We also have moral teachings and a set of laws. So we curb them, inhibit them, and complicate them greatly. For example, take the food-seeking instinct. We are here now because of that instinct. It's all dressed up by society. If we followed instinct, we would go into a butcher shop and take a steak and eat it. But we don't want to take the consequence of stealing. [*The conference leader then lectured briefly, and the trainees offered comments, on the sex instinct, paternal and maternal instincts, and the gregarious instinct.*] That's enough on instincts, I think. Do you think instincts are important in handling industrial relations?

T: No, they're governed by society.

CL: Let's turn to emotions. We are all a bundle of emotions. It doesn't mean getting disturbed or excited. Emotions are the moving force behind us—the moving fuel. Some of the emotions are beneficial and others are detrimental. Take anger, does it have a good effect or a bad effect? Do you think it can be controlled?

T: Yes.

CL: Under all conditions?

T: No.

CL: Some conditions can make us real angry—all of us—to varying degrees. The exhibition of anger is dangerous. We shouldn't try to say to ourselves, "I'm not angry." Recognize anger, and try to control your actions. If one supervisor bawls a man out in front of others and insults him, what would be the reaction on you and me? What would happen to your respect for him?

T: You'd lose it. You'd side with the worker.

CL: What about the worker?

T: He'd get mad too.

CL: What about the chance of solving the problem? The exhibition of anger is out of place. Is there any exception to that?

T: If it's handled properly, it can be put to good use.

T: There are some cases where you do everything to make things run smoothly; and if you show anger, it might help a bit—if the people are spiteful after reasoning and they're still doing wrong.

T: Would you try to find out what's wrong, not overlooking yourself?

T: But anger might help if the people are being spiteful.

T: In some emergencies, you have to blow your top.

CL: [*Cites an example of getting angry at his son.*]

T: That's merely an exhibition of anger.

CL: That's important. Suppose you have a shortage of parts. An exhibition of anger might get results. The same thing applies to buyers in the purchasing department when they deal with vendors. You have to use the right approach, and anger is useful in certain instances. To summarize anger, you have to control it. If you can't, wait, cool down until you are yourself again. Sometimes to get things done you have to put on an act of anger.

Now take ambition. [*Ensuing remarks on "ambition" were in much the same vein as those on "anger." Then there was a similar treatment of "fear." Then one of the trainees interrupted the discussion, and the following exchange took place.*]

T: Back to attendance, and talking about fear, I would like to cite a case. Management put out a pamphlet that they would notify you in case you were to work on Saturday. Someone in management in a high capacity comes over and says, "If you're not in tomorrow, you're out!" What do you think of that?

CL: It's bad. What do you think?

T: The same thing about overtime. You're told you have to work.

CL: That's wrong. You may have to talk to some that way, but it's the exception.

T: Do you believe that a supervisor should make the statement that he knows what goes on all the time, and also give a display of muscles? "I'm a pretty tough boy."

CL: That's obvious.

Running throughout this training conference were at least four approaches to supervisory training, namely, to provide background knowledge, to evoke desirable attitudes, to teach rules of supervision, and to inspire confidence. Furthermore, there were implicit in these approaches certain assumptions concerning supervisors' training needs, as follows:

(1) Supervisors need to have some background knowledge of psychology as a prerequisite for understanding human behavior and for more effective supervision on the job.

(2) Supervisors should have certain attitudes which can be evoked in the training environment.

(3) There are rules of supervision which are known, and the supervisors will behave more effectively on the job if they learn these rules in the training meetings.

(4) Supervisors should have confidence in the company, in its policies, and in their superiors, and such confidence can be developed in the training environment through an inspirational appeal.

From an examination of these training approaches and their underlying assumptions within the framework of the administrative situation presented earlier, it is difficult to see how these training conferences could have any effect on supervisors' behavior on the job. There is little that the trainees can take away from the conference that will help them with work problems.

How would familiarity with the definition of "instincts," "emotions," "introvert-extrovert," and so forth, help Harry to become aware of the fact that his behavior in the situation of the technical change affected other people? In the concrete work situation he did not apply this abstract knowledge of a nonclinical character because it was impossible to apply. As the technical change incident presented earlier indicates, administrative problems are *situational*, that is, they are made up of interdependent variables consisting of what people do, how they deal with one another, how they perceive their relationships, and how they feel about their work situations. We are asking the impossible of administrators when we expect them to "learn" some definitions and then to apply them. The definitions have no relevance, as such, to supervisors and therefore cannot be *learned* in the sense of the kind of learning which modifies behavior.

Similar questions might be raised concerning some of the other conventional training approaches. The same difficulty is likely to appear in all of them, namely, that the traditional lecture-conference concerned with abstract knowledge is not helpful to administrators in meeting job problems. Can favorable attitudes toward his supervisors be expected from Tony in view of the way he was dealt with in the matter of the technical change? No amount of either abstract discussion or inspirational appeal in training conferences can overcome what Tony learned about his superiors from that experience on the job. From his point of view, Tony's bosses were threats to his goals rather than sources of help.

What is the possibility that the case approach might accomplish more useful results?

SOME POSSIBILITIES OF THE CASE METHOD

Some of the assumptions behind the case method which suggest its possibilities for human relations training in industry are the following:

(1) Participants examine concrete situations from their own experience and are therefore provided an opportunity to reflect on, and modify, the lessons that experience has taught them.

(2) Through this reflective process, new assumptions and ideas about their own job, their behavior, and the behavior of others are evolved and carried over into actual work problems.

People like Harry, Dan, and Tony are asked to examine concrete situations involving people in administrative relationships similar to their own. During the discussion, their own "blind spots" will reveal themselves, possibly setting off a line of reflective thinking which may alter, if only slightly, their behavior on the job.

For purposes of illustration, a case suitable for discussion in an industry setting is given below.

SAULTER MANUFACTURING COMPANY

The following conversations took place a few weeks after an incentive payment plan had been introduced in the Saulter Manufacturing Company. The plan had been announced to workers at a series of meetings, none of which had resulted in much discussion. The plan involved some changes in worker activities, although none of these changes had sounded significant to the workers at the time they had been announced. The first of the conversations reported occurred when the man in charge of installing the incentive plan was walking through the plant.

OPERATOR: Say, would you tell me what our jobs are under the new system?

HEAD OF INCENTIVES: Sure, want me to write it down so you'll have it?

OPERATOR: Yeah, that would be fine.

HEAD OF INCENTIVES: Here's a piece of paper. It isn't big enough. Wait, I'll have it typed up in the office and bring it out.

OPERATOR: Here [he finds another sheet], this piece will do. Don't trouble about it.

HEAD OF INCENTIVES: O.K. [He writes.] Here you are.

Some days later the head of incentives was called out to the factory floor by a work stoppage. He found that the same operator with whom he had talked was involved. The conversation follows:

HEAD OF INCENTIVES: What's the trouble?

FOREMAN: The operators won't clean up around the machines.

HEAD OF INCENTIVES: Why not?

FOREMAN: They say you said it wasn't their job. They've always done it.

OPERATOR: You said the helpers were supposed to do it.

HEAD OF INCENTIVES: Yes, that's right. That's the way the job descriptions read now.

FOREMAN: It won't work that way. The helpers have too many machines; they aren't around enough.

In the discussion of this case it may be useful at the outset to ask for opinions and ideas about the situation. The conferees will probably begin by expressing value judgments about the people and events described. For instance, a methods man is likely to say, "The trouble here is, the foreman doesn't know how to organize his job. The work assignments are scientific, and it's up to the foreman to follow them." Another methods man may add, "Another thing, it shows you how ignorant supervision is about incentives. The whole thing in running a department is to follow the methods." At this point a foreman may interject, "That isn't it at all. Methods comes in, sets up a job, and leaves the foreman holding the bag. It's the foreman who's got to live with it." Another foreman may say, "And another thing, methods never tells you what they're up to. The foreman runs the department, but methods acts like they run the show. It shouldn't be that way." A methods man may reply, "What I think the trouble is, is that workers are lazy. Always griping about having too much to do." At this point a foreman may add, "Boy, that's no dream. Always looking for ways of getting out of work." Another foreman, "People aren't lazy. They want to know what's going on" or "This is an example of how people go over your head. The methods man should never have written that job description out and bypassed the foreman."

At this point in the discussion, the conference leader may be tempted to say, "Boys, you've got the thing all wrong. Nobody wants to take away anybody's authority. If you follow a few simple rules, things like this would never happen. Now in our company, the rules are, first, always work through the foreman; second, follow the job description; third, if there's a disagreement, talk it over among yourselves, and if you can't settle it, take it up with the man above you; fourth, don't argue in public because it doesn't look right for a methods man, a foreman, and a worker to argue where other people can hear you. These rules are common sense. If you follow them, you don't run into problems." (The conference leader might even write these "rules" on the blackboard.)

Such a response on the part of the conference leader would presuppose that rules are meaningful and that learning is simply "teacher tells, trainee absorbs, trainee has learned." It is not so simple as that. One of the objectives of supervisory training is to facilitate learning from experience; and this involves the development of skills both in dealing with concrete situations and in thinking about them. Rather than respond in this way, therefore, the skillful conference leader will, depending on the trend and flavor of the conference, either (1) say nothing, but listen and encourage, or (2) reflect the feelings and judgments being expressed, with comments such as "You feel the foreman is to blame," "You're saying the workers are lazy," or "You're worried about your authority." These comments are neutral and carry no traces of the conference leader's judgments.

A training conference which starts at the value judgment level serves as a medium for draining off hostile feelings. The conference leader's restatement of these feelings helps the trainees to become aware of them. But the discussion cannot remain at this level and still provide the maximum opportunity for learning. At some point, the expression of value judgments will peter out, probably of its own accord, and the trainees will slow down to catch their breath. Then the trainees will be ready to enter another level of discussion.

The next level of discussion, which for want of a better word we will call the "meaning" level, consists of some verbal introspection: "What is the meaning of what we have been hearing and saying?" The conference leader may stimulate this discussion by perhaps summarizing what he has been hearing. For instance, he may comment, "This is very interesting. The methods man has been saying, 'The foreman is to blame; methods is scientific!' The foremen have been saying, 'We should be informed; our authority is being undercut. We don't like it!' I wonder what this means?"

The trainees will probably become very self-conscious and confused. They are not used to examining their own reactions, and their confusion is likely to result in remarks to the conference leader such as "Well, what do *you* think it means?" If the conference leader is able once again to mirror the feelings underlying the remarks, he turns the burden of the learning process back to the trainees, where it belongs. The conference leader might say, "You want me to settle this. Is it as simple as all that?" The discussion can then turn to considering the roles of the trainees and the conference leader; and if the conference leader can hold his responses to "You want me to hand down the answer. Is it as simple as all that?" and if at the appropriate times he is able to keep quiet and let a period of uncomfortable silence prevail, the trainees will be encouraged to think about themselves and the meaning of the feelings and conflict expressed in the discussion.

The next step is to return to the situation in the case and to explore questions such as "What was the head of incentives saying, and how did he feel about the situation?" "What was the foreman trying to say, and what feelings was he expressing?" "What about the worker? Why do you suppose he wanted the head of incentives to write out his job? What did his action imply?" This third level is one of diagnosing the concrete situation, and the questions encourage exploration of the meaning of words and behavior in the situation. It may prove helpful in developing an interest in skills of listening and observing,[1] because the trainees may become aware of the fact that it is impossible to learn how people feel, or why they behave as they do, without listening and observing.

A fourth and very difficult level for discussion would be the action level. "How would you handle the situation if you were head of incentives? What would you say and do in this situation?" "Suppose you were the foreman here. You came onto the floor and found the work stoppage. The head of incentives came up. What would you say? What would you do?" At this point the trainees might explore further the skills involved in action and the implications for their own behavior. Attempts to oversimplify would be cut short by other trainees.

The foregoing will suggest some of the possibilities of the case method approach in helping executives and supervisors to develop administrative skills. When we re-examine the work incident described previously, the striking characteristic that suggests the case method as an approach to supervisory and executive development is the persistent tendency of the administrators involved to act as though they were unrelated to other people. On the contrary, by virtue of modern technology, administrators live and function within a system of relationships. Their behavior affects, and in turn is affected by, the behavior of other people. Concrete cases present problems of administrators as they behave in a network of relationships. Supervisors and executives who come together to study and discuss these cases will begin, we believe, to re-examine their own relationships and derive new meanings from their own experience. Despite the difficulties involved in collecting cases, developing skilled instructors, and facing up to the uncertainties which plague trainer and trainee alike, experimentation should begin. Our widening research experience suggests that, in the industry setting, new approaches must be tried in helping administrators to develop social skills.

[1] An approach to training which holds possibilities for practicing the skill of listening is role playing. For a discussion of role playing as a training method, see Alex Bavelas, "Role Playing and Management Training," *Sociatry*, Vol. 1, No. 2, June, 1947.

Following his retirement as Dean of the Harvard Business School in 1942, Wallace B. Donham turned with energy and enthusiasm to a new career as a teacher of undergraduates in the field of human relations, serving both in Harvard College and in Colgate University. With his great interest in the case method, which he had so long championed in graduate education for business, Professor Donham naturally sought to explore the possibility for the use of the case method in undergraduate teaching of the social sciences. His ripened observations on the case system, as a result of this experience, appear in the following paper. *

The Case Method in College Teaching of Social Science
WALLACE B. DONHAM

In the world today the kind of security that existed in England and in this country in the last century has disappeared, and disappeared for a long period ahead. With it disappeared the last excuse for the old educational system. It may have been well adapted to what Elton Mayo refers to as an established society, where it seemed permanently worth while to learn theoretical principles, rules, and precepts because they would continue to be pertinent to men's needs. We no longer live in such a society, but we have yet to work out educational objectives and methods adapted to present needs. The impact of pure science and more particularly of applied science imposes on the world rapid and accelerating social change as the most significant fact with which we must struggle. These changes involve all aspects of our lives. With continual and accelerating change goes a lessening of the capacity for foresight and, for vast numbers, a heightening of that sense of insecurity which leads easily to the sort of *anomie*, planless, pointless living, which Durkheim discusses in his book *Le Suicide*. Our problem becomes that of learning how to deal with change, how to develop, in Elton Mayo's language, an adaptive society. In education content becomes less significant than habits and skills. As time passes, content is eroded and changed in form like an ocean sand dune in winter gales. If particular content is not used, memory fails or the mind gets clogged with inert ideas.

Skills, on the other hand, generally improve with use, expand and give confidence in power to deal with successive novel situations. The case system, by utilizing carefully selected concrete situations as the basis for training and practice, gives useful content to the student, not as inert knowledge, but with the freshness and vitality that come with use. Skills in action develop. Each new situation comes to the student with the same freshness and novelty that his ever-changing experiences in life will exhibit.

The major problem of education, it seems to me, is to give men a sense of internal security, assurance in their capacity to get on with people collaboratively and to deal successfully with the unpredictable future, which will take the place of the type of security provided by the established society of our ancestors. Without going into the part of this task which must be done by philosophy and religion, I emphasize the fact that a great deal can be done by methods of teaching and by training in social science which simulates the active life men will enter after they leave college, with its unforeseeable variety of experience and the necessity for making constant responsible interpretations of new concrete situations. Such interpretations will, of course, be influenced by the past and by the traditions of the old established order, but they will generally be dominated by unpredictable change. Without a sense of security in the midst of change, the task of philosophy and religion becomes almost impossible.

I believe that teaching by the case system can be an important factor in giving students this sense of security and in preparing them to enter active life in this democracy to their own greater satisfaction, and so that they can make a larger contribution to the common weal. To make my point of view clear, it is necessary to present first some aspects of current conditions and of the background of students which affect problems of general education.

It is often assumed that college life is a cloistered period necessarily affording very limited experience. This same assumption is made about the home and school life preceding college. Again it is assumed, at least in our behavior, that since the student's experience before and during his college course is narrowly limited, it is necessary to teach a great deal of theory in college, almost wholly without any corresponding development of such practice or experience as would make the theory fully meaningful. We know that the divorcement of theory from practice is very generally accepted in Liberal Arts Colleges here and in England. For example, a distinguished Britisher, Sir Richard Livingstone, President of Corpus Christi College, Oxford, in his stimulating book *On Education*,[1] after wisely and effectively pointing out the essentiality of cross-fertilization between theory and experience,

[1] New York: The Macmillan Company, 1945.

reaches the conclusion that in secondary schools and, notwithstanding the greater maturity of the students, in the undergraduate universities as well theory and practice are of necessity kept separate. While he makes an exception and emphasizes strongly the significance of extracurricular experience in residential schools and colleges, he takes a pessimistic view about the capacity of the school or of the university in its undergraduate instruction to combine theory and practice and to expand the students' experience in ways which relate theoretical education to the lives they will lead after they leave college. He suggests that for outstanding students the best results of undergraduate university education will be attained after they finish their formal university instruction and have a good deal of experience in life. Then he thinks a certain fraction of them will come to see retroactively the real meaning of the theory which they learned as undergraduates and to realize the importance of theory in their practical experience.

For this reason, among others, he stresses the overwhelming importance of adult education undertaken by men and women after they have a substantial background of experience in their particular worlds of affairs. He illustrates the feasibility and importance of education at this stage by citing the extraordinary success of the Danish People's High School system, where residential school life and liberal arts study are combined by students who already have a substantial background of experience, ordinarily four years or more since completion of their formal compulsory education. Admission to such schools is open only after an interval of practical experience. To these students theory and practice come together easily and enthusiastically.

I am in complete agreement as to the importance of adult education, and I also think that the Danish system presents most attractive possibilities. I am convinced that this country needs much more attention to adult education and the way in which it is given. I am not, however, convinced that the obstacles Livingstone sees to more experiential education in the undergraduate years in college, and to some extent in the secondary schools, are necessarily insuperable.

For something over a quarter of a century I have been engaged in efforts to discover and put into effect under academic conditions ways of developing experience along with theory, to the end that each may continuously fertilize the other, and that to a large extent theory useful in life may be drawn from experience and practice even if it lacks nice logical elaboration. Although most of my experience has been in a graduate school, in recent years I have been applying and expanding my experience by teaching a course in Human Relations, open to undergraduates in Harvard College and Radcliffe College [1] Here we have found not only that we can relate the student's experience to theory but that, to a substantial degree, we can lead the student to draw generalizations from such experience. We have learned how to expand the student's experience, into orientations with which he is not and cannot be directly familiar while the educational process is going on, effectively enough so that he can use this expanded experience as the basis for generalizations much as does a skillful man of affairs when he interprets his experience in life. This process is based on the discussion of a succession of selected cases, factual reports which the student deals with as he must deal with tomorrow's factual situations when he meets them in life.

True, the expansion of experience just referred to does not literally bring to the student the same kind of *knowledge of acquaintance* that he would get from actual participation in tomorrow's problems, but it comes so close to doing this and follows so naturally on his actual experience that the knowledge obtained is far nearer to *knowledge of acquaintance* than it is to the usual generalized *knowledge about*. When the student leaves school, he still needs an "internship" in the job he takes; nevertheless, the similarity to living is close enough so that it actually makes the transition from formal education to life very much easier than the transition which the student must make if he has been studying theory *per se* rather than evolving theory from concrete situations. This is true even when theory is expounded by his lecturer or by the textbook and then illustrated by reference to concrete situations. It is even true if the reference by the lecturer is to the same cases which the student and the class group might have used in evolving theory at their own initiative. The case system as it has grown under constant trial and error has little or no place for the use of cases by the instructor to illustrate his theories. So used it fails to simulate actual firsthand experience.

The difference between *knowledge of acquaintance* and *knowledge about* is of first importance in education. The one becomes a part of a man because it is part of his personal experience. He uses it. The other is taken and often accepted because of the teacher's authority and prestige but is rarely related to the student's life. Since we all have the habit and, under many conditions, should have the habit of questioning authority, the instructor's point of view ought often to be taken with at least a grain of salt. In fact, the best teacher encourages differences of opinion. This habit of questioning authority applies, of course,

[1] See Wallace B. Donham, "An Experimental Course in Human Relations," *The Journal of General Education*, Vol. II, No. 1, October, 1947.

to theories built up logically from assumptions or selected premises, but unless such theories are constantly checked by fresh examination of concrete facts, the logics are often so neat and convincing that the invalidity of assumptions and the omissions in the choice of premises are easily overlooked. Even when the student accepts the theory, since theories frequently fail to fit his experience after he leaves college he comes to see, or should come to see, that in a rapidly changing world new developments will constantly make obsolete much of what he accepted without question. As a result he often unwisely dismisses large portions of academic subject matter as having no significance in his life. In the nature of things, social theory, since it always involves people and complex novel situations, should, except as it draws limited but vastly useful generalizations from recurring types of concrete situations, change far more rapidly than theories of natural science, which deals with material things. Social theories can rely far less than the natural sciences on the accumulative process of building brick on brick. For this reason, social science should rely more on keeping in touch with concrete experience and less on elaborate logical theories. As cumulative theory develops, I believe it must continue to be based on and constantly checked against actual situations. The complexity and changing nature of the facts will in general keep the logical structure of theory on a simple basis.

Contrary to the assumption that childhood is a time of little experience on which education can be built, I submit that the first 18 years of life are filled with immensely diversified and long-lasting activities and experiences. Indeed I question whether there is any other period in life where so much activity and so much experience is crowded into so few years as between the ages of two and eighteen. There is no period where experience has so much effect in moulding whole lives as in this early period.

Unfortunately, when the youth goes to college, although he has this immense background of experience, he has almost no training in interpreting it. Interpretation up to this time has been by parents or other close relatives of an earlier generation, by religious leaders, or by teachers. The reasons for the interpretations have rarely been disclosed to the child in ways which place on him responsibility for the interpretations or for action which follows on the interpretation. This is another way of saying that he has had little practice in the *conscious process* of abstracting generalizations from the facts of his experience. Yet in his immediate surroundings he makes abstractions at a very early age, e.g., in his accurate use of the word "chair" in spite of multifarious differences in shape, form, and material which differentiate chairs. When he abstracts, and he continuously abstracts from facts, he never seems to formulate his generalizations consciously. Moreover, he learns readily from the experience of others in his own age group, who like him reach abstractions without conscious effort. He quickly picks up abstractions from them even though he often seems to resist learning from his teachers and his parents. Perhaps this is because his contemporaries are less didactic, usually less authoritarian, although he often learns in this period to follow leaders in or near his own age group. His group experience is frequently large. The widely diversified backgrounds of college students plus this habit of learning easily from contemporaries make the varied kinds of experience represented in a typical college classroom great potential assets to the teacher.

When the student leaves home and secondary school for the university, he enters what should be a great new adventure both socially and intellectually. For the first time, in most instances, he is really on his own as a human being. His social activities, being in a wholly new environment, have all the freshness that comes with novelty. Unfortunately, especially in his Freshman year, his organized educational activities, unlike his social activities, too often lack emotional appeal. They come to him as a mere continuance of secondary school. Consequently he fails to find intellectual stimulus and a sense of adventure. He spends his time in college mainly being told by his teachers or by his textbooks, as he was in school, "what he ought to think about what he ought to think about."[1] He rarely has an opportunity, under traditional college methods, to take the initiative or to behave responsibly in academic situations involving discretion until well along in his college course. Yet his life outside the classroom up to this time has presented many such opportunities, and his social life in college does so increasingly. His classroom activities or responsibilities are rarely if ever related to his life, and little is done to expand these responsibilities beyond asking him to meet academic requirements whose significance as training for life he often fails to understand. Indeed, too often the academic requirements are of doubtful value for this purpose, and the undergraduate is apt to look on them as necessary evils and to acquire a "gentleman's C" complex which often lasts through college.

These observations do not apply to the student's extracurricular activities, including his whole social life, where the lasting educational results are often the greatest. Note, however, that in his social activities he is judged on his actions by his contemporaries, not graded on examinations which are generally designed, not so much to test his

[1] Quotation from a college Senior.

power and his skills in action, as to find whether or not he has learned what he was told to learn. Moreover, stimulating social experiences start on the opening day of the Freshman year, and in many colleges the period extending nearly to the end of the football season coincides with the period preceding the first scholastic check-up, i.e., late October or November hour examinations. These early months are a period when it is easy to unlearn even good study habits established in secondary school. Curiously enough, methods which ignore the importance of giving intellectual work an immediate imaginative and emotional appeal to newcomers are often defended as putting students on their own and making them responsible. The introduction to college is very effective for the normally adjusted boy on the social and athletic sides, where men try to get the respect and esteem of their fellows, but it is not so successful on the intellectual side, where there is little corresponding stimulus. Discipline and enforced minimum standards are poor substitutes for interest. On the other hand, the boy who comes to college with an inadequate background in getting on with his fellows often retreats into isolated intellectual work as a way of avoiding the social contacts and decisions which appear necessary to a well-adjusted life. An intellectual life which excludes or unduly minimizes social contacts and experience is dangerous. It often leads to inability to cope with the everyday problems of life and to great unhappiness. Most colleges pay far too little attention to this problem.

In this country we take pride in the fact that college training is primarily intellectual. Yet the lives we lead are primarily emotional. Indeed, in perspective, the intellectual side of life, which we all value so highly, is a recent veneer on an age-long evolutionary process where emotions long wholly dominated behavior and man only gradually learned in self-defense to be a social animal. Emotions still dominate much of behavior, yet we continuously decry their importance. Too little effort is made, by those responsible for education, to tie the logical and intellectual subject matter taught to the student into his active life and the entrancing adventure of independence which he is experiencing in his new social and intellectual environment, and thus to arouse his emotional interest in education. Under our customary methods the burden of responsibility is not put on the student, and the initiative is not transferred from the teacher to the student in ways that make his intellectual work become part of his total life experience.

It is precisely at this critical point that I feel we at the Harvard Business School in the past thirty-five years have made real progress through the development of the case system in the field of business administration.

When the case system is used there is a great increase in student interest and a ready acceptance of the burden of responsibility by students under conditions which are relatively free from the danger to other people that comes when responsibility in active life is assumed prematurely. Students are clearly not ready for the type of responsibility that a politician incurs when he attempts to solve some political problem where if he makes a mistake many other people are affected adversely, or for the type of responsibility that a man of affairs takes when he makes decisions which if mistaken react against many others than himself. The competition among students, i.e., the desire to stand well with one's peers in open discussion, is an effective burden of responsibility on the intellectual side, just as community life and athletics are on the social side. Under college conditions the danger to others resulting from responsibility assumed by students is happily slight. Indeed this insularity of experience offers one of the greatest unused opportunities for the college and one of the great reasons for college education for the student. But to use this educational opportunity effectively the college must transfer the burden of intellectual responsibility to the student. When this is done, interest is aroused and discussion of classroom problems comes to claim its full share in undergraduate "bull sessions."

Enough evidence already exists to indicate that the capacity of the case approach to arouse interest does not depend merely on the vocational appeal of professional training. I am fully convinced that the case approach is widely applicable to undergraduate work in college. In the whole social science field, to a considerable extent in the sciences, and to a large extent in the humanities, I believe it possible to tie the development of theory responsibly into the lives of men—the life they led before they came to college, and the life that surrounds them in the university, as well as the life that they realize they must be prepared to struggle with soon after they leave college. If college education is tied effectively into life so that it is recognized by students as preparation for life, it develops an appeal much like the vocational appeal of professional training.

At Harvard we have experimented on a considerable scale with methods of tying theory into life experience by cases in social science, for business administration is a social science involving many other social sciences. The cases which we have developed are concrete situations, segments of actual life, reported as closely as we can reproduce them. They are not as readily available as are law cases in the reported decisions of the Courts of Appeal, but they are far more effectively related to life situations as they actually happen. The profession of law suffers by reason of the detachment of law training from concrete reality in its universal complexity and the consequent overstressing of legal theory when men come to practice law.[1] On the one hand, our cases are not so good as the patient on the cot in a medical clinic because we cannot bring a social situation into our clinic. Where the medical student can see, hear, and feel the patient, we must rely on reports of facts, portrayals of people, presentations of opinion. On the other hand, our cases are better than the medical cases in that the very immediacy of the medical case on the cot easily leads the doctor to ignore the fact that patients have families, that they have economic problems, human responsibilities, jobs, and a whole complex of social surroundings. In some respects we have made more progress in getting together effective material because our cases cannot be so easily acquired as law cases or so realistically presented as the patient on the cot in the medical clinic. We have learned to bring in many more of the surrounding circumstances than law schools or the medical professions have yet learned to bring in effectively.

Furthermore we make an effort to arrange cases in such a manner that we secure an orderly expansion of the student's experience. When this is done, the steps which the student must take in assimilating and interpreting factual material no longer place an impossible burden on his capacity to think of himself as a component part of the situation and as an actor in it. This does not mean that we should start with easy cases and build up to hard ones. Rather it means watching the expansion of experience and not proceeding too fast. Then students respond with a sense of responsibility, and long steps can be taken toward developing both skills in interpretation of their expanding experience and skills in action. With case instruction skillfully organized, there need be little of that sense of frustration which we all feel when we must jump too far beyond our experience and deal responsibly with problems where we see no promising mode of attack.

To meet pedagogical necessities some cases used in a social science will necessarily be so reported as to leave out obviously important factors which do not fall within the usual category of the particular social science. In this situation the nature of the omissions can often be stated. The student should be cautioned as to the inconclusive nature of analyses based on a partial selection of facts. On the other hand, in others of the cases used a more inclusive reporting based on the "total situation" is important. Then the instructor should expand the analysis beyond the concepts of the particular social science and seek to deter-

[1] See Karl N. Llewellyn, "The Current Crisis in Legal Education," in *Education for Professional Responsibility* (Pittsburgh, Pa.: Carnegie Press, 1948), p. 101.

mine questions of policy and action with reference to the total situation. One of the difficulties about situations as they develop in real life is their refusal to stay within tidy intellectual schemes. This proclivity of life to cut across rational boundaries should be made clear. Of course, the choice of descriptive matter in any social situation is in itself an abstraction, but it is an abstraction made with reference to the situation and not with reference to arbitrary assumptions or to conventional limitations on the scope of things embraced in a particular category of learning. Such specialized choices of things to be considered in a given category of learning are accepted largely for historical reasons by individuals and groups of social scientists who work in that special field. Yet in many instances experience shows that rationally defined problems in such a special field easily become isolated from the concrete situations in ways which make the resulting theories wholly unrealistic as applied to concrete facts. Then there often arises an instance of Whitehead's "fallacy of misplaced concreteness," mistaking the abstract for the concrete.

Social science clearly needs much reconstruction, and its classifications much restudy, to bring them in touch with reality. We have made progress in such restudy by using cases, particularly in administration and fields allied to administration. As I use the term "administration," it includes human relations, because these are always an important factor. Administration properly taught can be the great integrating subject in the social sciences, in part because its emphasis on action focuses attention on the present. Of course, understanding of the present needs to rely on a constant study of the past and on a continuous forecast of the future, recognizing all its uncertainties. The administrator almost inevitably gets into trouble if in thinking about his concrete problems he finds significance in and takes into account only facts chosen within the traditional limitations of some academically isolated subject, whether in natural science or in social science. Administration is one of the most neglected fields in social science. Note what Brooks Adams says in *The Theory of Social Revolutions:*[1]

Administration is the capacity of coordinating many, and often conflicting, social energies in a single organism so adroitly that they shall operate as a unity. This presupposes the power of recognizing a series of relations between numerous special social interests, with all of which no single man can be intimately acquainted. Probably no very highly specialized class can be strong in this intellectual quality because of the intellectual isolation incident to

[1] Pages 207–208. Quoted by permission of the publisher, The Macmillan Company, New York, 1913.

specialization; and yet administration or generalization is not only the faculty upon which social stability rests, but is, possibly, the highest faculty of the human mind.

Of course, we all become specialists, and, as Whitehead says, outside our own specialties, ignoramuses; but that fact need not lead us to believe that our specialized conclusions are futile, provided we use them for what they are worth, i.e., as valuable but partial illuminants of problems. Contrariwise, we should be skeptical about depending primarily on specialized conclusions whenever we are faced by the necessity of decision and action. Then we must seek to expand our areas of thought. Where our individual human limitations intervene as controlling factors, we should realize the need for experts, not so often to decide the question before us as to help us expand our premises. We need to know how to use experts without being abused by them.

Such an educational program in the social sciences is difficult to carry so far as we wish it could be carried, but this limitation results from the nature of the field. I have seen it stated that Fermi, the atomic physicist, as a young man seriously debated whether he should choose economics or physics as a career and chose physics because it was so much easier. Surely he was right. In social science it will be a long while, in determining policy at the point of action, before we can get beyond the stage where we must rely on skilled judgments of social phenomena. Controlled experiments and accurate measurements are generally impossible, as are most methods of natural science. Quite as important, one of the ways to break down the dogmatism of science and its assurance in its deterministic methodology is to show, even in the teaching of science and its consequences, and certainly in the world in which we live, the vast range of human activities which depend on judgment rather than on quasi certainties such as those of physics, chemistry, and applied mathematics. But if judgments rather than certainties are all that we can attain in most human affairs, education certainly should be designed to develop the habits and skills needed as a foundation for judgment.

I know that at the Business School we are succeeding with a large percentage of students in building the habit of consciously interpreting experience to the point where they carry it over into life, and I know we do much to start the lifetime job of developing skilled judgments dealing with novel facts and of developing the skills needed for administrative action. I talked during a recent Commencement season with several groups of men who graduated from the Business School twenty to twenty-five years ago. Without suggesting the response I wanted, even by the terminology I used, I found that to them the most important thing they got out of the School, phrased in one way or another, was their ability to look at new problems, as they met them in life, in the light of work they did in the School and the incipient skills they then acquired, even though the factual content met in their careers was always different from their School cases and the judgments reached always had to be related to the new facts. This ability to deal competently with new problems they picked out as the thing that had been accomplished in the Business School which had not previously been developed in their undergraduate work.

As one man ten years out phrased it to me, "You didn't teach us anything in the Business School."

I said, "I will accept that, but in which sense do you mean it?"

"Well," he said, "I studied a great number of cases with care, sought my own interpretations of them, discussed them with other members of the class, went into the classroom, where we argued them with the instructor, modified my conclusions, and reached what I thought were good working conclusions not only on the cases but on the subject matter we were discussing. In ten years of experience I have never met a problem on all fours with any case I studied, or reached any conclusion that was controlled by the class discussion."

I said I would accept that, but "What did the School do for you?"

"That," he said, "is simple. It gave me a sense of assurance that I could tackle any problem, either because I had the experience to justify handling it myself or because I knew in what direction to turn in situations where my experience was inadequate."

Almost all faculty members at the Harvard Business School engage in case research and prepare some of the teaching material for their classes. But case research is a time-consuming task, and most professors find it quite impossible to do as much case research as they would like. In order to increase the number and scope of the cases which can be obtained, much of the case collecting is done by research assistants. These men typically are recent graduates of the School who are assigned to work under the guidance of a particular faculty member.

The job of a research assistant is to collect and prepare the teaching material to be used by the teachers. This process is usually referred to as "collecting cases," but the phrase is misleading unless it is interpreted broadly.

The research assistant plays a vital part in the case method because to a large extent it is he who must be relied upon not only to prepare the teaching material which is used but also, by his accurate reporting of facts as he finds them, to bring back from the field to the teachers and to the School in general a recognition and an appreciation of the constantly changing realities of business.

The following paper embodies pertinent instructions and suggestions to case research assistants, i.e., "case collectors," prepared by James W. Culliton at the time when he was Assistant Director of Research in charge of case gathering at the Harvard Business School.

Writing Business Cases JAMES W. CULLITON

The job of the research assistant collecting cases is a demanding one. It requires not only ability but also enthusiastic interest in the case method, plus an understanding employment of the techniques and procedures which have proved useful in the past. The purpose of the material which follows is, so far as possible, to familiarize the new research assistant with some of the proven procedures and routines and to pass along certain "helpful hints" which may be useful.

THE CASE COLLECTION PROCESS

Collecting cases, as it is practiced at the Harvard Business School, usually involves interviews with people outside the School. At times cases are written exclusively from published sources; but experience indicates that, by and large, they are not so satisfactory as cases secured in whole or in part from personal interviews. Consequently the process of collecting cases centers around the interview, and many of these comments on the case collection process naturally have to do with preparing for, carrying on, and writing up interviews.

256

Even when cases are based upon personal interviews, however, all the material in the final case usually is not secured solely from the interview. It therefore becomes important that research assistants be well prepared not only to get the most out of the interview but also to secure *all* the pertinent information from whatever source it is available.

Both the finished product (the case) and the interview (which in effect is the central core of case collection) will be better if the interview is preceded by thorough preparation and followed by efficient use of the information received. Some of the more effective techniques of case collection accumulated by the School from its past experience are given below. While these suggestions are addressed directly to those of you who will engage in case collection, they may also be of interest to others who would like to know more about the case collection process of the School.

BEFORE THE INTERVIEW

Expand Your Own Background Knowledge. If you have a working knowledge of business generally and a familiarity with the current business problems most likely to be perplexing to business executives, you stand a better chance of securing the helpful cooperation of businessmen.

Find "Leads." There is no one best or usual way of finding leads to follow in order to make appointments for getting case material. Frequently the professor will have in mind several leads which have come to his attention through his contacts with personal friends, business associates, trade associations, and other business organizations; at other times he may be searching for a special kind of problem (e.g., salesmen's compensation, reciprocity, pricing, or refinancing), and a lead can be developed among some companies which may be presumed to have a problem in that area.

People using the case system, however, seem to develop a knack of spotting case leads; the things they read in magazines, books, newspapers, advertisements, company reports; the people they meet, visitors to the School, speakers, friends; the things they see, factory buildings, new products, changing business practice—all are instinctively examined as possible case leads.

In the constant search for good case material, it is well to remember that the foundation of the case system rests not on the unusual situations faced infrequently by businessmen but on the specific and typical situations which confront people in administrative positions. Surely, if the School is to assume any leadership, it needs cases dealing with newly developing practices and with problems not yet recognized by most businessmen. Yet, if only to keep proportionate emphasis realistic, most cases report typical problems.

Make Appointments. For research assistants to drop in on businessmen unannounced has not proved satisfactory. It is better to make an appointment in advance so that the person to be interviewed knows (1) when you are coming and (2), in a general way, what is the purpose of your visit.

Start with Top Executives. The first contact with a company should always be through a responsible top executive. The higher, the better. Sometimes officers of lower rank can help; but the farther you go from the top, the greater is the possibility of failure, and also the greater is the possibility of setting off internal frictions within the company which may eventually harm the School.

Establish a Routine for Making Appointments. In consultation with the professor for whom you are working, select the person or persons to see. (A professor appreciates constructive suggestions on your part, but before you see anyone for case collection purposes—even friends—check with your boss.)

Then check the card contact file to find out whether anyone from the School has recently visited the firm or person you intend to see. This is important for two reasons: (1) It is embarrassing to the School to have particular companies "pestered" by too frequent visits; there is danger also that executives may get the impression, if they are visited independently by two or more School representatives, that the School does not know what it is doing. (2) If someone else from the School has visited anyone in the company and is still available, you may be able to pick up some valuable tips about what to look for, how to act, and what to avoid.

After these steps have been completed, by letter or by telephone, as the circumstances warrant, ask for and arrange an appointment.

Learn All You Can about the Person, Company, and Industry You Are Visiting. Frequently the interview does not contribute the major part of the material included in a case; almost always, however, it sets the stage, clarifies the issue, or finally crystallizes the business situation into a real problem. It is therefore helpful to know as much as possible before the interview takes place. Know the person, know the company, know the industry—even have a pretty good idea of the company's problems. Then what you hear in the personal interview will have more meaning for you. (For suggested sources, see Exhibit 1.)

Know What You Want, but . . . You should talk over prospective case trips with the professor; make sure you have a real understanding of what he wants, where he expects you to find it, and how he expects to use it. Experience shows that if such consultation results in written "specifications" the cases produced are more satisfactory. Either get written specifications from your professor or put some in writing yourself.

EXHIBIT 1
SUGGESTED SOURCES OF PERSONAL AND COMPANY INFORMATION
(Not complete—add your own)

Contact files, *plus* discussion with members of the School staff who have already visited the company

Case file—cases already written

Employment files, especially to find out whether the company employs any Business School graduates

Harvard Alumni Directories, both Harvard Business School and Harvard College—if the man you are going to visit is a Harvard man, it is well to know it

Directory of Directors

Who's Who

Trade journals in the industry

Company reports and documents

Standard & Poor's

Moody's

New York Times Index

Thomas' Register

New York Stock Exchange listing statements

It is also helpful to jot down, more briefly than in case specifications, some key questions you would like to ask; then, if conversation lags or memory fails you, you can pick up the interview on important questions rather than trivia.

But, in the process of knowing what you want, do not overlook other things, including the possibility that what you thought you wanted either does not really exist or is in fact quite different from what you supposed. Research is looking for facts, not looking for evidence to support a preconceived notion while evidence to the contrary is ignored. Keep alert for evidence that may force you and the professor to re-examine your current thoughts and beliefs; keep alert for situations other than those which you set out to explore. If you see leads for material which might be useful in other courses, pass them along to the people concerned with those courses.

DURING THE INTERVIEW

The exact conduct of an interview will be determined by many things which cannot be forecast. The businessman whom you will be interviewing is probably the most important unpredictable factor; his personality, position, and authority, as well as whether he happens to be very busy or relatively free, are important. The extent of his knowledge of the work of Harvard and of the purpose of your visit will determine how much introductory information you will have to give. The following suggestions are intended to be complete, and parts can be eliminated when they are obviously unnecessary.

Explain the School's Case Collection Policies. As briefly as possible, tell of the case method of instruction and the collection of teaching material. It is the policy of the School not to offer anything specific, such as consultation services or commentaries on company action, in return for the privilege of writing up a company's experience as a case for teaching material. Avoid promising or even implying that the company might expect any service in return for helping the School—it is a pure donation to education. Make it clear that we expect to receive confidential information and that we always have treated it as such, and always will. Indicate the use to which cases are put and the fact that many are eventually published. If necessary, explain that company identity can be disguised. If it is not necessary, however, do not offer to disguise; greater flexibility is retained if the decision regarding disguise is left to the School.

Explaining the policy of the School is frequently easier if you are able to show a copy of a completed case. Be prepared by carrying a few mimeographed cases with you.

Get the Material You Need. In general it is a good procedure to ask for what you want, especially if it is a factual record such as a profit and loss statement. It is better to let the executive know what you want and to have him give it to you than to get it by other means and have him wonder later how you got it. You will soon learn, however, that there are various subtle ways of getting information legitimately and that frequently intelligent guesses about undisclosed information will produce the real and authentic information. In brief, experience indicates that you should be direct, but tactful and resourceful.

Successful experience in getting the information needed for good case material indicates that the following are useful rules to bear in mind: (1) Do not ask businessmen, "Have you any problems?" Rather ask for the benefit of their experience. (2) Be prepared to guide the conversation with intelligent questions, but do not preplan the interview to such an extent that you prevent the executive from giving you ideas or pertinent information which you may not have anticipated. (3) Do not be argumentative. The job of a research assistant is to discover and report facts and opinions, not to change them.

There can be no general rules as to whether you should take notes during an interview. Most of the time it is unsatisfactory to take notes *sub rosa;* either take them openly, with or without asking permission, or do not take any. Except when exact figures are involved, many research assistants have found it best to refrain from taking notes during an interview; rather they center their attention solely on the topics being discussed, and then make notes immediately after the interview is concluded. Jotting down key words during an interview is sometimes a useful technique.

Whether or not notes are taken during an interview, it is good practice, especially when on an extended trip, to make notes covering the day's work before the day has passed. Some case writers find it advisable, even on local calls, to make rather extensive notes before returning to the office.

Get Some Material You May Not Need. In addition to the necessary material for a specific case, almost always you will find information which apparently has no bearing on your problem. Do not accept such material indiscriminately, but learn to accept some odds and ends of information. It is amazing how and when you will find them useful.

Observe. Make mental notes, consciously and subconsciously, of the things you see. Is the office neat, or gaudy? Does the man act as if he were interested? Is he constantly interrupted? Is his secretary efficient? Where is the plant or office located with respect to the rest of the town?

Accept, where time permits, invitations to look around. If the opportunity arises, lunch with people connected with the company, and let them guide the conversation. Do not worry about what such random information adds to the particular case; it may add nothing, but, unless such observation is overdone to the extent that you take time from your immediate job, you add to your appreciation of the business.

After the Interview

After the interview, the research assistant's primary concern is the writing of the case. There are, however, certain administrative requirements which also must be observed in the interests of adequate control of the case collecting procedure.

The following five requirements are essential:

(1) The fact that an interview was held should be reported in the contact files.[1]

----

[1] The actual work of case collection at the Harvard Business School is carried out on a decentralized basis. Because of the dimensions of the program, a central contact file is maintained for the use of research assistants, as well as a central file of all cases collected and a record of the source of every case obtained.

(2) All confidences must be kept strictly.

(3) Cases must be disguised if disguise either was promised or is necessary to maintain confidences.

(4) Cases must be numbered and entered in the case files.

(5) All cases, with few exceptions, must be released, i.e., the School must secure written permission to use them.

Each of these requirements is discussed briefly below.

Report of Contact. Each interview should be reported on a contact slip within 24 hours. (The form of contact slip is reproduced in Exhibit 2.) This record must be complete with name of firm, kind of

EXHIBIT 2
CONTACT SLIP

Firm Name	
Street Address	
City State	OUTSIDE CONTACT INFORMATION
Kind of Business	
Name and position of person interviewed	
Subject of Interview	
Remarks	
Date of interview Signature	

business, person interviewed, degree of cooperation received, and date of interview. Sufficient detail should be given so that the next interviewer may know what cooperation to expect or what approach to take. Facetious or sarcastic comments are to be avoided; unsatisfactory interviews should be reported in a dignified, helpful statement.

Maintaining Confidences. The research assistant constantly should have in mind the reputation of the School for keeping facts confidential. If company executives consider it necessary, all figures and confidential information may be disguised so that the identity of the individual companies will not be revealed.

No material may be used in the classroom or published without written permission of some responsible executive in the company. (See *Release*, page 263.)

It is important not to give to one businessman the names of others from whom information has been received.

Under no circumstances should cases be discussed with individuals not on the School staff in such a way as to reveal the identity of the firms from which the information was secured.

A research assistant should discuss strictly confidential information secured from individual companies *only* with the professor for whom he is working. At times there may even be information which should not be reported to the professor.

In all events, *company confidences must not be violated.*

Disguise. The name of the case should be a fictitious company name unless permission is given to use the actual name. In disguised cases do not use the name of any executive in the company giving the information. Avoid facetious names or those difficult or tiresome to use in the classroom and in the case books.

Before assigning a fictitious name to a case, check the name in order to be sure that it is not the name of an actual company or one that already has been used for a case in some other course.

Ordinarily no attempt should be made to disguise the industry; a case in which the industry is disguised may prove not to be useful for teaching purposes.

Figures may be changed by multiplying by a constant or by applying some other mechanical device that does not destroy essential relationships.

Case Numbering. Every case collected by the School is assigned an identifying number, and at least one copy of every case is put into the central files. It is essential for control and maximum usefulness of the cases that this procedure be continued.

Release. It is expected that all cases secured will be released for publication. With the exceptions indicated below, it is necessary to obtain the release from a responsible person. A written memorandum regarding the release or a letter granting permission to use the material must be in the School file. This is a most important rule and should be followed in spirit as well as to the letter. There are two reasons why signed releases are insisted upon. The first is to protect the company itself from the misinterpretation of facts or from the uncontrolled use of material given in confidence; the release card assures the company that the case will be used only in the form in which it was released. The second purpose is to protect the School by providing written evidence that permission has been granted to use the material in question. (The form of release card used by the School is reproduced in Exhibit 3.)

EXHIBIT 3
RELEASE CARD

GRADUATE SCHOOL OF BUSINESS ADMINISTRATION
HARVARD UNIVERSITY
SOLDIERS FIELD, BOSTON 63, MASSACHUSETTS

Gentlemen: We have read the case entitled_____

_____

which was sent us for verification and approval.   We hereby
authorize the use of this material

without change   .   .   .   .   ☐
with corrections indicated.   .   .   ☐

It is understood that this material will be used for educational
purposes only.

Signature of Executive_____

Date_____   Firm_____

If a case is revised after a release has been given, great care must be
exercised to be sure that no changes are made which might violate the
release privilege.

Even though a case is based wholly on published information,
it frequently is advisable to obtain a release or verification from
an executive of the company. Such a release from the company
or companies concerned should be obtained under the following
circumstances:

(1) Where part of the material or all of it is taken from sources not
authorized by the company, such as articles in the *Wall Street Journal*
or the *Commercial and Financial Chronicle.*

(2) Where the author of the case has not used published material
verbatim but has paraphrased or condensed to a substantial degree.

For a case based on published material, the circumstances under
which it does not appear essential to obtain a formal release from an
executive of the company or companies concerned are the following:

(1) Where the entire case is based on material quoted verbatim
from a source fully authorized by the company, such as the company's
annual reports, letters to stockholders, or financial and operating
statements published in *Standard & Poor's, Moody's,* or similar manuals.
Such cases should carry a footnote stating the source. When such
cases involve highly controversial issues, careful consideration should
be given to the desirability of sending a copy of the case to someone in
the company, requesting correction of any errors it may contain.

(2) Where the case consists of court and commission decisions, with or without the briefs presented.

(3) Where the material quoted or paraphrased is of a wholly general character not pertaining to any particular company, such as cases on government price control, the Federal fiscal policy, and so on.

For obvious reasons, cases which are written and sent for release within a short time after the original interview have a better chance of being released promptly.

After the case collection process has been completed with a particular company, good taste suggests that the research assistant or the professor drop a note to the company executive, thanking him for his cooperation.

TECHNIQUES OF CASE WRITING

The quality of a case is ultimately measured by its usefulness as teaching material. Experience has indicated, however, that certain literary standards are necessary, and certain accepted forms of presentation go a long way toward assuring acceptable cases.

Case writing is fundamentally no different from other writing. The fact that it is primarily reportorial suggests various techniques and dictates at times the proper order of presentation.

One essential requirement is that the case must be in thoroughly good English and free from defects in organization and errors in grammar, punctuation, or the use of words. This requirement is particularly necessary in view of the fact that so many cases now go directly into mimeographed casebooks. For this reason, most professors have found it desirable to have all new cases edited by a member of the staff trained in that type of work before they are copied in final form. The editing may be done by the professor's secretary or by any other competent editor who is available. Some professors have found that reading a case aloud with the research assistant speeds effective editing.

This section is devoted to certain techniques which have proved helpful in writing useful cases. Since the techniques of case writing vary somewhat from case to case, from course to course, and from time to time, the following are for the most part only suggestions. They are, however, suggestions based upon past successful (and unsuccessful) experience and should be disregarded only with sufficient reason.

1. ORGANIZING YOUR MATERIAL

a. If you have not already done it in the field, write everything down.

b. Prepare an outline of the case, and use it in writing.

2. Suggestions for Writing

a. Statement of the Issue. It is frequently helpful to start a case with a statement of the issue. For some years this was the accepted practice at the School. With the more widespread use of "diagnostic" cases, starting each case with a clear-cut issue became more difficult. Nevertheless it is still effective if the first paragraph sets forth a lead to the theme of the case, an issue (real or nominal), or some other "excuse" for writing the case, against which the rest of the material can be interpreted. Many cases, for instance, include an account of the founding and development of a company. Such an account, however, is given not merely for the sake of history but rather for background to analysis of the current situation. If the first paragraph gives a clue to the use to which such historical material should be put, the case not only is more effective but also carries much more reader-interest.

No matter what outline is adopted, it is well to remember that most cases, to be useful in teaching, should deal with an administrative situation and should not be memoranda merely relating interesting facts.

b. Dictating. In most instances case writing can be speeded if the first draft is dictated rather than written in longhand. Practice in dictating is also good training. Experiment to find the combination of dictation and longhand writing that is most effective.

c. Topic Sentences. The development of topic sentences can also speed the process of getting cases dictated and typed, and at the same time ensure a well-planned case. If an outline is expanded to the extent that each topic sentence is sketched out, the research assistant will be able to dictate the case directly from his outline without writing it in longhand himself.

3. Generally Accepted Procedures

a. Use of the Past Tense. Ordinarily cases at the School are written in the past tense. This device is used in order to protect the company from which the information was received; it forestalls any implication that the facts as of one day will be the same at a later date. Experience at the School indicates, too, that cases written in the past tense retain their usefulness for teaching longer than cases in the present tense. A little practice develops techniques of using the past tense without making all the facts seem dead. If the past tense is not used, it may be necessary to indicate that the case was written as of a specified date.

b. Tabulations. Tabulate all data that can be presented in table form.

c. Exhibits and Appendices. Tables, charts, balance sheets, forms, and maps may be used as exhibits in cases. These should be *numbered* consecutively in the order of their appearance in the case. Specific reference to the source or sources of the material should be given at the bottom of each exhibit. Material not an integral part of the case or too long for inclusion in the text may be given in appendices. Appendices are usually designated by *letter* ("Appendix A").

d. Checking Figures and Disguises. All figures included in a case must be checked for accuracy.

To facilitate checking, make it a practice to record complete and specific source references. (For instance, include exact page numbers and other details which will enable the person checking your work to refer immediately to the same source that you used.) Source references noted on work sheets and rough drafts frequently should be more comprehensive than those which will appear in the published version.

It is essential that any disguises be completely executed so that the case is fully consistent.

e. Facts. All relevant facts that are available ought to be included. In most instances, each case should present only the plans which the company reviewed for the particular situation. When certain facts are not available, it is often significant to say so.

Research assistants are essentially reporters of facts. Opinions of the writer should not be included in a case. Opinions of others should be labeled as such and should not be reported as facts.

Recalling his own experience as a student, the research assistant should scrutinize his cases carefully to be sure that students will have no difficulty in understanding the situation.

f. Decisions. Inclusion of decisions actually arrived at by company executives frequently adds interest to a case and helps crystallize the student's thinking. Whether decisions are to be included, however, depends largely on the use to which the case is to be put.

g. Published Sources. When an entire case, written under the real name of the company, is based on published material such as the annual reports of a company or its financial statements as reported in *Moody's*, a footnote from the case title should indicate the source.

h. Reprinting. When substantial quotations are used, permission to reprint must be secured from the publisher. Exact indication of the source, including title of article, as well as author, publisher, and date of publication, must accompany each quotation.

Newspaper articles, not syndicated, and advertisements may be used without the formality of securing a release from the company, provided due credit is given to the source from which the material is taken.

i. Use of "Notes to Instructor." Additional information that is not essential to the case but that the professor may want to offer the student as background material may be written up in the form of notes and filed with the instructor's copy of the case. All information pertaining to the particular situation and all the facts which are to be used in the discussion of the case should, of course, be included in the case so that the students will not feel that the teacher has an unfair advantage over them so far as facts are concerned.

Explanation of the disguise used and other "historical notes" on how the case was secured and written may usefully be included in a Note to Instructor.

j. Miscellaneous. It is a good practice to put an identifying title, your name, and the date on all work sheets, notes, and the like.

For your own information and satisfaction as well as for the purpose of enabling you to report on your activities, you may wish to keep a list of the names of the people and companies which you visit, a copy of each of the cases that you write, and similar bits of personal history.

A summary of the case routine, listing the steps in the order in which they are usually followed, is given in Exhibit 4.

4. "Armchair Cases"

At times when the case collection process does not unearth the kind of business problem which a professor has been seeking, a research assistant may be tempted to write a case which is a composite of several different real situations. Such cases (known at the Business School as armchair cases) should be used with caution. They are among the most difficult to write because the absence of outside facts against which they can be checked may lead to inconsistencies within the case and to the inclusion of unreal and unrealistic business problems. The use, and especially the excessive use, of armchair cases may defeat one of the prime purposes of the case system, which is not to illustrate theories but to force professors and students alike to face real business facts.

Exhibit 4
Case Routine

1. The first draft of a new case is prepared by the research assistant and disguised if necessary. (If a fictitious name is to be used, it should be checked by the research assistant before the case is written.)
2. Two copies of the case are typed by the Stenographic Department and returned to the research assistant.
3. The case is discussed with the professor, and changes or additions are made.
4. The case is edited.
5. Any necessary checking of figures in the case is done, and the disguise is checked if necessary. This is the responsibility of the editor.
6. The case is approved by the professor, who is to note his approval on the case.

7. The case as approved is sent by the research assistant to the Stenographic Department.

8. The case is typed in final form and read back in the Stenographic Department.

   a. Five copies are made when a company release is needed. The number may vary with the individual requirements of professors.

   b. Two copies are made when most of the case is to be copied from published material which can be given directly to the stencil cutter.[1] Under these circumstances the carbon need be only a skeleton; it will serve as a temporary file copy until replaced by the mimeographed case.

   c. When a case is to be planographed, the rough draft will serve as a temporary file copy, to be replaced as soon as possible by the planographed case.

9. All copies of the case, including the rough draft, are sent by the Stenographic Department to the person in charge of the case files for numbering.

10. Copies of the case are then distributed as follows: one copy to the research assistant for the company, four copies to the "Hold" file until a release is secured.

11. The case is sent by the professor, or by the research assistant after consultation with the professor, to a responsible executive in the company for release.

12. The company executive does one of three things:

   a. Releases the case without corrections by sending a signed release card or an authorizing letter.

   b. Releases the case with corrections by returning the case and a signed release card or other authorization.

   c. Refuses to release the case.

13. Depending on the executive's action, the procedure is as follows:

   a. If the case is released, the release card and all correspondence are sent to the case files.

   b. If the case is released with corrections, the corrections are incorporated in the case by the research assistant. (If corrections are substantial, both the professor and the editor should be consulted.) The release card, all correspondence, and the corrected copy are sent to the case files. A corrected copy is returned to the company.

   c. If the case is not released, the situation should be discussed with the professor. Further contact with the company may be undertaken to see whether the case may be released after further changes are made. If the professor decides to abide by the management's decision or if further negotiations fail to secure a release, all copies of the case and the correspondence are filed in the "Dead" file of the case files.

---

[1] At the Harvard Business School new cases commonly are used several times in mimeographed or planographed form before they are published in printed case books. —ED.

The following paper presents the observations made by a research assistant on the work of the case writer. To a certain extent it is a commentary on some of the suggestions made by Professor Culliton in the course of his paper "Writing Business Cases." The material reproduced here is taken from the essay submitted by John Fayerweather, then a research assistant, in the competition of 1947–48 referred to on page 76.

The Work of the Case Writer   JOHN FAYERWEATHER

The function of the research assistant is to produce cases. It is not his part to establish teaching objectives. But in the frequent conferences between the case writer and the professor the teaching objectives and the means of achieving them necessarily are always in the background.

The job of the research assistant is not unlike that of the television cameraman. He must poke about the business world, picking subjects, choosing views, and bringing them into focus for the inspection of the students. The story of the growth of a case from inception to completion is the story of the case writer's work.

When looking for a case which will pose a specific problem, it is natural to seek out a company to which that problem is of genuine concern. For instance, when a case on foreign trade-mark protection was needed, the quickest and most obvious solution was to approach an export executive who had written several articles on the subject. He was glad to help, and he narrated an interesting experience on which to base the case. But the weakness here was as patent as the gain. In his awareness of the dangers of trade-mark piracy and in the protective policies which he had devised, the executive was far in advance of many of his competitors. Thus the case, though excellent in most respects, may have given the students an unrealistic picture of actual business practice.

The case writer's job is especially difficult when the company is having a hard time solving the particular problem. The natural tendency for the researcher is to avoid such situations, partly out of consideration for the feelings of the company executives and partly out of a desire to simplify his own work. But business life must not be represented as a bed of roses; hence the case writer does seek out such companies. It is a great credit to American businessmen that so many of them are willing to bare their toughest problems in order that young men may profit from their experiences.

As a practical matter the research assistant, in seeking a case, learns to avoid certain industries and companies which he knows are habitually reluctant to give out information. One of the interesting aspects of American industry is the wide variation in this respect. Some companies are wary about discussing even general policies, while others are frank to a fault. The many factors which contribute to this condition would make interesting case studies in themselves, but they are not something the case writer can change.

A third consideration which the research assistant needs to take into account when he is seeking a case is the manner in which the welfare of the company may have been affected by the particular problem. To take a simple example, the researcher usually obtains information more readily from the company that won the lawsuit than from the company that lost. Of course, it is not always feasible to get cases from the companies which won the lawsuits; and it may be unwise, in any event, to concentrate on such firms, since their experience may over-stress the successful aspects of business negotiations. The consideration is, nevertheless, a helpful one for the case writer to keep in mind.

After he has chosen a subject, the next phase of the television cameraman's job is to persuade the subject to pose. If the case writer is fortunate, his professor or some other faculty member will introduce him to an executive high in the company who is able and willing to provide the information needed for his case. The simplicity of this type of approach presents a dangerous pitfall for the hard-pressed researcher. He may find himself taking an undue proportion of cases from companies already known to him, without venturing sufficiently into other concerns.

If the case writer knows some man in the lower reaches of an organization, he may obtain a valuable understanding of the company from talking with him. Except for this kind of informal talk, however, it is rarely wise to use such a connection as the initial point of contact for gathering case material. Since the information desired is often detailed and confidential in nature and may not be available, in the ordinary course of business, to the junior executives, the case writer cannot expect his friend to jeopardize his own career by asking for help from his superiors. And quite apart from this personal consideration, the researcher will almost invariably find a much better reception if he approaches the president directly, even when he has no more introduction than the Harvard Business School letterhead. The case writer is constantly surprised at the willingness of busy executives in a position of authority to take time to further his work.

In writing to executives to ask for interviews, the research assistant is helped by an insight into the reasons for the interest of these busy men. Without a doubt, much of it stems from the interest of the School in them and their work. Many businessmen argue, with some justification, that professors in their ivory towers cannot educate men for business, that two years spent in apprenticeship would profit a young man far more than two years in business school listening to professorial preaching. The letter from the research assistant stating that the school is interested in the way in which the executive dealt with some situation is to him a signal of academic recognition of these arguments. It is his opportunity to tell the students how business really operates. And, in truth, the effectiveness of the case method depends to a large degree on its success in transmitting the experience of many individual businessmen.

In his approach, the researcher can offer no monetary inducement, no free advertising, nothing, in fact, beyond the satisfaction of contributing to education. To the credit of the business community, this inducement alone has been sufficient to carry forward the case-collecting process.

A word must be injected here about the use of secondary sources of information. Much time is saved in the writing of a case if magazine articles, newspapers, and other reports are used. Experience has shown, however, that these sources may be grossly inaccurate or unrealistic; hence the research assistant cannot safely base his material upon them alone.

The use of secondary sources as preliminary information to aid the case collector in preparing for interviews is another matter and one whose value can scarcely be overstressed. To write a good case, the research assistant needs a thorough understanding of the company's history and operations. By familiarizing himself with such materials as he can find in company reports and other printed sources, he saves his limited interviewing time for the more vital issues; he is able to conduct the interview with far greater intelligence; and he encourages the cooperation of the executive by evincing a knowledge of, and an interest in, the activities of the company.

Since the initial approach by letter or telephone must be brief if it is to receive the attention of a busy executive, the next stage, the interview, will usually start with a fairly complete description of the case method and the immediate interest of the case collector. After that, the researcher proceeds as best he can toward the accumulation of the information needed for his case. A few aspects of the interviewing technique used in case collecting are worth noting. The first is that of holding the interview to the subject. It is easy to wander into areas not related to the case. Within limits, however, this wandering may be useful, for it gives the researcher a chance to see what matters are most on the executive's mind, what the relations between him and his assistants are, and a myriad of other things which will contribute to the "pluses" of his case.

Sometimes the research assistant finds that the executive is not willing to disclose information essential for the case. One solution for this problem is to give up. Pressing for information that is not willingly given can damage the reputation of the School and jeopardize the efforts of other case collectors. Another solution is to go off into channels in which information is available. Only rarely can the researcher know before an interview the nature of all a company's problems; and, as the interview progresses, he should be alert for different, and possibly better, subjects for discussion.

In utilizing statements made during interviews, the case writer tries to label facts and opinions as such, leaving the students to evaluate the latter. The border line between facts and opinions is never clear, however. One man may state as a fact what another says was an opinion. To ensure accuracy, the researcher tries to check the story, particularly those parts upon which the main issues depend, through a number of sources.

Should the case writer take notes during an interview? Some do; some do not. The controlling factors are usually the nature of the material—whether human problems or statistics, for instance—and the capacity of the research assistant's memory. Two other considerations are worth noting. It is hard to think and write at the same time. The case writer does not merely record surface facts. He has to explore the situation being discussed and to do it with the same penetration that a management consultant would apply. Every statement made by the executive must immediately be analyzed by the research assistant for clues of further matters to be explored. To free his mind for such constructive activity, the researcher can take only the sketchiest of notes. On the other hand, taking notes has a unique value in focusing the conversation. For example, the executive watching the research assistant trying to formulate an organization chart is led to concentrate on the essential basic information. Interesting ramifications of channels of authority and flow of work are relegated to their proper position as supplementary information.

In order to obtain confidential information, the research assistant may agree to disguise the case by means of fictitious names, figures, and so forth. Depending upon the nature of the case, much may be done in this direction. It is possible to preserve the heart of the problem even though the identity of the actual situation may be virtually destroyed. Sometimes also the disguise may be improved if the story is cut off without a statement as to the decision which was actually reached.

There are, nevertheless, limitations on the use of disguise. The television cameraman, wishing to show how a football player makes a tackle, is not concerned about the uniform of the players. But if he is describing the offensive strategy of one of the powerful Notre Dame teams, he must describe the qualities of the stars and their coach. In so doing, he will disclose the identity of the team, no matter what its uniform. Likewise, in business management cases, the past history and nature of a company are often so essential a part of the story that adequate disguise would greatly reduce the value of the case. Even so, a fictitious company name may be used merely to avoid the involvement of the actual company name in class discussion.

Now comes the cameraman's most difficult job: picking and choosing from his material, ordering it into a coherent whole, and presenting it as an effective story. To complete his cases as efficiently as possible, the research assistant tends to develop a routine, of which the following is an example. As soon as possible after his interview, he dictates a summary of the interview, filling in from memory parts on which he did not make notes. He then draws up an outline of the proposed case and discusses the outline and interview notes with the professor. Next he writes a draft of the case, observing as he does so that he will need additional material in certain places. The draft is read by the professor, who raises further questions. Then the draft is revised, and a copy is sent to the executive interviewed, with a request that he read it over and note any changes needed. Unless the company is at a great distance from the School, the case writer visits the executive a few days later to receive his comments and acquire missing information. Then he returns to the School and rewrites and polishes the case.

The choice of material for inclusion in the case is always a compromise between the voluminous information necessary to give a full picture and the comparatively brief statement which the student can be expected to digest in the time that he has allotted to the study of one case. The businessman in whose shoes the student is supposed to be placed can draw on a vast store of experience with past and present circumstances in solving his problems. The fact that this background material cannot be set forth in the case does not preclude a useful and intelligent discussion of the problem. It does result, however, in the student's sharpening his analytical powers on compartmentalized problems without considering them as parts of much larger operations. Since training in the broader area is vital for business success, the case writer introduces as much information as he can about personalities and company policies.

What quantity of irrelevant material should be included cannot be stated categorically. Certainly it is important to develop a student's ability to discriminate between useful and unnecessary information. Thus some extraneous data need to be given. The student's training is most effective, however, if the volume of such data varies from considerable to none—hence the absence of any fixed policy. There is one serious risk in including extraneous material, namely, that the class may be thrown completely off the track or may never get to the main point because of the profusion of surplus information.

The use of live material, such as reports and letters obtained from company files, poses a further problem. Such material adds substantially to the reality of a case. Still, the students may have to wade through a mass of details and technicalities to get at the heart of the problem. Thus, in the interests of expedition, the case writer usually does much of the wading for the students and presents the material in condensed form.

Many cases include material which is not part of the description of the business situation but is necessary for a proper understanding, such as a summary of stock-issuing procedure. The material may be in a separate technical note or an appendix, or may be part of the body of the case.

The next step is organization of the case, and here again there must be a compromise between time limits and training objectives. Unless the material in a case is ordered to some degree, the students are unable to get at the meat, and the resulting class discussion is quite unsatisfactory. Thus most cases present a somewhat systematized description of the company in general and the specific aspects being considered.

Whether the statement of the case should be carried to the point of presenting the issue and discussing the pros and cons is another matter. Both the problem-finding and the stated-problem types of cases have their place in the system. Cases in the latter category include two types: those in which the problem is merely posed and those in which the company's decision and the reasons behind it are given. The choice between these types is made on the basis of the ability of the students to discern the significant issues. In the early stages of an unfamiliar course, the best strategy may be to take a complete solution and pick it apart. As their experience grows, the students develop the ability to arrive at reasonable solutions independently, and the presentation of a company decision may curb their imagination.

The actual writing of a case, like all writing, is the often tedious process of creating a description which is readable and accurate. Some ingenuity is required in seeding essential facts and figures through the body of the case, to be ferreted out by the students. The case writer has to be skillful lest the students fail to pick up the scent and miss the point of the case.

The story must also be presented without implying that the actions of the company are either right or wrong. A detached and accurate presentation is achieved only by the most careful editing. Where time permits, it is often helpful for the case writer to read the case aloud with someone else, determining that it is clear and correct in every part and makes an integrated whole. The research assistant looks to his professor and to experienced editors for help, but his officemates and other case writers are excellent guinea pigs on which to test his writings.

The final draft of the case, with a release card, is sent for approval by the chief executive and any others, such as the public relations officer, who may be interested. Until the case is released the case writer keeps in touch with the executive, asking whether there are any questions he may answer and generally indicating his interest.

So ends the "collecting" of one case, a process which may have taken from one to six weeks of work time spread over a period of several months.

A good way to summarize these observations on the case method is to consider the effect on the case collector himself. In the course of his work, the research assistant receives in more intensive form the same type of education that the students do. Visiting here and there through an industry, he becomes oriented to the companies, people, and activities of which the industry is composed. In gathering the material for his cases, he acquires considerable specific information. From the remarks of the executives whom he interviews and from his own thinking, he learns much about the principles upon which the operation of the industry is based. Of most value to him is his close contact with the problems of individual companies. In writing up these problems as cases, he necessarily analyzes them himself. Through this process and through the thought he must apply to practical matters all along the case-gathering procedure, his analytical abilities are stimulated and strengthened.

Finally, among the numerous questions about the case method still remaining unanswered, there is sure to be that large and important one, "How much does it cost, and how do you finance those costs?" In the last paper in this volume Arthur H. Tully, Jr., addresses himself to this question.

The Financing of Case Collection

ARTHUR H. TULLY, JR.

The great success of the Business School during the war years in training supply officers for the armed services and analyzing many logistic problems might be said to justify those who see this faculty of the University as the one academic group which knows how to teach "administration." I realize, of course, the strenuous objections that many graduates of our Law School now serving the Government in administrative posts would make to any such contention.

Interesting evidence, however, is afforded by the brilliant record of the Advanced Management course of thirteen weeks offered to business executives in the last ten years. Furthermore, the testimony of employers and alumni is almost unanimous as to the value of the regular two-year course for those who are going to enter business. As one who has done little more than observe and applaud this Harvard development, I suggest the key to the success has been the insistent and persistent use of the highly expensive case method of instruction.—JAMES B. CONANT

The foregoing quotation from James Bryant Conant's final report as President of Harvard to the Board of Overseers, for the year 1951–52, seems an appropriate setting for this paper on the costs of the "highly expensive" case method and the means by which they have been defrayed. Administrators of schools or university departments who contemplate adoption of the case method frequently ask, "How much per case does it cost?" No categorical answer to that question is feasible, unfortunately, but an effort will be made to show that case collection *is* costly, to indicate roughly how expensive it is, to explain how the costs have generally been met in the past, and finally to describe the current vital role of The Associates of the Harvard Business School as financial sponsors of case and project research.

Gathering complete case histories of actual business problems faced by specific companies has been a continuous process supported by a variety of sources in the past but currently financed entirely through funds provided by The Associates of the Harvard Business School. These cases are the lifeblood of the School's method of instruction, under which the student gradually acquires the ability to recognize the existence of problems, to apply the reasoning needed for analysis, and to develop the experience essential for making business decisions.

Whereas a medical school has hospitals for clinical studies, a law school has reports on the decisions of the courts, and the scientific schools have their laboratories for experimentation, an effective clinical study of decision-making in industry calls for firsthand observations in the field. At the Harvard Business School these firsthand observations are provided by the collected cases.

Over the past thirty years it has cost upwards of $5,000,000 to gather this case material, which requires constant revision and replacement in order to keep abreast of modern business trends, practices, and facts. Not only has this teaching material been vital to the training of over 16,000 alumni of the Harvard Business School and over 2,000 graduates of the Advanced Management Program, but many of the cases in a number of courses have also been utilized by over 260 other institutions for business education. Thus, through supporting the training of research personnel and the case-gathering activities of the Harvard Business School, The Associates presently are in fact aiding the production of realistic teaching material for nationwide use.

As Dr. Copeland has described earlier in this volume,[1] the initial gathering of cases was undertaken with an allocation of $5,000 in the academic year 1920–21. The recorded expenditures debited to case collection rapidly grew to $139,000 in 1924–25 and thereafter ranged between $70,000 and $125,000 annually for the next dozen years. The early objective was to compile an inventory of "timeless" cases that could be taught year after year, but this concept proved unrealistic. As business methods and situations changed, a considerable proportion of the cases had to be discarded and replaced. This experience led Dean Donham to make the following statement in his 1938 Annual Report:

Quality instruction in business turns out to be much more expensive than we had assumed in the first fifteen or twenty years of our existence. In this respect it compares more nearly with medical training than it does with the work in many departments of the Faculty of Arts and Sciences or in the Law School. Training of doctors and businessmen, if it is to be realistic, and nothing unrealistic is adequate, must be given by faculties who not only are in close touch with their respective fields but use teaching material drawn from actual experience. For the medical profession this means much instruction in small groups in hospitals. For our field it means teaching material which is costly to obtain because it must be obtained by field agents who visit industry for

[1] See Melvin T. Copeland, "The Genesis of the Case Method in Business Instruction," supra, pp. 25–33.

the purpose, and teachers whose time is free enough so that they may maintain constant contacts with groups of businessmen. There is nothing in our field comparable with the published cases of law which we can use as teaching material. We must collect such material ourselves. For these reasons high quality can be established and maintained only through the expenditure of considerable sums not paralleled in most educational areas.

The historian and the accountant will both necessarily be disappointed in the following account of "the expenditure of considerable sums" for case research, because the records have real limitations. Education, and particularly the financing thereof, is not like ordinary business; and in the Business School the accounting has frequently been influenced by the exigencies of the moment, which called for applying the available funds to the activities deemed currently most important. The figures actually recorded for case research often have been only the bare bones of the real costs. Funds to pay for replenishment of the lifeblood bank of case material have in the past frequently been diverted on a recurring emergency basis from other, so-called "unrestricted," sources.

Also the costs themselves are not clear cut. When a research assistant is definitely assigned to a single professor solely for the purpose of gathering cases, his salary, travel, and other expenses can be charged to the case research account. On the other hand, an instructor assisting a professor in teaching a course and thus debited to the instruction account may, and frequently does, devote a part of his time to case collection. Though currently such hidden costs are more or less revealed by an allocation method evolved over the years, such an approach to accounting accuracy has not always prevailed. And when it comes to reckoning the time and effort chargeable to case gathering on the part of the professor responsible for a course, limitations on accounting accuracy apply even more fully. The professor's own case-gathering activities are frequently incidental to his other direct relationships with business—in his consulting work, in his activities as a member of various professional societies, in his speaking engagements, or in the course of missions of public responsibility which he may undertake on behalf of the School.

Another factor minimizing the practical significance of any answer to the unit-cost-per-case question is the extreme variety in the cases themselves. On the one hand, there are the cases drawn entirely from published sources, as well as the "armchair cases," written with comparatively little time, effort, or travel. At the other extreme are the complicated cases, for instance those for the Business Policy course, that may take months of checking and repeated visits to a distant company to ensure accurate reporting of as many as possible of the relevant factors bearing upon important policy decisions. Likewise, to assemble a realistic description of involved interactions in a case for the course in Human Relations may also require months of company visits in order to get to know all the people involved and to obtain their full confidence. With such variety in the conditions of gathering cases there is a correspondingly wide divergence in the costs.

In the relatively short time-period of a year, which is the usual fiscal measuring unit, the mix of the long and the short cases, the simple and the involved cases, those distantly obtained and those from nearby sources, inevitably leads to wide annual fluctuations in the number of cases gathered, the expenses incurred, and hence the cost per case. The simple arithmetic of dividing total case expenditures for a year by the number of cases completed in that year therefore furnishes only the roughest guide for budgeting and planning purposes.

Thus no answer to the question "How much per case does it cost?" can be strictly accurate. Of one fact the reader can be confidently assured: the recorded cost has always been *less* than the properly allocable expenses. The following figures, therefore, are to be taken with this grain of salt.

After case gathering had been initiated with the allocation of $5,000 in the fiscal year 1920–21, the records show that $26,466 was used for the collection of cases in 1921–22. In those two academic years 1,577 cases were prepared. The indicated unit cost, averaging just under $20, was by far the lowest ever attained. In the remainder of the 1920's, the indicated annual average cost per case ranged from $52 to $276. In the 1930–1940 decade the range narrowed, with a low of $145 and a high of $241. The jaggedness of the curve, however, permits no clear derivation of a trend.

Because of the dislocation of the war years, and especially because instruction largely for the armed services involved unrecorded expenditures for case gathering directly assumed by the services, the figures for the fiscal years 1941 through 1946 have no real significance with reference to the cost of case collection.

The five-year postwar period ending with fiscal 1952 began with an indicated average cost per case of $130, the low for the period, and ended with the high of $234 for the last year. As might be expected for that inflationary period, there was a trend, and it was clearly upward. However, the fact that the indicated average cost of gathering a case was not even higher may be attributed in considerable degree to greatly increased activity in the School's other major type of field investigation, the research *projects*. Financed through their own individual budgets and accounts, these projects frequently produce material that can be adapted and used as cases. Thus the by-product may be usable for instruction with little direct cost to the case-gathering account, and, to the extent that this is so, the average case-gathering cost is lowered.

As a final caveat against a simple mathematical application of these empirically derived and roughly indicated average costs per case to any educational program contemplating use of the case method, let it be repeated that in some courses, especially those that are interdisciplinary in character, the costs of a good case are frequently far above the average. As already indicated, complex cases for the courses in Business Policy or Human Relations, just for instance, may properly require very large expenditures of manpower, travel, time, and hence money. Though their effect upon the averages is apparently not great, the aberrations are wide, not unusual, and to some extent foreseeable when complex or subtle cases are to be secured. Predictable or not, experience shows that the cost of some of these cases may be as high as $1,000 or $2,000.

In terms of aggregates rather than unit costs, the record of this thirty-odd-year educational experiment is impressive not only in total amount but also in diversity of sources and types of money-raising. Quite apart from the organized financing through The Associates, about $500,000 was received for general or specific case research purposes between 1920 and 1941. Thus $215,000 was collected in the Fund for the Development of the Case System (including $40,000 by transfer from the Harvard Endowments Fund); and more narrowly designated contributions during this period included $36,000 given for the collection of cases in Retailing, $48,000 for cases in the field of Advertising, and $131,000 for cases in Public Utility Management.

Up to the end of fiscal 1952 the School's research expenditures had amounted to more than $7,000,000. Specifically recorded as having been devoted to case research were expenditures of $2,650,000. But to this figure should be added some part of the $3,650,000 classified as having been spent either for "special" or for "project" research.[1] Considering the case by-product results of research projects and a number of other factors already briefly touched upon, it seems fair to estimate that, all in all, about $5,000,000 has been devoted directly and indirectly to the production of material to support the School's case method of instruction. As a test of that estimate of inclusive costs

[1] The remaining $700,000 of the $7,000,000 was spent for the cost studies made by the Bureau of Business Research, beginning with the study of the cost of doing business in shoe stores in 1911 and including the annual studies of operating results in department stores and in variety chains, now carried on for more than thirty and twenty years, respectively. Funds for these Bureau cost studies have been furnished principally by trade associations.

the unit cost of over 20,000 cases collected since 1921 works out to
about $240, a figure which seems close to observed realities.

Such a sizable sum as $7,000,000 for educational research purposes
is of course not easily obtained even over a period of three decades.
Some idea of the difficulties and administrative effort involved may
be gained from excerpts from the initial pamphlet setting forth in 1930
the plan for organization of what was originally known as "The Two
Hundred Fifty Associates of the Harvard Business School." From a
statement addressed by Dean Donham to the Organization Committee and included in its published proposal, the following paragraph
summarizes previous experience and the background of need for funds
"to stabilize and promote research and the collection of material for
the teaching of business," the Committee's own stated purpose:

Nearly all of our research in the past has been financed by annual gifts of
businessmen. There are distinct disadvantages in this hand-to-mouth financing. The heavy burden on the administrative officers of the School, arising
from the necessity of raising this money, has been a constant source of interference with plans for the internal development of the School. Moreover, the
financial uncertainty and the fact that donors have often restricted the use of
funds to particular projects have destroyed the possibility of organizing either
subject matter or personnel to accomplish long-time programs. The continuation of research work even with these limitations is now jeopardized because
our present methods of financing have become so burdensome that they are
affecting our efficiency. I therefore welcome the organization of The Two
Hundred Fifty Associates of the Harvard Business School, for it offers
stabilization of the support business is already giving us.

The trusteeship of The Two Hundred Fifty Associates was assumed
by the Visiting Committee appointed by the Board of Overseers of
Harvard College to report on the activities of the Graduate School of
Business Administration. The chairman in 1930, the late Jesse Isidor
Straus, who was also an Overseer, devoted a large part of his time to
the organizing effort that resulted in a membership of 199 in the first
year. Though the number of Associates was to decline during the
depression, the backlog of faithful contributing members gave
invaluable support to the continuation of case research through the
lean years.

Early membership in The Two Hundred Fifty Associates was held
largely by individuals. When the Trust Agreement was redrawn in
1943 and the name shortened to "The Associates of the Harvard
Business School," the Trustees supported Dean David in the effort to
emphasize membership by business corporations. Since then the number of Associates has more than doubled, and as of 1953 a majority of
the 335 memberships are held in corporate names. The project

research publications of the School's Division of Research and the *Harvard Business Review* are sent to all members of The Associates; and in cases where the members are corporations the publications go not only to the presidents but to other key administrative personnel as well. The comprehensive mailing list of The Associates is roughly 1,400. There is thus wide dissemination of research findings based on concentrated study of special problems of broad significance to the business community.

Though The Associates has existed during only the latter half of the School's total research program and during only two-thirds of its case-gathering period, this organization has furnished almost 40% of the School's forty-year research funds and is currently financing well over half the research budget. Case research, providing the lifeblood of the School's instruction, receives its sole support from Associates' funds. Undertakings in project research, on the other hand, are often initiated by underwriting from The Associates and carried on until, having become going concerns, they attract special financing by foundations, groups of companies, government agencies, trade associations, or others.

When substantial research activities are financed in the manner that has been described, there is an obvious necessity for establishing and enforcing certain ironclad policies to govern the acceptance of projects and the conduct of the work. Thus all research carried on by the Harvard Business School must conform to the following policies:

(1) The School undertakes only research projects of sufficient breadth and importance (*a*) to be of significant use for the purposes of teaching and of Faculty development, (*b*) to be of substantial concern to business generally, and (*c*) to be of general value in helping the School to meet its professional obligations to society. The School does not undertake studies which are of interest primarily to a single business enterprise.

(2) Research programs are ordinarily approved only when there is reasonable expectation that the results will be published. Decisions regarding publication and distribution lie with the authors and the Dean.

(3) The conclusions reached and the opinions expressed in any study are those of the individuals responsible for the particular project. Neither the School nor the Faculty as a group reaches conclusions or makes recommendations on results of research.

Independence in research, the freedom to report the facts as they are found and to draw such conclusions as are supportable by the evidence, is strongly buttressed by the aggregate financial support of the many sponsors who constitute The Associates.

Notes on the Contributors

KENNETH R. ANDREWS, A.B. (*Wesleyan Univ.*) 1936, A.M. (*ibid.*) 1937, Ph.D. (*Univ. of Illinois*) 1948. Associate Professor of Business Administration. A member of the group at the Harvard Business School which has concerned itself especially with the use of the case method in teaching Administrative Practices, and editor of the symposium published by the Harvard University Press in 1953 under the title *The Case Method of Teaching Human Relations and Administration.* Consultant to industry on the use of cases in executive development. Publications include *Nook Farm: Mark Twain's Hartford Circle,* "Product Diversification and the Public Interest" and "Executive Training by the Case Method" (both in the *Harvard Business Review*), and several articles in other journals. Currently teaching the Administrative Practices course in the Advanced Management Program at the Harvard Business School.

NEIL H. BORDEN, A.B. (*Univ. of Colorado*) 1919, M.B.A. (*Harvard Univ.*) 1922. Professor of Advertising. On the staff of the Harvard Business School since 1922. Closely concerned, throughout this period, with case research and the development of instruction by the case method. Recipient of research award (1946) of Kappa Tau Alpha, national journalism fraternity, for his research on national advertising in newspapers; Medal for Distinguished Service given by Syracuse University School of Journalism (1949); Charles Coolidge Parlin Award (1949) and Paul D. Converse Award (1951) for outstanding contribution to the development of the science of marketing. Publications include *Advertising: Text and Cases* and two editions of the predecessor *Problems in Advertising; The Economic Effects of Advertising;* cases and commentaries comprising two specialized volumes in the *Harvard Business Reports* series; several monographs in the series of Harvard Business Research studies; *National Advertising in Newspapers;* and a long list of periodical articles. Currently is President of the American Marketing Association.

W. WALLER CARSON, JR., A.B. (*Princeton Univ.*) 1946, M.B.A. (*Harvard Univ.*) 1947. Assistant Professor of Business Administration at Northwestern University. After completion of work for M.B.A. degree, was Instructor in Business Administration at the Harvard Business School and assisted in preparation of Professor Tosdal's two-volume study of *Salesmen's Compensation.* Joined the staff at Northwestern in the summer of 1951.

C. ROLAND CHRISTENSEN, A.B. (*Univ. of Iowa*) 1941, M.B.A. (*Harvard Univ.*) 1943, D.C.S. (*ibid.*) 1953. Assistant Professor of Business Administration.

285

Experience includes more than three years on Research and Procurement Control for the Army. Author of *Management Succession in Small and Growing Enterprises*. Currently teaching in the second-year required course in Business Policy.

MELVIN T. COPELAND, A.B. (*Bowdoin Coll.*) 1906, A.M. (*Harvard Univ.*) 1907, Ph.D. (*ibid.*) 1910, S.D. (hon.) (*Bowdoin Coll.*) 1931. George Fisher Baker Professor of Administration, Emeritus. Director of Research, Harvard Business School, 1942–1953. Pioneer in the study of marketing, authority on the cotton textile industry, and analyst of the development and performance of executives. Publications include *Problems in Marketing, Principles of Merchandising, Cotton Manufacturing Industry in the United States, Raw Material Prices and Business Conditions, International Raw Commodity Prices and the Devaluation of the Dollar, A Raw Commodity Revolution,* and *The Executive at Work.* Co-author of *Merchandising of Cotton Textiles—Methods and Organization* and *The Board of Directors and Business Management.* Long record of public service, including post of Executive Secretary of the Commercial Economy Board, Council of National Defense, during World War I, and chairmanship of the Advisory Council, U.S. Senate Trade Policies Committee, in 1947. Member of Board of Overseers, Bowdoin College, 1934–1947; Trustee since 1947.

JAMES W. CULLITON, A.B. (*Canisius Coll.*) 1932, M.B.A. (*Harvard Univ.*) 1934, D.C.S. (*ibid.*) 1941. Administrative Head of the Experimental Program for Administrators at the University of Notre Dame. Following graduation from the Business School in 1934, spent three years in business in New York and during this period served as Lecturer at Fordham University. Joined staff of the Business School in 1937 to collect cases for courses in Economics and Marketing. Head of Department of Management at Boston College School of Business Administration, 1941–42. Executive Director of Massachusetts Committee on Post War Readjustment, 1942–1944. At the Business School, 1944–1948, as Assistant Director of Research, in charge of case collection. Was Associate Professor of Business Administration at time of resignation in 1952. Author of *Make or Buy, The Management of Marketing Costs,* and a number of periodical articles.

DEWITT C. DEARBORN, A.B. (*Gettysburg Coll.*) 1940, M.B.A. (*Harvard Univ.*) 1948. Administrator, Program for Executives, Graduate School of Industrial Administration, Carnegie Institute of Technology. Assistant Professor of Finance, University of Kansas, 1948–1951. Research Associate at the Harvard Business School, 1951–1953. Co-author of *Spending for Industrial Research, 1951–1952.*

ARTHUR STONE DEWING, A.B. (*Harvard Univ.*) 1902, A.M. (*ibid.*) 1903, Ph.D. (*ibid.*) 1905. Formerly Professor of Finance, Harvard Business School. Currently serving as President and/or Treasurer and/or Director of a dozen public utility companies (including Albion Gas Light Company, Portland

Water Company, Illinois Gas Company, Coastal Public Service Corporation of South Carolina, Granite State Gas and Electric Company, Florida Home Gas Company, and International Hydroelectric System) and several other businesses. Publications include *Financial Policy of Corporations, Corporation Finance, The Corporation—A Study of Its Financial Structure, Promotion and Reorganization of Industrial Corporations,* and *History of National Cordage Company.*

WALLACE B. DONHAM, A.B. (*Harvard Univ.*) 1898, LL.B. (*ibid.*) 1901, LL.D. (hon.) (*ibid.*) 1939, LL.D. (hon.) (*Juniata Coll.*) 1941, LL.D. (hon.) (*New York Univ.*) 1943, L.H.D. (*Colgate Univ.*) 1943. George Fisher Baker Professor of Administration, Emeritus, since 1948. Old Colony Trust Company, 1901–1919 (Vice President from 1906 on). Dean of the Harvard Business School from 1919 to 1942, during which period the case method of instruction in business administration became a practical reality. After resignation as Dean in 1942, devoted himself to exploring the possibilities of undergraduate instruction by the case method, first in Harvard College and then as Visiting Professor in Human Relations at Colgate University. Publications include *Business Adrift, Business Looks at the Unforeseen, Education for Responsible Living,* and *Administration and Blind Spots,* in addition to a large number of articles.

ALBERT H. DUNN III, A.B. (*Amherst Coll.*) 1943 (1947), M.B.A. (*Harvard Univ.*) 1947. Assistant Professor of Business Administration. War service as cryptographer with the Signal Corps. Special work in 1950 with Mobilization Analysis Center in Washington. In 1952 and 1953, 18 months of research and writing on manufacturers' point-of-sale promotion activities; findings are scheduled for publication by Division of Research, Harvard Business School. Has taught Sales Management, Advertising, and Written Analysis of Cases, and currently is teaching Marketing.

JOHN FAYERWEATHER, S.B. in Engineering (*Princeton Univ.*) 1943, M.B.A. (*Harvard Univ.*) 1948. Assistant Professor of Business Administration. Following graduation from Princeton, worked for U.S. Geological Survey. Then served three years with Army Engineer construction units. On completing work for M.B.A. in 1948, joined staff of Business School as Research Assistant. Taught Written Analysis of Cases; was recalled to duty with the Army; and since returning to the Business School has taught Foreign Trade Management.

CHARLES I. GRAGG, A.B. (*Univ. of Rochester*) 1918 (1920), M.B.A. (*Harvard Univ.*) 1921, D.C.S. (*ibid.*) 1928. Professor of Business Administration. Concerned, since the early 1920's, in development of cases and the case method. Editor of the series of *Harvard Business Reports;* co-author of several case collections, including *Introduction to Business—A Case Book* and *Problems in Retailing;* author of numerous articles in the field of education as well as in business. Involved, at one time or another, in course development in several areas, including Marketing, Public Relations and Responsibilities, Business Economics, Business and the American Society, Administrative Practices, and the required work in Written Analysis of Cases. During World War II served with War Production Board; was adviser to Salary Stabilization Board; and was chairman of the seven-man committee appointed to study the New England economy and consult with the President's Council of Economic Advisers. Currently teaching the course on Business and the American Society in the Business School's Advanced Management Program.

HARRY L. HANSEN, S.B. (*Haverford Coll.*) 1933, M.B.A. (*Harvard Univ.*) 1935, D.C.S. (*ibid.*) 1939. Professor of Business Administration. Began post-graduate association with the Business School as Research Assistant writing cases for Sales Management and Foreign Trade. In years immediately preceding World War II, served as Assistant Dean and taught Marketing. During the war, instructed in Statistical School for the Army Air Forces at the Business School, and in 1944–45 was Civilian Director of Academic Training for the Army Air Forces War Adjustment Course at the Business School. Since February, 1946, has taught Marketing. Author of several articles in professional journals, and co-author of *Problems in Marketing* and *Readings in Marketing*.

JOHN LINTNER, A.B. (*Univ. of Kansas*) 1939, A.M. (*ibid.*) 1940, A.M. (*Harvard Univ.*) 1942, Ph.D. (*ibid.*) 1946. Associate Professor of Business Administration. Began teaching Economics in 1939–40 as Assistant Instructor in Economics and Government at the University of Kansas. At Harvard as Teaching Fellow in Economics, 1941–42, and Junior Fellow, Society of Fellows, 1942–1945. Member of staff of National Bureau of Economic Research, 1941–1943. Joined the Faculty of the Business School in 1945 and taught first-year course in Finance. Currently teaching Advanced Economic Analysis, and Business Responsibilities in the American Society. Author of *Mutual Savings Banks in the Saving and Mortgage Markets*. Co-author of *Effects of Federal Taxes on Growing Enterprises* and *Effects of Taxation on Corporate Mergers*. Several articles in *Harvard Business Review*, *Review of Economics and Statistics*, and *American Economic Review*.

JOHN G. MCLEAN, S.B. (*California Inst. of Technology*) 1938, M.B.A. (*Harvard Univ.*) 1940, D.C.S. (*ibid.*) 1948. Professor of Business Administration. During World War II taught in the Navy War Adjustment Officers Course administered by the Business School for the Navy Supply Corps. Taught in Surplus Disposal Indoctrination Course, which he was instrumental in setting up for the Navy Supply Corps at the Business School. Currently in charge of second-year course in Advanced Production Problems. Adviser to various industrial organizations, and has also been a consultant to the United States Navy and the United States Air Force. Co-author of *The Growth of Integrated Oil Companies*.

MALCOLM P. MCNAIR, A.B. (*Harvard Univ.*) 1916, A.M. (*ibid.*) 1920. Lincoln Filene Professor of Retailing. On the staff of the Business School since 1920.

Engaged over this period in teaching, course development, and case collection, primarily in Retailing and Marketing but also to some extent in Business Economics and Business and Government. During World War II, Civilian Director of Army Supply Officers Training School and Navy War Adjustment Course at the Business School. Since the 1920's in charge of studies made by the Harvard Bureau of Business Research on operating costs in various retail and wholesale trades. Director of several corporations. Recipient in 1952 of gold medal of National Retail Dry Goods Association for distinguished service to retailing, and in 1953 of Paul D. Converse award for contribution to advancement of marketing. Author of numerous articles in professional journals; co-author of many Harvard problem books, including *Problems in Marketing, Problems in Business Economics,* and *Problems in Retailing;* author of *The Retail Method of Inventory* and co-author of *The Retail Inventory Method and Lifo.*

ROBERT W. MERRY, A.B. (*Harvard Univ.*) 1934 (1935), M.B.A. (*ibid.*) 1939, D.C.S. (*ibid.*) 1943. Professor of Business Administration. Fields of particular interest, Finance and Production. In business, 1932, 1935–1938. During World War II taught in courses given at the Business School for Army Supply Officers Training School and for Navy Supply Corps Midshipmen-Officers School and Navy War Adjustment Course. President (1953–1954) of Boston Chapter of Society for the Advancement of Management. Currently in charge of first-year course in Production.

POWELL NILAND, S.B. (*Univ. of Scranton*) 1942, M.B.A. (*Harvard Univ.*) 1948, D.C.S. (*ibid.*) 1953. Assistant Professor of Business Administration. Four years' service in the Navy. Work at the Business School initially in the field of Taxation. Assisted in preparation of two of the volumes in the study of Effects of Taxation, namely, *Corporate Mergers* and *Inventory Accounting and Policies.* Currently teaching in first-year course in Production.

THOMAS J. RAYMOND, A.B. (*New Jersey State Teachers Coll.*) 1942, M.B.A. (*Harvard Univ.*) 1947. Assistant Professor of Business Administration. Before World War II, in cost accounting and investment banking. During the war served with the Air Force. In 1951–1952, special work as administrative consultant to the State Department. Chairman of Finance Department at Boston College School of Business Administration, 1947–1949. Currently in charge of first-year work in Written Analysis of Cases at the Harvard Business School.

DONALD R. SCHOEN, A.B. (*Lehigh Univ.*) 1941, M.B.A. (*Harvard Univ.*) 1948. Assistant Professor of Business Administration. Experience includes three years with the Army, and a period as design engineer for the Bell Telephone Laboratories. Has assisted in course in Manufacturing; has served as Administrative Assistant to the Dean at the Business School; currently is teaching in second-year required course in Business Policy.

PHILIP A. SPRAGUE, A.B. (*Beloit Coll.*) 1946, M.B.A. (*Harvard Univ.*) 1948. In 1948–49 on Business School staff as Research Assistant in Advertising. Since that time, at The Hays Corporation, manufacturers of instruments and controls, at first as Advertising Manager and since 1951 as Executive Vice President.

ANDREW R. TOWL, A.B. (*Muskingum Coll.*) 1932, A.M. (*Columbia Univ.*) 1933, M.B.A. (*Harvard Univ.*) 1936. Director of Case Development, Assistant Director of Research, and Member of the Faculty of Business Administration. Work in investment analysis and organization for Provident Trust Company of Philadelphia from 1936 to 1944. Since 1944, on staff of the Harvard Business School. Co-author of *The Board of Directors and Business Management*. Author of several articles in professional journals. Currently supervising the work of case research assistants at the Business School.

ARTHUR H. TULLY, JR., A.B. (*Harvard Univ.*) 1924. In the investment banking business from 1924 to 1944. For two years Director of Aeronautics, Commonwealth of Massachusetts. Since 1946 on staff of the Harvard Business School. Currently Director of The Associates of the Harvard Business School, Assistant Director of Research, and Member of the Faculty of Business Administration.

A. ZALEZNIK, A.B. (*Alma Coll.*) 1945, M.B.A. (*Harvard Univ.*) 1947, D.C.S. (*ibid*). 1951. Assistant Professor of Business Administration. Interested especially in the improvement of human relations in industry and the use of the case method in supervisory and executive training. Has taught Production and second-year course in Advanced Production Problems at the Business School. In 1953 taught Human Relations at Atlantic Summer School of Advanced Business Administration (sponsored by the universities in the Maritime Provinces of Canada). Currently participating in Program for Advanced Training and Research in Human Relations at the Business School and assisting in administration of Doctoral Program. Author of *Foreman Training in a Growing Enterprise*.

List of Some of the Printed and Mimeographed Collections of Harvard Business School Cases

BOOKS IN PRINT

Lynn L. Bollinger and John S. Day, *Management of New Enterprises*, Irwin, 1954.

Neil H. Borden, *Advertising: Text and Cases*, Irwin, 2d ed., 1950.

Franklin E. Folts, *Introduction to Industrial Management*, McGraw-Hill, 4th ed., 1954.

John D. Glover and Ralph M. Hower, *The Administrator: Cases on Human Relations in Business*, Irwin, 2d ed., 1952.

Pearson Hunt and Charles M. Williams, *Case Problems in Finance*, Irwin, 2d ed., 1953.

Howard T. Lewis, *Procurement: Principles and Cases*, Irwin, 2d. ed., 1952.

Malcolm P. McNair, Charles I. Gragg, and Stanley F. Teele, *Problems in Retailing*, McGraw-Hill, 1937.

Malcolm P. McNair and Harry L. Hansen, *Problems in Marketing*, McGraw-Hill, 1949.

Clarence B. Nickerson, *Cost Accounting: Text, Problems, and Cases*, McGraw-Hill, 1954 (in press).

Benjamin M. Selekman, Sylvia K. Selekman, and Stephen H. Fuller, *Problems in Labor Relations*, McGraw-Hill, 1950.

George Albert Smith, *Policy Formulation and Administration*, Irwin, 1951.

Harry R. Tosdal, *Introduction to Sales Management*, McGraw-Hill, 3d ed., 1950.

Harry R. Tosdal, *Problems in Sales Management*, McGraw-Hill, 1939.

MIMEOGRAPHED COLLECTIONS

Since case collecting is a continuing process, new cases are constantly being added to the Business School files. Before these new cases are included in printed case books, they commonly are distributed in mimeographed form for discussion in the several courses. In 1953–54, mimeographed collections were in use in the following courses, either to supplement existing printed material or to furnish the basis for all the case discussion.

First-year courses:
    Administrative Practices
    Business Responsibilities in the American Society
    Control
    Finance
    Marketing
    Production
Second-year courses:
    Administration and Review of Accounts
    Advanced Economic Analysis
    Advanced Production Problems
    Analysis of Markets
    The Business Administrator and Government Policy
    Business History
    Business Policy
    Collective Bargaining
    Factory Management

Financial Accounting
Financial Management
Foreign Trade Management
Human Relations
Industrial Accounting
Industrial Procurement
Investment Management
Legal Aspects of Business
Management of Financial Institutions
Management of New Enterprises
Personnel Administration
Retail Distribution
Sales Management
Statistical Controls for Company Management
Taxation
Transportation